Constructing
Dialogue

Constructing Dialogue

From *Citizen Kane* to *Midnight in Paris*

MARK AXELROD

BLOOMSBURY
NEW YORK • LONDON • NEW DELHI • SYDNEY

Bloomsbury Academic

An imprint of Bloomsbury Publishing Inc.

1385 Broadway　　　50 Bedford Square
New York　　　　　London
NY 10018　　　　　WC1B 3DP
USA　　　　　　　UK

www.bloomsbury.com

Bloomsbury is a registered trade mark of Bloomsbury Publishing Plc

First published 2014

Library of Congress Cataloging-in-Publication Data
A catalog record for this book is available from the Library of Congress.

ISBN: HB: 978-1-4411-7425-3
PB: 978-1-4411-0851-7
ePDF: 978-1-4411-6980-8
ePub: 978-1-4411-2191-2

Typeset by Fakenham Prepress Solutions, Fakenham, Norfolk NR21 8NN
Printed and bound in the United States of America

Contents

Introduction vii
Author's Note x

1 *Citizen Kane* (1941) Herman J. Mankiewicz, Orson Welles 1

2 *Casablanca* (1942) Julius J. Epstein, Philip G. Epstein, Howard Koch 11

3 *Sunset Boulevard* (1950) Billy Wilder 33

4 *North by Northwest* (1959) Ernest Lehman 53

5 *Jules & Jim* (1962) François Truffaut, Jean Gruault 65

6 *Lolita* (1963) Vladimir Nabokov, Stanley Kubrick 87

7 *Goldfinger* (1964) Richard Maibaum, Paul Dehn 109

8 *The Graduate* (1969) Calder Willingham, Buck Henry 121

9 *Midnight Cowboy* (1969) Waldo Salt 133

10 *Chinatown* (1973) Robert Towne 153

11 *Annie Hall* (1977) Woody Allen, Marshall Brickman 167

12 *Breaking Away* (1979) Steve Tesich 177

13 *When Harry Met Sally* (1989) Nora Ephron 187

14 *The Fisher King* (1991) Richard LaGravenese 197

15 *Thelma & Louise* (1991) Callie Khouri 209

16 *Toy Story* (1995) Joss Whedon, Andrew Stanton, John Lasseter, Pete Docter, Joe Ranft, and Alec Sokolow 227

17 *Good Will Hunting* (1997) Matt Damon, Ben Affleck / *Ordinary People* (1980) Alvin Sargent 241

18 *American Beauty* (1999) Alan Ball 267

19 *Midnight in Paris* (2011) Woody Allen 279

CONTENTS

Dialogue: A Trailer 297
Dialogue Exercises 299
Bibliography 305
Index 307

Introduction

This is the fourth book I've written devoted to the craft of screenwriting. The first three covered a variety of areas. *Aspects of the Screenplay* (Heinemann, 2001) dealt with the overall structure of feature screenplays including notions of mythic structure used by Joseph Campbell Northrop Frye, Jessie Weston among others; *Conflict and Character* (Heinemann Drama, 2004) focused on those two aspects using several case studies including *Good Will Hunting, Driven*, and *Amélie*; and *I Read it at the Movies* (Heinemann Drama, 2006), focused on adaptation and the adaptation process including *Lolita, Death in Venice, Bladerunner*, and *Il Postino*. *Constructing Dialogue* is the natural extension of what I've already written in that it's specifically devoted to the construction of dialogue writing and how that aspect of screenwriting is fundamental to creating a viable scene.

What I intend to present in this book is why and how dialogue is the fundamental catalyst for any successful scene using excerpts from original screenplays from *Citizen Kane* to *Midnight in Paris* a span of some seven decades. Whereas *Aspects of the Screenplay* treated several features of screenwriting in a general way, this book will be devoted to a more analytical treatment of certain individual scenes of films and how those scenes were constructed to be the most highly dramatic *vis à vis* their dialogue.

Choosing specific scenes to analyze was not easy given the range of choices one has, but I decided to choose a number of films written by writers, whom I consider to be or have been some of the finest screenwriters in Hollywood, covering a span of almost three-quarters of a century. With that in mind, I have chosen a wide range of films from that time period from writers as diverse as Billy Wilder and the late Nora Ephron, Waldo Salt and Woody Allen, just to name a few.

In *Aspects of the Screenplay* (an earlier book), I alluded to Aristotle's *Poetics* and to one important item in particular that he wrote about; namely, how the "end is linked to the beginning with inevitable certainty." In that book, I was referring to the overall structure of the screenplay and how, in the end of the film, one discovers how it links to the beginning; however, if we can look at the overall structure of the script on a "macro" level, we can ask ourselves: Might the same things apply on a "micro" level? In other words, if we can look at the overall structure of the screenplay, from beginning to end, as being at the "macroscript" (my invented term) level to see if the end is linked to beginning with inevitable certainty (e.g. *Citizen Kane*, *Rain Man*, etc.) can we not look at the individual scene at the "microscript" (another invented term) level to see if the same thing applies? By microscript I mean individual scenes and how they function within themselves and within the context of the film as a whole.

That particular idea came to me after watching *The Graduate* for the nth time and in particular two very critical scenes in the film. I returned to the script and studied it as well to see what Buck Henry did to make those particular scenes work so effectively and, in fact, the scenes or the sequence of scenes were so tightly written that there was never a doubt the end was linked to the beginning with "inevitable certainty." I then began to look at other films, from other time periods to see if, in fact, the same thing applied. If the screenwriters were conscious (or unconscious) of the fact they were structuring scenes with a beginning, middle, and end that worked at the microscript level which inevitably led to me choosing the writers I've chosen.

As a writer, I have my own favorites whether those are novelists, or playwrights, or screenwriters. I have selected these films because the writers who wrote them are or were truly gifted at their craft, but what I wanted to focus on was how each of them specifically utilized dialogue to make those scenes work as effectively and dramatically as possible. Some of those writers, such as Steve Tesich and Billy Wilder, had previous dramatic experience. Others, such as Buck Henry, had television experience; regardless, each of these writers was aware of how dialogue needed to be written in order to create the best possible scene.

To that end, I need to summarize a few things I alluded to in previous books; namely, what elements each scene must include in order to work effectively and how the dialogue augments that process.

I once suggested (and still do) that the optimum scene needs to do the following things that fit into what I call the **M-A-D-E** formula:

1 **M**aintain scenic integrity

2 **A**dvance the storyline

3 **D**evelop character

4 **E**licit conflict and engage emotionally

Unless one is writing a purely experimental film (and that would have its own rules) the vast majority of narrative films would be obligated to work with these components. In addition, the techniques that the best writers employ in writing dialogue include the following:

- Question & Answer;

- Question/Statement Interrupt;

- Question/Statement Lead; Question/Question Lead;

- Statement/Statement Lead.

But the most important technique is the use of **Dialogic Links** or that bit of dialogue that links one character's dialogue with another character's dialogue by repeating the same or similar phrases or words in such a way they contribute to the four aforementioned items.

What should become fairly apparent after reading and analyzing all these excerpts from screenplays is the fact there is a consistent repetition in what's being accomplished. For some, that repetition may seem to be a failure of execution. In fact, it's just the opposite. From *Citizen Kane* to *The Fisher King* there is a transition of a half-century of filmmaking. From *Goldfinger* to *Annie Hall* there is a transition of genre. From *Jules & Jim* to *Lolita* there is a transition of film culture. And yet there is an uncanny consistency not only in the way the scenes in these films are constructed, but also in the way dialogue is an instrumental part of that construction. Having analyzed hundreds of films, I have found that the most well-crafted, well-written scripts are those scripts that employ these techniques. Are these the only techniques? Perhaps not, but as you'll see in a half-century of filmmaking, from *Citizen Kane* to *The Fisher King* they still work and if one utilizes them I can guarantee that the script you write will be a script you can be proud of.

Author's Note

Every attempt has been made to gain permissions from studios and/or producers to use excerpts from all of these screenplays many of which appear to be easily available online.

1

Citizen Kane (1941)

Screenplay by Herman J. Mankiewicz and Orson Welles

As with all the films I'm using, the number of scenes to choose from is limitless and what one writer might choose to write about may not be what another writer chooses to write about. But since I'm the writer here, I've decided to discuss the projection booth scene. The shooting script of *Citizen Kane* is dated July 16, 1940, produced in 1941 with a running time of 119 minutes.

The script is written in extreme detail, but we can summarize the opening scenes accordingly. Through a series of ten dissolves in the first 13 scenes, the reader is moved from the space outside Kane's palatial estate of Xanadu to inside Xanadu and specifically to Kane's bedroom. There is an increasingly *deductive movement* from an expansive landscape outside the confines of the estate to a narrower one within the estate leading, finally, to the one main focus, that is, the very tiny light that emanates from Kane's chambers.

Approximately two minutes into the film we hear the word "*Rosebud*," at two-and-a-half minutes, Kane is dead. For approximately the next ten minutes what follows is the "News on the March" segment that is essentially divided into 15 separate, but integral, components that summarize and highlight the entire storyline as follows.

"News on the March" segments

1　Kane's funeral and Xanadu

2　History of Kane's news empire

3　Kane's association with famous people

4　Kane's first news building

5　Kane's corporate empire and its holdings

　Kane's youth

7　Kane's association with Thatcher, his guardian

8　Assorted Comments about Kane

9　Kane's marriage to Emily Norton

10　Kane's marriage to Susan Alexander

11　Kane's building of the Chicago Opera House

12　Kane's construction of Xanadu

13　Kane and politics

14　Kane and scandal

15　Kane's death

Mankiewicz has written an engaging and compelling opening hook and in the first two minutes has clearly alluded to what I've written about in previous books: the QBA or "the question to be answered," which very simply is …

What is Rosebud?

The QBA can be defined as "that implied question posited at the beginning of the script that, in some way, must be answered by the end of it." In effect, it is the thread that is tied into the storyline, which, in this script, is really a multiple storyline made of four individual character perspectives. Unlike a film such as *Rocky* in which a character who begins in deprivation and ultimately attains a kind of "hero-hood" at the end while following a single, sustained character arc, Kane's character arc goes through an alteration that is mediated by the points of view of four different people and those four different points of view make up his overriding arc.

We initially meet Kane on his deathbed and move to how he got there, but not before the storyline is summarized through the "News on the March" segment which, itself, is a linear progression of events tracing Kane's life from 1895–1940, thus summarizing his character from an impoverished child to a financial tycoon.

Imbedded within the "News on the March" segment is a variety of scenes that comment on Kane's character and allude to the "secret of Rosebud." The clearest example of that is when Walter P. Thatcher recalls the journey he took to visit Kane's family in 1870 and was asked by someone in the room: "Is it not a fact that on that occasion the boy personally attacked you after striking you in the stomach with a sled?" (Kael, 2002, p. 106). The others in the room laugh, but, not coincidentally, this is the first scene that includes any non-Voice-Over dialogue other than Kane's last word, "Rosebud." Clearly, if the question were irrelevant why would Mankiewicz have included it as dialogue and the first bit of dialogue to be stated?

But it's only after these sequences of scenes that encapsulate Kane's life that one of the most critical scenes is developed; namely, the scene in the projection room. From the script we get the following text:

> During the entire course of this scene, nobody's face is really seen. Sections of their bodies are picked out by a table light, a silhouette is thrown on the screen, and their faces and bodies are themselves thrown into silhouette against the brilliant slanting rays of light from the projection room.

At this point, the dialogue begins that essentially shapes the entire story both in terms of the storyline and in terms of Kane's character. Someone says it's difficult to do, "seventy years of a man's life" Mankiewicz is very careful in his scene directions even though Welles changed it.

But, at this point, there's a major change in how the scene is developed. From the original script, the dialogue is reduced from four-plus script pages to about two pages. The reason for the revision is quite evident in that the original dialogue tended to retard the flow of the scene and by so doing tended to reduce the dramatic impact of the scene as well as the need to emphasize the content. There were numerous allusions to Kane as having the talent of a mountebank, the morals of a bootlegger, the manners of a pasha and that he succeeded in transforming the noble profession of journalism into something without security. Those Kanesean "virtues" didn't have any critical impact on the construction of the scene in that they merely repeated a lot of what was seen in the opening of the film.

The question one must ask at that point is: why repeat them? In clear, Aristotelian terms, what would make for a better, more succinct, more integrated scene would be to eliminate the repetitive or redundant dialogue and to establish a *scenic arc*. By that I mean, the scene should have an opening, middle, and end, and that the end should, in some fashion, integrate with the beginning so that it reveals a completely unified and somewhat seamless scene. Although this was not necessarily done in the script, it was clearly done in the final cut and the results of that revision tend to link the beginning with the end in the manner in which Aristotle talks about in his *Poetics.*

At the conclusion of the "News on the March" segment we have the scene in the projection room from which the newsreel has been screened and the word "Rosebud" is not only discussed by several shadowy reporters in the projection booth, but also the word becomes the primary focus of the scene. Of course, we have to suspend our disbelief, since there was no one in the room to hear Kane whisper "Rosebud," and unless the nurse had super-hearing she wouldn't have heard it either, but the word has significant importance not only in terms of establishing Kane's character arc, but also in initiating the question to be answered.

At that point, Rawlston, the managing editor of the newspaper, begins his dialogue when he says, what it needs is an end. "All we saw on that screen is that Charles Foster Kane is dead. I know that. I read the papers. It isn't enough to tell us what a man did. You've got to tell us who he was. Wait a minute. What were Kane's last words? Do you remember boys? What were the last words he said on earth? Maybe he told us all about himself on his death bed?"

Thompson, the reporter who will finally get the assignment to uncover the mystery of Rosebud, says yes, and maybe he didn't. Ironically, the beginning of the scene is the end of Kane's life, but it is also the beginning of Thompson's quest to uncover who the real Kane was and what, in fact, is the meaning of the word, "Rosebud." I suspect that Mankiewicz could have made the projection room "un-smoky," but it's a brilliant nuance to "cloud" the fact that there's a mystery behind the word Rosebud and it's going to take someone like Thompson to "clear" it up.

The dialogue continues:

                    RAWLSTON
        All we saw on that screen was a
        big American -

                    A VOICE
        One of the biggest.

> RAWLSTON

But how is he different from Ford?
Or Hearst for that matter? Or
Rockefeller — or John Doe?
I tell you, Thompson — a man's
dying words — When Charles Foster
Kane died he said just one word.

> THOMPSON

Rosebud.

> RAWLSTON

Yes, Just that one word. But who
is She? Here's a man who might have
Been President. Who was as loved
And hated and talked about as much as
any man in our time — but when he
comes to die, he's got something
on his mind called "Rosebud."
What does that mean?

> ANOTHER VOICE

A racehorse he bet on once,
probably, that didn't come in -

> RAWLSTON

All right. But what was the race?

There is a short silence.

> VOICE

Rosebud.

> RAWLSTON

Thompson!

> THOMPSON

Yes, sir.

                    RAWLSTON
(decisively)
Find out about Rosebud. Get in touch
with everybody who ever knew him. Oh,
knew him well. That manager of his -
Bernstein, his second wife. Is she
still living?

                    THOMPSON
Susan Alexander Kane.

                     VOICE
She's in a nightclub in Atlantic
City.

                    RAWLSTON
See them all. Get in touch with
everybody that ever worked for him
whoever loved him, whoever hated his guts.
(pauses) I don't mean go through the City
Directory, of course -

                    THOMPSON
I'll get to it right away, Mr.
Rawlston.

                    RAWLSTON
Good! Rosebud. Dead or alive.
It'll probably turn out to be a
very simple thing.

At that point, there is a smash cut to a photo of Susan Kane Alexander and the story continues. But what's revealing about the script is what Mankiewicz writes: "(NOTE: Now begins the story proper—the search by Thompson for the facts about Kane–his researches—his interviews with the people who knew Kane)" (Kael, 2002, p. 126). Thompson then begins a kind of "quest" to discover who Kane actually was. I choose the word "quest" because, as we'll see, many, many films are tied into this notion of the quest and of someone discovering something. One certainly can see the impact of how the quest operates in film by reading any one of a number of excellent books including Joseph Campbell's, *The Hero With a Thousand Faces*, Northrop Frye's,

Anatomy of Criticism, Jessie Weston's, *From Ritual to Romance* or Arnold Van Gennep's, *The Rites of Passage* since those texts clearly deal with the notion of the quest in terms of narrative.

In terms of how Mankiewicz establishes the arc of the scene, it's fairly clear. The scene begins with the "death" of Kane, the end of the scene is an attempt to discover his "life" and a specific thing about his life; namely, what "Rosebud" means. Of all the things to look for in a man's life, the editor decides on Rosebud and so the dialogue advances that discovery.

> RAWLSTON
> All we saw on that screen was a
> **big** American -
>
> A VOICE
> One of the **biggest.**
>
> RAWLSTON
> But how is he different from Ford?
> Or Hearst for that matter? Or
> Rockefeller — or John Doe?
> I tell you, Thompson — a man's
> dying words -When Charles Foster
> Kane died he said just **one word.**
>
> THOMPSON
> **Rosebud.**
>
> RAWLSTON
> Yes, Just that **one word.** But who
> is she? Here's a man who might have
> been President. Who was as loved
> and hated and talked about as much as
> any man in our time — but when he
> comes to die, he's got something

on his mind called **"Rosebud."**
What does that mean?

ANOTHER VOICE
A **racehorse** he bet on once,
probably, that didn't come in -

RAWLSTON
All right. But what was the **race?**

There is a short silence.

VOICE
Rosebud.

RAWLSTON
Thompson!

THOMPSON
Yes, sir.

RAWLSTON
Hold this thing up for **a week.**
Two weeks if you have to ...

THOMPSON
Don't you think right after his
death …

RAWLSTON
(decisively)
Find out about **Rosebud.** Get in touch
with everybody **who ever knew him.** Oh,
knew him well. That manager of his -
Bernstein, **his second wife. Is she
still living?**

THOMPSON
Susan Alexander Kane.

VOICE
She's in a nightclub in Atlantic
City.

RAWLSTON

See them all. Get in touch with
everybody that ever worked for him
whoever loved him,
whoever hated his guts.
(pauses)
I don't mean go through the City
Directory, of course -

THOMPSON

I'll get to it right away, Mr.
Rawlston.

RAWLSTON

Good! **Rosebud.** Dead or alive.
It'll probably turn out to be a
very simple thing.

The dialogue links neatly advance Hitchcock's notion of what constitutes the MacGuffin—a term popularized by director/producer Alfred Hitchcock. In a 1939 lecture at Columbia University, Hitchcock stated: "[We] have a name in the studio, and we call it the 'MacGuffin. It is the mechanical element that usually crops up in any story. In crook stories it is almost always the necklace and in spy stories it is most always the papers. Interviewed in 1966 by the New Wave French director, François Truffaut, Hitchcock illustrated the term "MacGuffin" with this story: It might be a Scottish name, taken from a story about two men in a train. One man says "What's that package up there in the baggage rack?", and the other answers, "Oh, that's a MacGuffin. The first one asks "What's a MacGuffin?" "Well," the other man says, "it's an apparatus for trapping lions in the Scottish Highlands. The first man says, "But there are no lions in the Scottish Highlands," and the other one answers, "Well, then that's no MacGuffin!"[1]

In this case, the MacGuffin is Rosebud. One can see that the links advance the scene to its natural conclusion, since the entire focus of the scene is related to Rosebud. After all, the word is mentioned five times in the scene. What is it? A racehorse? If not a racehorse, then what? The dialogue reinforces the mystery of what Rosebud might be and Rawlston's demand that Thompson discover the meaning of Rosebud ties up the scene, especially when he states, and ironically, that "It'll probably turn out to

---

[1] http://en.wikipedia.org/wiki/MacGuffin [accessed May 2013].

be a very simple thing." The dialogue maintains scenic continuity while, at the same time, advances the storyline, develops something about Kane's character, and elicits conflict. In this case, the conflict is something about the mysterious Rosebud.

Likewise, it is not coincidental, then, that by the time we get to Scene 116, the interior of the Great Hall at Xanadu, as all of Kane's worldly goods are being catalogued, the reporters in attendance, many of whom may have been there at the outset, begin discussing Kane's life with Thompson. And, not coincidentally, the word "Rosebud" once again emerges even though, by that time, no one can account for its meaning. If the ending relates to what Aristotle has said about the relationship between endings and beginnings, then there should be a natural link between them. In Scene 117, Mankiewicz writes: "The sled is on top of the pile. As [the] camera comes close, it shows the faded rosebud and, though the letters are faded, unmistakably the word "Rosebud" across it. The laborer drops his shovel, takes the sled in his hand and throws it into the furnace. The flames start to devour it" (Kael, 2002, p. 294).

Clearly, the mystery of Rosebud initiated at the outset of the film, is answered by the conclusion of it and, in fact, the ending is linked to the beginning with inevitable certainty just as Aristotle suggested. What Mankiewicz did was to divide the story arc into four specific flashback segments, all of which comment on Kane through individual points of view as they reflect on their individual relationships with Kane: Bernstein, his accountant; Leland, Kane's best friend and a drama critic; Susan Alexander, Kane's second wife; and Raymond, Kane's butler. Thompson interviews all four of them with one thing in mind: to discover what Rosebud means. In the process of trying to uncover that "mystery," Thompson learns a lot about Kane the man and the final comment about Rosebud comes from Thompson himself who says: "Maybe Rosebud was something he couldn't get or something he lost, but it wouldn't have explained anything—Rosebud is just a piece in a jigsaw puzzle—a missing piece" (Kael, 2002, p. 294).

Rosebud is the thread that keeps the entire script together and it's Thompson's quest to discover the meaning of Rosebud and through that quest we see how Kane's character arc has been shaped, but, in terms of dialogue and scene, what's of interest here is how Mankiewicz has incorporated dialogue links in order to advance the scene. What we'll see is that this linking technique is one of the most vital techniques in constructing a scene and is a major tool in the screenwriter's craft. And although there are only about 17 links in this brief scene as compared to dozens in some other films, from *Citizen Kane* to *Midnight in Paris* the use of dialogue links is mandatory not only in unifying the scene, but in unifying the entire script.

2

Casablanca (1942)

Screenplay by Julius J. Epstein, Philip G. Epstein and Howard Koch Based on the play "Everybody Goes to Rick's" by Murray Burnett and Joan Alison

In Aljean Harmetz's book, *Round Up the Usual Suspects: The Making of Casablanca: Bogart, Bergman, and World War II* (1993), the Warner Brothers' story analyst who read the play, Stephen Karnot, called it "sophisticated hokum" or something like pretentious nonsense. Regardless, the rights were purchased for $20,000 and no one knew how well that bit of hokum was going to do either short-term or long-term. But beyond the Rick and Ilsa love story (you must remember that) what about the script itself? How did this screenplay by committee finally get finished? Practically the entire film takes place in Rick's Café. Except for the Paris flashback, the scenes at the Blue Parrot, the Prefect's office, and the airport, the entire film is isolated to one setting as one scene dissolves into another. What that restriction does in terms of setting is to make this film almost totally dialogue dependent, and that dependence on dialogue makes the film that much more remarkable in its ability to maintain an audience's interest and sustain the story.

The opening of the film essentially begins with the discovery that Ugarte has killed German couriers for their "letters of transit." Since those letters are the only legitimate way anyone can leave Casablanca, their possession is paramount. In Hitchcockian terms, the letters are the MacGuffin and their appearance, either in name or form, manifests throughout the film. After Ugarte gives the letters to Rick for safekeeping, he is arrested and subsequently murdered. The question then becomes: what will Rick do with the letters? Without summarizing the entire film (which doesn't do justice to the film itself) I would like to focus on four specific scenes: (1) Rick and Ugarte; (2) Rick and Renault outside the café; (3) Rick and Laszlo before the latter's "arrest"; and (4) the airport scene.

This particular scene is preceded by the voice over information about the war and how Casablanca is the way out for those people who want to avoid the war. It's also been established that two German couriers have been killed. We enter Rick's café and soon we see Rick meeting Ugarte (Peter Lorre) who walks back to Rick's private table.

                         UGARTE
            Huh. You know, Rick, watching you
            just now with the Deutsches Bank,
            one would think you'd been doing
            this all your life.

                          RICK
            Well, what makes you think I haven't?

                         UGARTE
            Oh, nothing. But when you first came
            to Casablanca, I thought—

                          RICK
            —You thought what?

                         UGARTE
            What right do I have to think?

                         UGARTE
            May I? Too bad about those two German
            couriers, wasn't it?

                    RICK

They got a lucky break. Yesterday
they were just two German clerks.
Today they're the 'Honored Dead'.

                   UGARTE

You are a very cynical person, Rick,
if you'll forgive me for saying so.

                    RICK

I forgive you.

A waiter comes up to the table with a tray of drinks. He
places one before Ugarte.

                   UGARTE

Thank you.
(to Rick)
Will you have a drink with me please?

                    RICK

No.

                   UGARTE

I forgot. You never drink with ...
(to waiter)
I'll have another, please.
(to Rick, sadly)
You despise me, don't you?

                    RICK

If I gave you any thought, I probably
would.

                   UGARTE

But why? Oh, you object to the kind
of business I do, huh? But think of
all those poor refugees who must rot
in this place if I didn't help them.
That's not so bad. Through ways of
my own I provide them with exit visas.

                    RICK
For a price, Ugarte, for a price.

                   UGARTE
But think of all the poor devils who
cannot meet Renault's price. I get
it for them for half. Is that so
parasitic?

                    RICK
I don't mind a parasite. I object to
a cut-rate one.

                   UGARTE
Well, Rick, after tonight I'll be
through with the whole business, and
I am leaving finally this Casablanca.

                    RICK
Who did you bribe for your visa?
Renault or yourself?

                   UGARTE
Myself. I found myself much more
reasonable.

takes an envelope from his pocket and lays it on the
table.

                   UGARTE
Look, Rick, do you know what this
is? Something that even you have
never seen. Letters of transit signed
by General de Gaulle. Cannot be
rescinded, not even questioned.

Rick appears ready to take them from Ugarte.

                    UGARTE
One moment. Tonight I'll be selling
those for more money than even I
have ever dreamed of, and then, addio
Casablanca! You know, Rick, I have
many friends in Casablanca, but
somehow, just because you despise me
you're the only one I trust. Will
you keep these for me? Please.

                    RICK
For how long?

                    UGARTE
Perhaps an hour, perhaps a little
longer.

                    RICK
I don't want them here overnight.

                    UGARTE
Don't be afraid of that. Please keep
them for me. Thank you. I knew I
could trust you. Oh, waiter. I'll be
expecting some people. If anybody asks for
me I'll be right here.

                    WAITER
Yes, Monsieur.

The waiter leaves. Ugarte turns to Rick.

                    UGARTE
Rick, I hope you are more impressed
with me now, huh? If you'll forgive
me, I'll share my good luck with
your roulette wheel.

He starts across the floor.

                        RICK
Just a moment.

Ugarte stops as Rick comes up to him.

                        RICK
Yeah, I heard a rumor that those
German couriers were carrying letters
of transit.

Ugarte hesitates for a moment.

                      UGARTE
Huh? I heard that rumor, too. Poor
devils.

Rick looks at Ugarte steadily.

                        RICK
(slowly)
Yes, you're right, Ugarte. I am a
little more impressed with you.

Rick then leaves the gambling room and walks into the main room. This particular scene is critical to the entire film since it focuses on what will be the most important item of interest throughout the story; namely, the letters of transit. The scene gives us the vital information about what they are, how Ugarte got them, and why he gives them to Rick. But the dialogue also establishes what kind of character Rick is that he would even deal with someone like Ugarte. We discover that Rick isn't above the law and that aspect of his character links to the end of the film as well. But as we've seen with other films, the screenwriters' ability to use the dialogue links in the process of moving the scene along is apparent.

                    UGARTE
Huh. You know, Rick, watching you
just now with the Deutsches Bank,
**one would think you'd been doing
this all your life.**

                    RICK
Well, **what makes you think I haven't?**

                    UGARTE
Oh, nothing. But when you first came
to Casablanca, **I thought—**

                    RICK
—You thought what?

                    UGARTE
What right do I have **to think?**

                    UGARTE
May I? **Too bad about those two German
couriers,** wasn't it?

                    RICK
They got a lucky break. Yesterday
they were just two German clerks.
Today **they're** the 'Honored Dead'.

                    UGARTE
You are a very cynical person, Rick,
if **you'll forgive me for saying so.**

                    RICK
I forgive you.

A waiter comes up to the table with a tray of drinks. He
places one before Ugarte.

                    UGARTE
Thank you.
        (to Rick)
Will you have a drink with me please?

                    RICK
No.

                    UGARTE
I forgot. **You never drink** with ...
(to waiter)
I'll have another, please.
(to Rick, sadly)
You despise me, don't you?

                    RICK
**If I gave you any thought, I probably
would.**

                    UGARTE
But why? Oh, you object to the kind
of business I do, huh? But think of
all those poor refugees who must rot
in this place if I didn't help them.
That's not so bad. **Through ways of
my own I provide them with exit visas.**

                    RICK
For a price, Ugarte, **for a price.**

                    UGARTE
But think of all the poor devils who
cannot meet Renault's **price.** I get
it for them for half. Is that so
parasitic?

                    RICK
I don't mind a **parasite.** I object to
a cut-rate one.

UGARTE
Well, Rick, after tonight I'll be
through with the whole business, and
I am leaving finally this Casablanca.

RICK
Who did you bribe for your visa?
Renault or yourself?

UGARTE
Myself. I found myself much more
reasonable.

He takes an envelope from his pocket and lays it on the
table.

UGARTE
Look, Rick, do you know what this
is? Something that even you have
never seen. **Letters of transit** signed
by General de Gaulle. Cannot be
rescinded, not even questioned.

Rick appears ready to take them from Ugarte.

UGARTE
One moment. Tonight I'll be **selling
those** for more money than even I
have ever dreamed of, and then, addio
Casablanca! You know, Rick, I have
many friends in Casablanca, but
somehow, just because you despise me
you're the only one I trust. **Will
you keep these for me? Please.**

RICK
For how long?

UGARTE
**Perhaps an hour, perhaps a little
longer.**

                              RICK
          I don't want them here overnight.

                              UGARTE
          Don't be afraid of that. Please keep
          them for me. Thank you. I knew I
          could trust you. Oh, waiter. I'll be
          expecting some people. If anybody asks for
          me I'll be right here.

                              WAITER
          Yes, Monsieur.

The waiter leaves. Ugarte turns to Rick.

                              UGARTE
          Rick, I hope you are **more impressed
          with me** now, huh? **If you'll forgive
          me,** I'll share my good luck with
          your roulette wheel.

He starts across the floor.

                              RICK
          Just a moment.

Ugarte stops as Rick comes up to him.

                              RICK
          Yeah, I heard a **rumor** that those
          German couriers were carrying **letters
          of transit.**

Ugarte hesitates for a moment.

                              UGARTE
          Huh? I heard that **rumor,** too. Poor
          devils.

Rick looks at Ugarte steadily.

                    RICK
        Yes, you're right, Ugarte. I am a
        little more impressed with you.

Rick leaves the gambling room and goes into the main room.

Because so many of the scenes deal with Rick and Renault, it is difficult to
select just one. What each of those independent scenes does is to reinforce
their respective characters. Rick and Renault know each other very well. They
know their strengths and their weaknesses and they know each of them is
capable of being deceived by the other. That ability is the foundation for their
mutual respect which is established in their first dialogue and concludes with
Rick's famous last line: "Louis, I think this is the beginning of a beautiful
friendship." The scene I've chosen is the first scene in which Renault, the
Prefect, is introduced as Rick has just "stuffed" an inebriated ex-lover,
Yvonne, into a cab.

                    RENAULT
        How extravagant you are, **throwing
        away women** like that. Someday they
                may be scarce.

Rick sits down at the table.

                    RENAULT
                    (amused)
        You know, I think now I shall pay a
        call on **Yvonne**, maybe get **her** on the
                rebound, eh?

                    RICK
        When it comes to **women,** you're a
                true democrat.

As they talk, Captain Tonelli and Lieutenant Casselle
walk by toward the entrance of the cafe. Casselle talks
non-stop and Tonelli tries. They both stop, salute
Renault, and walk into the cafe.

                    RENAULT
        If he gets a word in it'll be a major
                Italian victory.

There is a certain irony in Renault's comment about women since Rick is very
democratic when it comes to women. He's also very moral when it comes to
women as the film suggests.

```
Rick laughs. Rick and Renault look up when they hear the
BUZZ of a plane taking off from the adjacent airfield.
The plane flies directly over their heads.
```

> RENAULT
> The **plane** to **Lisbon.**
> You would like to be on it?

> RICK
> (curtly)
> Why? What's in **Lisbon?**

> RENAULT
> **The clipper to America.**

```
Rick doesn't answer. His look isn't a happy one.
```

> RENAULT
> I have often speculated on why you
> don't **return to America. Did you**
> **abscond with the church funds? Did**
> **you run off with a senator's wife? I**
> **like to think you killed a man.** It's
> the romantic in me.

```
Rick still looks in the direction of the airport.
```

> RICK
> **It was a combination of all three.**

The plane to Lisbon is really the lynchpin of the entire story since it's the
only way out of Casablanca to America. Lisbon, in combination with the
letters of transit, becomes a recurrent motif throughout the film and, of
course, becomes the focus of the finale of the film. What's of interest is
how the writers linked Lisbon to America, and America to Rick, and Rick's
apparent reasons for not returning to America. The three things Renault
alludes to (i.e. stealing money, adultery, murder) Rick doesn't deny, but says

it was a "combination." That may or may not have been true about why he left America. What is true is that he is guilty of all three of those things in Casablanca which leads Renault to question why Rick is in Casablanca. We can suspend our disbelief that Renault has never asked Rick that question before, especially since they know each other so well, but the dialogue links continue to propel the story forward.

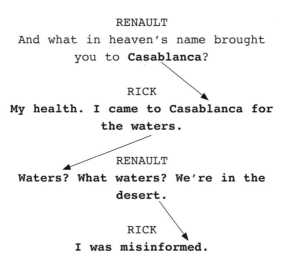

RENAULT
And what in heaven's name brought
you to **Casablanca?**

RICK
**My health. I came to Casablanca for
the waters.**

RENAULT
**Waters? What waters? We're in the
desert.**

RICK
I was misinformed.

Once again, the dialogue links advance something about Rick. In this case, it accents Rick's sense of irony which is something that is replete throughout the film. Rick is very much a private person and he uses his sense of irony in order to cover up that sense of who he is. More than once does Renault use the word "romantic" in relation to Rick, and Rick uses the word in relation to Renault. He also calls Rick a "sentimentalist" at least twice during the course of the film and his final action in the film tends to corroborate both aspects of his character.

EMIL, the croupier, comes out of the cafe and walks over to Rick.

> EMIL
> Excuse me, Monsieur Rick, but a gentleman inside has **won twenty thousand francs. The cashier would like some money.**

> RICK
> Well, I'll get it from the **safe.**

> EMIL
> I am so upset, Monsieur Rick. **You know I can't understand—**

> RICK
> —Forget it, Emil. **Mistakes like that happen all the time.**
> EMIL
> I'm awfully sorry.

This particular dialogue, which ends the scene, may appear to be insignificant, but, in its own way, it ties the end of the scene with the beginning. The "gentleman" may, in fact, be Ugarte who, in his own way, is as deceitful as Rick. Emil declares he can't understand how that happened and Rick replies that mistakes happen. Of course, Emil's comment begs the question: Why? Why might he not understand? Why would he be sorry? Of course, the answer is that the games are rigged and we see how they're rigged in other scenes. So, the scene is neatly framed by the notion of "deceit." In the first instance, Rick has, from Yvonne's point of view, deceived her into letting her think Rick was in love with her. In the second instance, Rick has been deceived by someone who actually gamed the system. But if one reads the scene closely, then it becomes fairly apparent that the entire scene is predicated on the notion of deceit and the notion of deceit plays a major role throughout the entire film.

INT. RICK'S CAFE—MAIN ROOM—NIGHT

Rick comes down the stairs. Laszlo wraps one of the small bar towels around his cut wrist. Rick looks questioningly at the injured hand.

                         LASZLO
          It's nothing. Just a little cut. We
                had to get through a window.
       Rick walks to the bar, picks up a bottle, and pours a
                          drink.

                          RICK
            Well, this might come in handy.

                         LASZLO
                       Thank you.

                          RICK
                 Had a close one, eh?

                         LASZLO
                      Yes, rather.

       Laszlo takes a drink.

                          RICK
            Don't you sometimes wonder if it's
            worth all this? I mean what you're
                    fighting for?

                         LASZLO
            We might as well question why we
         breathe. If we stop breathing, we'll
         die. If we stop **fighting** our enemies,
               the world will die.

                          RICK
         What of it? **Then it'll be out of
                     its misery.**

       Rick reaches in his jacket for his cigarette case, opens
       it, and takes out a cigarette.

       This is first significant scene between Rick and Laszlo, the Czech resistance
       fighter who has sought asylum in America via Casablanca. Laszlo has injured
       himself after escaping through a window when a meeting of the Resistance

was interrupted by the Nazis. That injury leads to Rick's comment about "fighting," and Laszlo links on the same word. If the "fighting" stops the "world will die," and Rick links on that by stating "it" (the world) would then be put out of its misery. That presumed indifference on Rick's part prompts Laszlo to bring up the word "destiny."

                    LASZLO
         You know how you sound, Monsieur
         Blaine? Like a man who's trying to
          convince himself of something he
          doesn't believe in his heart. **Each
        of us has a destiny, for good or for
                      evil.**

                      RICK
              Yes, I get the point.

Rick lights his cigarette.

                    LASZLO
          I **wonder if you do.** I **wonder** if you
            know that **you're trying to escape
          from yourself and that you'll never
                    succeed.**

                      RICK
          You seem to know all about my **destiny.**

After Laszlo brings up the word "destiny," Rick links on his dialogue by stating he gets the point, the point being about one's destiny. Laszlo links on that by stating Rick will never succeed in escaping from himself (i.e. escaping one's destiny) and that prompts Rick to link again with the word. The notion destiny is critical not only to the scene, but to the entire storyline, since one cannot escape one's destiny. One might be able to escape one's future, because the future is often within one's control, but destiny is never within one's control and in that conflict between one's future and one's destiny lay the foundation for the entire film. At that point, Laszlo says what he's known all along and what Rick has only recently discovered.

                    LASZLO
I know a good deal more about you
    than you suspect. I know, for
instance, that you are in love with
a woman. **It is perhaps strange that
we both should be in love with the
same woman.** The first evening I came
here in this cafe, I knew there was
something between you and Ilsa. Since
no one is to blame, I, I demand no
explanation. I ask only one thing.
You won't give me the letters of
transit. All right. But I want my
wife to be safe. I ask you as a favor
to use the letters to take her away
            from Casablanca.

                    RICK
You love her that much?

                    LASZLO
Apparently you think of me only as
the leader of a cause. Well, I am
        also **a human being.**

                    LASZLO
    Yes, **I love her that much.**

The whole notion of destiny plays out here. It was destiny that Rick would
have met Ilsa in Paris and fallen in love with her; it was destiny that she would
have left him; it was destiny that Rick would end up in Casablanca; it was
destiny that Laszlo and Ilsa would come to Casablanca to escape the Nazis;
and it was destiny that the three of them would meet there. As they discuss
the notion of destiny, destiny itself intervenes.

Suddenly there is a CRASH at the door of the cafe, followed
by the forced entry of several gendarmes. A French officer
walks in and addresses Laszlo.

                    FRENCH OFFICER
                    Mr. Laszlo?

> LASZLO
> Yes?

> FRENCH OFFICER
> You will come with us. **We have a
> warrant for your arrest.**

> LASZLO
> **On what charge?**

> FRENCH OFFICER
> Captain Renault will discuss **that**
> with you later.

> RICK
> It seems that **destiny** has taken a
> hand.

Laszlo looks for a moment at Rick, then in dignified silence crosses to the officer. Together they walk toward the door.

Rick's eyes follow them, but his expression reveals nothing of his feelings.

As we've seen, the entire scene is predicated on the notion of destiny, and, at that moment, Laszlo presumably becomes a victim to his destiny through Rick's apparent deceit. The dialogue links not only link their individual dialogues, but augment these two notions of destiny and deceit that are constantly being played out, which leads to the penultimate scenes of the film as Rick has apparently double-crossed Renault and offered safe passage to Laszlo and Ilsa instead of himself by signing their names to the letters of transit.

Renault stops dead in his tracks, and turns around. Both Ilsa and Renault look at Rick with astonishment.

> ILSA
> **But why my name,** Richard?

> RICK
> Because **you're getting on that plane.**

ILSA
(confused)
I don't understand. **What about you?**

RICK
I'm staying here with him 'til the
plane gets safely away.

Rick's intention suddenly dawns on Ilsa.

ILSA
No, Richard, no. What has happened
to you? **Last night we said—**

RICK
**Last night we said a great many
things. You said** I was to do the
thinking for both of us. Well, I've
done a lot of it since then and it
all adds up to one thing. **You're
getting on that plane with Victor
where you belong.**

ILSA
(protesting)
But Richard, no, I, I—

RICK
You've got to listen to me. Do
you have any idea what you'd have to
look forward to if you stayed here?
Nine chances out of ten we'd both
wind up in a concentration camp.
Isn't that true, Louis?

Renault countersigns the papers.

RENAULT
I'm afraid Major Strasser would
insist.

                    ILSA
You're saying this only to make me
                    go.

                    RICK
I'm saying it because it's true.
Inside of us we both know you belong
with Victor. You're part of his work,
the thing that keeps him going. If
that plane leaves the ground and
you're not with him, you'll regret
                    it.

                    ILSA
                    No.

                    RICK
Maybe not today, maybe not tomorrow,
but soon, and for the rest of your
                    life.

                    ILSA
But what about us?

                    RICK
We'll always have Paris. We didn't
have, we'd lost it, until you came
to Casablanca. We got it back last
                    night.

                    ILSA
And I said I would never leave you.

                    RICK
And you never will. But I've got a
job to do, too. Where I'm going you
can't follow. What I've got to do
you can't be any part of. Ilsa, I'm
no good at being noble, but it doesn't
take much to see that the problems
of three little people don't amount

```
          to a hill of beans in this crazy
          world. Someday you'll understand
                 that. Now, now ...
     Ilsa's eyes well up with tears. Rick puts his hand to
        her chin and raises her face to meet his own.


                         RICK
               Here's looking at you, kid.
                                              CUT TO:
```

One sees how the dialogue links play a major part in moving the scene to its natural conclusion. Not only do they link Rick's dialogue with Ilsa's dialogue, but they bring the film to its natural ending. Destiny prevails for Ilsa and Laszlo by virtue of Rick's deceit. His comment about not being "noble" is a refrain of a comment made earlier by Renault that Rick was "patriotic." Not only is he noble in how he has, at least for the moment, sacrificed his own escape, but when the Nazi Strasser arrives, Rick shoots him and is only saved by Renault who covers for him. Once again, the focus of the scene is almost exclusively dependent on the notion of deceit and what makes *Casablanca* such an excellent example to use in relation to dialogue and scene construction is that almost every scene in the film is predicated on the notion of deceit and that construction vividly reinforces the Aristotelian idea of how ends are linked inextricably with beginnings.

3

Sunset Boulevard (1950)
Screenplay by Billy Wilder

*S*unset Boulevard should be a must see (if not must read) for anyone who is or who has thoughts of becoming a screenwriter. Not because it predates *The Player* by almost 50 years (and by virtue of that, really comments on what a screenwriter's life was, is, and, presumably, what it will be like for decades to come), but because of Billy Wilder's enormous talent as a writer and as a master of comedic dialogue. Even though his mentor was German director Ernst Lubitsch, and even though Wilder always kept a sign hanging in his office that asked, "How would Lubitsch do it?," his ability as a dialogist is purely his own and exceeded that of his mentor. Although he allegedly said his English was a mixture between Arnold Schwarzenegger and Archbishop Tutu (since English was Wilder's second if not third language), it's evident that Wilder's ear was more attuned to dialogue than a lot of other writers who were native speakers of English. His English may have been acquired, but his sense of humor must have been genetic.

I once invited Wilder to be a speaker at the university where I teach. He responded that he would, but at his age (he was 94 at the time) he didn't know if he had enough numbers left to book something a year in advance. When once asked what the purpose of making films was he responded, "Well, number one, it's too late for me now to change and to become a gardener. Number two is to get away from the house and the vacuum cleaner. I want to be in my office and think. And number three, it's very exciting. I like to tell stories. Ultimately it's interesting. You meet nice people, it's glamorous, and, if you get lucky, very profitable. You suffer a great deal, but to paraphrase President Truman, if you can't take all that crap, get out of the studio. Believe me, this is not a profession for a dignified human being. I can see the interest in pictures when I talk to you students [at the American Film Institute], especially now that almost every university has something connected with movies. But if I had a son I would beat him with a very large whip trying to make a gardener, a dentist or something else out of him. Don't do it. It's just too tough. It hurts, and the moments of glory are very far between. Well, it's too late for me to turn back, too late for me to become a gardener. I can't bend over the azaleas. Not anymore."[1] As I said, *Sunset Boulevard* is a must see for anyone who has aspirations of becoming a screenwriter.

The opening scene of the film establishes that Gillis (William Holden) has been murdered. The rest of the film deals with how Gillis got murdered so that in the end we understand (especially from an Aristotelian point of view) how it's linked to the beginning with absolute certainty. But if that's the *macroscript* to which I alluded to in the introduction, then we need to deal with the *microscripts* within.

The two subsequent scenes of *Sunset Boulevard* are both dramatically engaging and dialogically humorous. The scene opens with the impecunious Gillis typing. As Wilder writes it, the apartment is "dingy and cheerless." A buzzer sounds, then sounds again. Gillis goes to the door where two men, one with a briefcase, are waiting. They want Gillis's car since he's behind on payments. He creates a ruse to get rid of them and then the scene shifts as Gillis goes on in a voice over about how he needs $290 or he'll lose the car since it's not in Palm Springs because he has anticipated the finance company coming after it and so he parked it behind Rudy's Shoeshine Parlor. Gillis continues talking as the scene shifts to the alley next to Sidney's Men's Shop.

Not only do these scenes establish Gillis's impecunious state, but the dialogue is written in such a way as to augment that condition. Of course, we know Gillis is lying about the car as would anyone who's come face to face with the Repo Man. The dialogue is written in such a way as to propel the storyline forward and develop character. Obviously, Gillis is forced to be one step ahead of the finance company if not one step ahead of everyone he owes. The beginning of the scene (which establishes his apparent penury) is linked to the end of the scene in which his penury is clearly defined and which naturally leads to his attempt to resolve his financial dilemma; namely, trying to sell a screenplay to Sheldrake.

Sheldrake is an important Hollywood producer and it's this scene that was reprised almost entirely in Altman's, *The Player*. Sheldrake's office is reflective of a Paramount executive: with mahogany desk, leather chairs, etc. The walls are dotted with autographed photographs of Paramount stars and an Oscar

---

[1] http://www.imdb.com/name/nm0000697/bio [accessed May 2013].

rests on a bookshelf. Piles of scripts are strewn on the floor. Sheldrake is in his mid-40s. He's smoking a cigarette when Gillis walks in.

                    SHELDRAKE
          All right, Gillis. You've got
          five minutes. What's your story
          about?

                    GILLIS
          It's about a ball player, a rookie
          shortstop that's batting 347. The
          poor kid was once mixed up in a hold-
          up. But he's trying to go straight—
          except there's a bunch of gamblers
          who won't let him.

                    SHELDRAKE
          So they tell the kid to throw the
          World Series, or else, huh?

                    GILLIS
          More or less. Only for the end
          I've got a gimmick that's real good.

                    SHELDRAKE
          Got a title?

                    GILLIS
          Bases Loaded. There's a 40-page
          outline.

                    SHELDRAKE
          (To the secretary)
          Get the Readers' Department and
          see what they have on Bases Loaded.

>   GILLIS
>   They're pretty hot about it
>   over at Twentieth, but I think
>   Zanuck's all wet. Can you see
>   Ty Power as a shortstop?
>   You've got the best man for it
>   right here on this lot. Alan Ladd.
>   Good change of pace for
>   Alan Ladd. There's another thing:
>   it's pretty simple to shoot. Lot
>   of outdoor stuff. Bet you could
>   make the whole thing for under a
>   million. And there's a great little
>   part for Bill Demarest. One of the
>   trainers, an old time player who
>   got beaned and goes out of his head
>   sometimes.

At that moment, Sheldrake's assistant, Betty Schaefer, early 20s, walks in with a folder of papers. She doesn't notice Gillis.

>   BETTY
>   Hello, Mr. Sheldrake. On that Bases
>   Loaded. I covered it with a 2-page
>   synopsis. (She holds it out)
>   But I wouldn't bother.

>   SHELDRAKE
>   What's wrong with it?

>   BETTY
>   It's from hunger.

>   SHELDRAKE
>   Nothing for Ladd?

>   BETTY
>   Just a rehash of something that
>   wasn't very good to begin with.

                    SHELDRAKE
I'm sure you'll be glad to meet
Mr. Gillis. He wrote it.

Betty turns towards Gillis, embarrassed.

                    SHELDRAKE
This is Miss Kramer.

                    BETTY
Schaefer. Betty Schaefer. And
right now I wish I could crawl
into a hole and pull it in after
me.

                    GILLIS
If I could be of any help...

                    BETTY
I'm sorry, Mr. Gillis, but I
just don't think it's any good.
I found it flat and banal.

                    GILLIS
Exactly what kind of material do
you recommend? James Joyce?
Dostoevsky?

                    SHELDRAKE
Name dropper.

                    BETTY
I just think pictures should say
a little something.

                    GILLIS
Oh, you're one of the message
kids. Just a story won't do.
You'd have turned down Gone With the
Wind.

> SHELDRAKE

No, that was me. I said, Who
wants to see a Civil War picture?

> BETTY

Perhaps the reason I hated Bases
Loaded is that I knew your name.
I'd always heard you had some talent.

> GILLIS

That was last year. This year
I'm trying to earn a living.

> BETTY

So you take Plot 27-A, make it
glossy, make it slick—

> SHELDRAKE

Careful. Those are dirty words!
You sound like a bunch of New
York critics. Thank you, Miss
Schaefer.

> BETTY

Goodbye, Mr. Gillis.

> GILLIS

Goodbye. Next time I'll write
The Naked and the Dead.

> SHELDRAKE

Well, seems like Zanuck's got
himself a baseball picture.

> GILLIS

Mr. Sheldrake, I don't want you
to think I thought this was going
to win any Academy Award.

> SHELDRAKE

Of course, we're always looking

for a Betty Hutton. Do you see
it as a Betty Hutton?

> GILLIS

Frankly, no.

> SHELDRAKE
> (Amusing himself)
> Now wait a minute. If we made
> it a girls' softball team, put
> in a few numbers. Might make a
> cute musical: It Happened in
> the Bull Pen—the story of a
> Woman.

> GILLIS

You trying to be funny?—because
I'm all out of laughs. I'm over a
barrel and I need a job.

> SHELDRAKE

Sure, Gillis. If something should
come along—

> GILLIS

Along is no good. I need it now.

> SHELDRAKE

Haven't got a thing.

> GILLIS

Any kind of assignment. Additional
Dialogue.

> SHELDRAKE

There's nothing, Gillis. Not
even if you were a relative.

> GILLIS
> (Hating it)
> Look, Mr. Sheldrake, could you

> let me have three hundred bucks
> yourself, as a personal loan?

                    SHELDRAKE
> Could I? Gillis, last year some-
> body talked me into buying a ranch
> in the valley. So I borrowed money
> from the bank so I could pay for
> the ranch. This year I had to
> mortgage the ranch so I could keep
> up my life insurance so I could
> borrow on the insurance so I could
> pay my income tax. Now if Dewey
> had been elected

                    GILLIS
> Goodbye, Mr. Sheldrake.

Once again, we can look at the arc of the scene. Gillis walks in, hopeful that he's going to sell a script. If not sell a script, score some cash from Sheldrake. In the end, he gets neither. As a *microscript*, it has a clear beginning, middle, and end, and the dialogue maintains scenic continuity, contributes extensively to Gillis's character, advances the storyline and offers conflict. If we break down the dialogue, one clearly sees how Wilder uses links to propel the storyline forward.

                    SHELDRAKE
> All right, Gillis. You've got
> five minutes. **What's your story**
> **about?**

                    GILLIS
> **It's about a ball player, a rookie**
> **shortstop that's batting 347.** The
> poor kid was once mixed up in a hold-
> up. But he's trying to go straight
> except there's a **bunch of gamblers**
> who won't let him.

                    SHELDRAKE
> So **they tell the kid to throw the**

World Series, or else, huh?

GILLIS

More or less. Only for the end
I've got a gimmick that's real good.

SHELDRAKE

Got a title?

GILLIS

Bases Loaded. There's a 40-page
outline.

SHELDRAKE

(To the secretary)
Get the Readers' Department and
see what they have on **Bases Loaded.**

GILLIS

**They're pretty hot about it
over at Twentieth,** but I think
Zanuck's all wet. Can you see
Ty Power as a shortstop?
You've got the best man for it
right here on this lot. Alan Ladd.
Good change of pace for
Alan Ladd. There's another thing:
it's pretty simple to shoot. Lot
of outdoor stuff. Bet you could
make the whole thing for under a
million. And there's a great little
part for Bill Demarest. One of the
trainers, an old time player who
got beaned and goes out of his head
sometimes.

So, Gillis is doing his best to pitch the story in five minutes which, by today's standards, is a lifetime. The dialogue links are clear with the "story" linking to the title, linking to Alan Ladd which is the current Paramount best seller. At that moment, Sheldrake's assistant, Betty Schaefer, early 20s, walks in with a folder of papers. She doesn't notice Gillis, but begins by linking on the title of the script.

> **BETTY**
> Hello, Mr. Sheldrake. On that **Bases**
> **Loaded.** I covered it with a 2-page
> synopsis. (She holds it out)
> **But I wouldn't bother.**
>
>   **SHELDRAKE**
> **What's wrong with it?**
>
>   **BETTY**
> **It's from hunger.**
>
>   **SHELDRAKE**
> **Nothing** for Ladd?
>
>   **BETTY**
> **Just a rehash** of something that
> wasn't very good to begin with.
>
>   **SHELDRAKE**
> I'm sure you'll be glad to meet
> **Mr. Gillis.** He wrote it.

Betty's lead explicitly states that she wouldn't bother "with it" (the script) because "it's from hunger," and being "from hunger" isn't for Ladd. Not only is there nothing for Ladd, but it (the script) is just a "rehash." Off the rehash line, Sheldrake, through an indirect link, introduces Betty to the re-hasher, Gillis, even though he doesn't know her name. Betty is embarrassed.

>   **SHELDRAKE**
> This is **Miss Kramer.**
>
>   **BETTY**
> **Schaefer. Betty Schaefer. And**
> **right now I wish I could crawl**
> **into a hole and pull it in after**
> **me.**
>
>   **GILLIS**
> **If I could be of any help ...**

                    BETTY
I'm sorry, Mr. Gillis, but **I
just don't think it's any good.
I found it flat and banal.**

                    GILLIS
Exactly what **kind of material do
you recommend? James Joyce?
Dostoesvsky?**

                    SHELDRAKE
Name dropper.

                    BETTY
I just think **pictures should say
a little something.**

                    GILLIS
Oh, you're one of the **message
kids. Just a story won't do.
You'd have turned down Gone With the
Wind.**

                    SHELDRAKE
No, that was me. I said, Who
wants to see a Civil War picture?

                    BETTY
Perhaps the reason I hated **Bases
Loaded** is that I knew your name.
I'd always heard you had some talent.

                    GILLIS
**That was last year. This year
I'm trying to earn a living.**

                    BETTY
**So you take Plot 27-A, make it
glossy, make it slick …**

> SHELDRAKE
> Careful. Those are dirty words!
> You sound like a bunch of New
> York critics. Thank you, Miss
> Schaefer.

> BETTY
> Goodbye, Mr. Gillis.

> GILLIS
> Goodbye. **Next time I'll write**
> The Naked and the Dead.

Rather seamlessly, Wilder has introduced Miss Schaefer and linked their dialogues together with the focus being the script, *Bases Loaded*. He's also created a conflict between them on both intellectual and pragmatic levels that will play out later in the film. On her departure, Sheldrake returns to what Gillis alluded to earlier; namely, that Twentieth Century (that is, Zanuck) was keen on the script. Here's where the bogus information undermines Gillis.

> SHELDRAKE
> Well, seems like **Zanuck's** got
> himself a baseball picture.

> GILLIS
> Mr. Sheldrake, **I don't want you**
> **to think I thought this was going**
> **to win any Academy Award.**

> SHELDRAKE
> Of course, we're always looking
> for a **Betty Hutton.**
>   SHELDRAKE (Cont'd)
> **Do you see it as a Betty Hutton?**

> GILLIS
> **Frankly, no.**

> SHELDRAKE
> Now wait a minute. If we made
> it a **girls' softball team,** put

in a few numbers. Might make a
cute musical: **It Happened in
the Bull Pen the story of a
Woman.**

                    GILLIS
You trying to be funny? -- because
I'm all out of laughs. **I'm over a
barrel and I need a job.**

                    SHELDRAKE
Sure, Gillis. **If something should
come along…**

                    GILLIS
Along is no good. I need it now.

                    SHELDRAKE
Haven't got a thing.

                    GILLIS
**Any kind of assignment. Additional
Dialogue.**

                    SHELDRAKE
There's nothing, Gillis. Not
even if you were a relative.

                    GILLIS
Look, Mr. Sheldrake, **could you
let me have three hundred bucks**
yourself, as a personal loan?

                    SHELDRAKE
Could I? Gillis, last year somebody talked me into buying a ranch
in the valley. So I borrowed money
from the bank so I could pay for
the ranch. This year I had to
mortgage the ranch so I could keep
up my life insurance so I could

```
       borrow on the insurance so I could
       pay my income tax. Now if Dewey
       had been elected
                        /
                      ↙
                               GILLIS
```

In addition to the exact links, Wilder uses "come along—along" "could you—could I," there are the analogue links associated with getting additional work with the ironic inclusion of the line "dialogue writing." But Wilder is a master at linking dialogue and linking those dialogues is instrumental in creating a scenic arc that works on both the storyline level and the character level. There is nothing wasted in the dialogue and except for Sheldrake's nine lines of dialogue and Gillis's voice overs, no dialogue is more than six lines long. So, not only does Wilder's dialogue create an arc that links the beginning of the scene with the end of the scene, but it continues to advance both the storyline and the character. Although we'll see that economic kind of dialogue writing almost 20 years later in *The Graduate*, it's something that clearly establishes Wilder as a master of dialogue writing.

One of the major devices that Wilder uses and that Hollywood has come to deplore is the use of the voice over (VO), but Wilder's use of the VO is something that has always been and continues to be a tradition in European film. As a matter of fact, the narrator in *Jules & Jim*, Michel Subor, was almost as famous as Truffaut himself. So, it wasn't surprising that Wilder used that dialogous technique numerous times throughout the film as a way of expanding the storyline.

However, one of the most effective scenes in the film comes when Gillis first meets Norma Desmond, the now obsolete silent film star, and we hear their conversation about writing and screenplays. Accidentally thought of as a mortician who has come to bury her pet chimpanzee, Gillis is effectively ordered to sit down and talk to Desmond about her script, a script she's been working on for decades.

```
                     NORMA
       How long is a movie script these
       days? I mean, how many pages?

                     GILLIS
       Depends on what it is—a Donald
          Duck or Joan of Arc.
```

                    NORMA
        This is to be a very important
        picture. I have written it
           myself. Took me years.

                    GILLIS
             (Looking at the piles
                  of script)
        Looks like enough for six impor-
             tant pictures.

                    NORMA
         It's the story of Salome. I
        think I'll have DeMille direct it.

                    GILLIS
                   Uh-huh.

                    NORMA
        We've made a lot of pictures
                 together.

                    GILLIS
          And you'll play Salome?

                    NORMA
               Who else ?

                    GILLIS
         Only asking. I didn't know
        you were planning a comeback.

                    NORMA
        I hate that word. It is a return.
        A return to the millions of people
        who have never forgiven me for
           deserting the screen.

                    GILLIS
               Fair enough.

> NORMA
> Salome—what a woman! What a
> part! The Princess in love with
> a Holy man. She dances the Dance
> of the Seven Veils. He rejects
> her, so she demands his head on a
> golden tray, kissing his cold, dead
> lips.

> GILLIS
> They'll love it in Pomona.

> NORMA
> (Taking it straight)
> They will love it every place.
> (She reaches for a
> batch of pages from
> the heap)
> Read it. Read the scene just
> before she has him killed!

> GILLIS
> Right now? Never let another
> writer read your stuff. He
> may steal it.

> NORMA
> I am not afraid. Read it!
> NORMA (Cont'd)
> (Calling)

> Max! Max!
> (To Gillis)
> Sit down. Is there enough light?

> GILLIS
> I've got twenty-twenty vision.

Max has entered.

NORMA
Bring something to drink.

MAX
Yes. Madame.

He leaves. Norma turns to Gillis again.

NORMA
I said sit down.

After being forced to read the script for hours, Gillis finally comments, albeit disingenuously given the fact he's now figured out that he may have a way to pay off the $290 and get his car back. Of course, the deal Gillis makes with Norma to edit the script is the deal Faust made with Mephistopheles, and, of course, her script of Salome has direct comparisons with their own relationship. Although Gillis's head doesn't end up on a platter it might as well have, since both he and John the Baptist end up the same way; however, when the dialogue in the scene is deconstructed, one sees why Wilder was not only a master of dialogue, but a brilliant comedic writer.

NORMA
How long is a **movie script** these days? I mean, **how many pages?**

GILLIS
Depends on what it is—a Donald Duck or Joan or Arc.

NORMA
This is to be a very important **picture.** I have written it myself. Took me years.

GILLIS
(Looking at the piles of script)
Looks like enough for **six important pictures.**

NORMA
It's the story of Salome. **I
think I'll have DeMille direct it.**

GILLIS
Uh-huh.

NORMA
**We've made a lot of pictures
together.**

GILLIS
And **you'll play Salome?**

NORMA
Who else?

GILLIS
Only asking. **I didn't know
you** were planning a **comeback.**

NORMA
I hate that word. It is a **return.**
A **return** to the millions of people
who have never forgiven me for
deserting the screen.

GILLIS
Fair enough.

NORMA
Salome—what a woman! What a
part! The Princess in love with
a Holy man. She dances the Dance
of the Seven Veils. **He rejects
her, so she demands his head on a
golden tray, kissing his cold, dead
lips.**

                    GILLIS
          They'll love it in Pomona.

                    NORMA
               (Taking it straight)
        They will love it every place.
              (She reaches for a
              batch of pages from
                  the heap)
        **Read it. Read the scene just
         before she has him killed!**

                    GILLIS
        Right now? Never let another
         writer read your stuff. **He
              may steal it.**

                    NORMA
          I am not afraid. Read it!

               NORMA (Cont'd)
                 (Calling)

                 Max! Max!
               (To Gillis)
        Sit down. Is there enough light?

                    GILLIS
          I've got twenty-twenty vision.

Max has entered.

                    NORMA
          Bring something to drink.

                    MAX
               Yes. Madame.
He leaves. Norma turns to Gillis again.

                    NORMA
            I said sit down.

In terms of scene construction, Gillis arrives by accident and stays by accident. In other words, the end is linked to the beginning by virtue of the fact that his arrival is contingent on *escaping* from the Repo Man and yet when given the opportunity to *escape* from Norma Desmond he opts not to. The longer he stays with her, the more he is co-opted into remaining since he's attracted by the "good life" and the material possessions he receives from her. The irony of that is it's the system that does him in. Not only that, but at one point in the script Norma says:

> Still wonderful, isn't it? And
> no dialogue. We didn't need
> dialogue. We had faces. There
> just aren't any faces like that
> anymore. Well, maybe one—
> Garbo.

For someone like Wilder, whose wit and mastery of dialogue are always apparent, that particular line sums up just how important dialogue is to the scene.

4

North by Northwest (1959)

Screenplay by Ernest Lehman

The original shooting script of *North by Northwest* was submitted by Ernest Lehman on August 12, 1958 and weighed in at a hefty 180 pages (a minimum of three hours of film time). Clearly, he and Hitchcock had a lot of material to cull. It wasn't as onerous a task as the task Kubrick had to do with Nabokov's 300-plus-page script, but it was something that needed to be done to reduce it to a manageable 131 minutes (slightly over two hours) of film time. There are some extraordinary scenes in the film to choose from, but I've selected two: the scene at Midway Airport, Chicago and the sequence of scenes at Mt. Rushmore.

The scene at Midway Airport is an excellent example to use for a number of reasons which I'll go into. The scene opens with Thornhill arriving at the airport in a police car. In the background is the sound of planes taking off. The police escort Thornhill to the Northwest ticket counter and tell him to wait. The professor comes rushing to the ticket counter out of breath. The professor leans over the counter and whispers something to the reservationist who nods and hands him an envelope presumably with plane tickets then the clerk points down the terminal. The professor returns to Thornhill and the police, and shows the police his identification. The police leave and the professor takes Thornhill by the arm. I've only included the dialogue and minimal stage directions in the following.

                    THORNHILL
        I don't think I caught your name.

                    PROFESSOR
        I don't think I pitched it.

                    THORNHILL
    You're police, aren't you? Or is it F.B.I.?

                    PROFESSOR
        F.B.I., C.I.A, O.N.I ... We're
        all in the same alphabet soup.

                    THORNHILL
    Well, put this in your alphabet soup:
        I had nothing to do with that
            United Nations killing ...

                    PROFESSOR
            We know that.

                    THORNHILL
                You do?
    Then what's the idea of the police
        chasing me all over the map.

                    PROFESSOR
    We never interfere with the police
        unless absolutely necessary.
        It has become necessary.

                    THORNHILL
    I take it, then, I'm to be cleared.

                    PROFESSOR
        I do wish you'd walk faster,
    Mr. Thornhill. We'll miss the plane.

                    THORNHILL
          Where are we going? New York
                or Washington?

                    PROFESSOR
          Rapid City, South Dakota.

                    THORNHILL
            Rapid City? What for?

                    PROFESSOR
            It's near Mt. Rushmore.

                    THORNHILL
          I've already seen Mt. Rushmore.

                    PROFESSOR
          So has your friend Mr. Vandamm.

                    THORNHILL
                  Vandamm?

                    PROFESSOR
          A rather formidable gentleman, eh?

                    THORNHILL
          And what about that treacherous
                tramp with him.

                    PROFESSOR
              Miss Kendall?

                    THORNHILL
                  Yeah.

                    PROFESSOR
          His mistress. We know all about her.

                    THORNHILL
            What's Vandamm up to?

PROFESSOR
Let's say he's a kind of ... importer-exporter.

THORNHILL
Of what?

PROFESSOR
Oh,you could say ... government secrets perhaps?

THORNHILL
Why don't you grab him?

PROFESSOR
Too much we still don't know
about his organization.

THORNHILL
Uh-huh. Well what's Mt. Rushmore
got to do with all this?

PROFESSOR
Vandamm has a place near there.
We think it's his jumping off
point to leave the country tomorrow
night.

THORNHILL
And you're going to stop him ...

PROFESSOR
No.

THORNHILL
Then ... what are we going there for?

PROFESSOR
To set his mind at
ease about George Kaplan.

THORNHILL
You, huh?

                        PROFESSOR
                        Eh?

                        THORNHILL
            You're George Kaplan, aren't you....

                    PROFESSOR (blandly)
             Oh no, Mr. Thornhill. There is
             no such person as George Kaplan.

                        THORNHILL
                Is no such person?

The professor tells Thornhill that they'll talk on the plane even though Thornhill
says he knows all about Kaplan—been in his hotel room, worn his clothes
(some of which had dandruff). But the professor insists that Kaplan doesn't
exist, but pleads with Thornhill to keep up the ruse for another day. At that
point, Thornhill points a finger at the professor. Just as he's about to speak
there is the sudden roar of engines as a plane prepares to taxi away from the
ramp. As the plane begins to taxi, its engines create a deafening roar. The two
men are trying to talk to each other, however we cannot hear what they're
saying and can only speculate what is being said based on their gestures. The
professor speaks calmly while Thornhill is arguing, denying, protesting, etc.
At the same time, the professor is tugging on Thornhill's arm trying to get him
towards the plane. Although we cannot hear the dialogue, we can assume
that the professor is telling him about the George Kaplan plot which was previously stated. As the two men approach another plane, the professor seems
to be appealing to Thornhill about something, while the latter shakes his head
vigorously. What's brilliant about this portion of the scene is that Lehman
allows the characters to "gesture" their dialogue rather than say it. While the
engines roar, one can see both Thornhill and the professor arguing, gesturing,
etc. about what the viewer already knows. Rather than re-state what's been
established, Lehman has the characters acting out the dialogue so that, when
the plane takes off, he can re-engage with the viewer with new dialogue.

                        THORNHILL
            Look, you started this crazy decoy
         business without me! Finish it without me!

                        PROFESSOR
            And well we might have if you
               hadn't stumbled into it.

                    THORNHILL
        I think you should give me a medal
          and a very long vacation instead
       of asking me to go on being a target
             just so that your Number One,
              or whatever you're call him,
                 doesn't get shot at!

                    PROFESSOR
       Not shot at, Mr. Thornhill found out.
    Once he's found out, he's as good as dead.
    And thanks to you clouds of suspicion are
                    forming.

                    THORNHILL
                 Thanks to me!

The professor encourages Thornhill to get on the plane, but Thornhill goes
into a diatribe about who he is, the wives and bartenders he has to support,
and how he doesn't want to play a cloak-and-dagger role. The professor asks
if that's his "final answer" to which Thornhill says yes. The professor looks
seriously at him and holds out his hand as if to say goodbye. Thornhill begins
to shake his hand.

                    PROFESSOR
                 Goodbye then,
        If I thought there was any chance
         of changing your mind, I'd talk
          about Miss Kendall, whom you
          obviously disapprove of for
                 good reason …

                    THORNHILL
           Yeah for using sex like some
          people use a fly-swatter … For
          trying to have me exterminated.

                    PROFESSOR
        I don't suppose it would matter to
        you that she was probably forced
           to do whatever she did ...
            in order to protect herself.

> THORNHILL
> Protect herself from what?

> PROFESSOR
> Suspicion ... exposure ... assassination.
> Forgive me for referring to our Number One
> as a man, Mr. Thornhill.
> It's about all I can do to help keep her
> *safe* while she's in all this terrible danger ...

At that point, Thornhill can't really believe what he's hearing as he attempts to come to terms with his ambivalent feelings.

> PROFESSOR'S VOICE (o.s.)
> I know you didn't mean to,
> but I'm afraid you have put her in a most delicate
> situation
> and much more than her life is at stake.

If we break down the scene into its component dialogic parts, a number of things become apparent. Certainly, we can see how the dialogue links play a major part in how the scene evolves.

> THORNHILL
> **I don't think** I caught your name.

> PROFESSOR
> **I don't think** I pitched it.

> THORNHILL
> You're police, aren't you? Or is it **F.B.I.**?

> PROFESSOR
> **F.B.I.**, C.I.A, O.N.I. ... We're
> all in the same **alphabet soup.**

> THORNHILL
> Well, put this in your **alphabet soup:**
> **I had nothing to do with that**
> **United Nations killing...**

> PROFESSOR
> **We know that.**

>   THORNHILL
>   You do?
>   Then what's the idea of the police
>   **chasing me** all over the map.
>
>   PROFESSOR
>   We **never interfere** with the police
>   unless absolutely necessary.
>   It has become necessary.

As I've indicated, the dialogue links are critical in moving the scene towards its natural ending and that's exactly what Lehman has done so far. At this point in the scene, Thornhill presumes he'll be cleared though the professor ignores the suggestion and asks him to walk faster or else they'll miss their plane.

>   THORNHILL
>   **Where are we going?**
>   New York or Washington?
>
>   PROFESSOR
>   **Rapid City, South Dakota.**
>
>   THORNHILL
>   **Rapid City?** What for?
>
>   PROFESSOR
>   It's near **Mt. Rushmore.**
>
>   THORNHILL
>   I've already seen **Mt. Rushmore.**
>
>   PROFESSOR
>   **So has your friend, Mr. Vandamm.**
>
>   THORNHILL
>   **Vandamm?**
>
>   PROFESSOR
>   A rather **formidable gentleman,** eh?

THORNHILL
And what about that treacherous
tramp with him.

PROFESSOR
Miss Kendall?

THORNHILL
Yeah.

PROFESSOR
His **mistress.** We know all about **her.**

THORNHILL
What's **Vandamm** up to?

PROFESSO
Let's say he's a kind of...**importer-exporter.**

THORNHILL
Of what?

PROFESSOR
Oh, you could say ... **government secrets** perhaps?

THORNHILL
Why don't you grab him?

PROFESSOR
Too much we still don't know
about his organization.

THORNHILL
Uh-huh. Well what's **Mt. Rushmore**
got to do with all this?

PROFESSOR
Vandamm has a place near there.
We think it's his jumping off
point to leave the country tomorrow
night.

Once again, the dialogue links not only move the scene towards a natural conclusion, but bring up the vital aspects of the scene; namely, where they are going, the introduction of Miss Kendall and her relationship with Vandamm and why Vandamm is so critical. Thornhill then asks the professor if they (i.e. the authorities) are going to stop him before he escapes. The professor says, "no" which prompts Thornhill to ask what's the reason for going to Mt. Rushmore.

> PROFESSOR
> To set his mind at
> ease about **George Kaplan.**
>
> THORNHILL
> **You, huh?**
>
> PROFESSOR
> **Eh?**
>
> THORNHILL
> You're **George Kaplan,** aren't you?
>
> PROFESSOR (blandly)
> Oh no, Mr. Thornhill. **There is
> no such person as George Kaplan.**
>
> THORNHILL
> Is **no such person?** (302)

Not only does this exchange focus on the mystery behind who George Kaplan is, but augments the mystery since Thornhill has been attempting to escape this "mistaken identity" throughout the film. At that point, Thornhill becomes a bit annoyed with how he's been "played."

> THORNHILL
> Look, you started this **crazy decoy
> business** without me! **Finish it** without me!
>
> PROFESSOR
> And well we might have **if you
> hadn't stumbled into it.**

                    THORNHILL
    I think you should give me a medal
      and a <u>very</u> long <u>vacation</u> instead
    of asking me to go on being a target
      just so that your **Number One,**
        or whatever you call him,
          doesn't get shot at!

                    PROFESSOR
    Not shot at, Mr. Thornhill found out.
    Once he's found out, he's as good as dead.
    And thanks to you clouds of suspicion are
                    forming.

Not only do the dialogue links maintain the integrity of the scene and move it along, but they augment Thornhill's apparent disdain for Miss Kendall who, at this point, Thornhill believes is Vandamm's mistress and that he has no intention of being involved any longer. With that, the professor "feigns" to end the arrangement.

                    PROFESSOR
                Goodbye then,
      If I thought there was any chance
      of changing your mind, I'd talk
        about **Miss Kendall,** whom you
          obviously disapprove of for
                good reason...

                    THORNHILL
      Yeah for using sex like some
      people use a fly-swatter ... For
      trying to have me exterminated.

                    PROFESSOR
      I don't suppose it would matter to
      you that **she was probably forced**
          to do whatever she did...
        in order to **protect herself.**

                    THORNHILL
      Protect herself from what?

> PROFESSOR
> **Suspicion ... exposure ... assassination.**
> Forgive me for referring to our **Number One**
>   **as a man,** Mr. Thornhill.
> It's about all I can do to help keep **her**
> *safe* while she's in all this terrible danger ...

This is the point that professor plays his "trump" card by telling Thornhill that "number one" is actually Miss Kendall. The revelation that Miss Kendall actually works for the authorities suddenly puts Thornhill in a rather precarious position and the professor tries to drive the point home in the last portion of dialogue in the scene.

> PROFESSOR'S VOICE (o.s.)
> I know you didn't mean to,
> but I'm afraid you have put **her** in a most delicate
> situation
> and much more than her life is at stake.

At that moment, another plane arrives with its landing lights illuminating Thornhill's rather puzzled face. The sound of the engines increases as if accenting the mounting determination within Thornhill and the pending decision he has to make. Lehman has done a brilliant job of linking the beginning of the scene with the end of the scene. In the opening, Thornhill arrives at the airport presumably to fly somewhere; in the middle, Thornhill refuses to fly somewhere; and in the end, Thornhill does fly somewhere. To that end, the scene maintains a certain amount of scenic integrity and, at the same time, reinforces the main foci of the scene, advances the storyline, develops character, and elicits conflicts which are the four items I mentioned that must be established and maintained in any well-balanced scene. These aspects are all unified through the use of the dialogue links that keep the dialogue flowing from beginning to end.

5

Jules & Jim (1962)

Screenplay by François Truffaut and Jean Gruault

I'm making a slight departure from the other films I've been writing about because *Jules & Jim* is different for several reasons: (1) it's a "foreign film"; (2) there is no English translation of the script; and (3) the way Truffaut uses dialogue (especially the preponderant use of voice overs which are really disliked by most American filmmakers) and scene construction is unique to European filmmaking and to French filmmaking in particular.

We can actually begin with the rapid cuts of scenes beneath the opening credits and before the actual onset of the storyline since those are the most critical collection of scenes in the film as they summarize what lies ahead. The film opens with *Voice Over #1* with Catherine saying:

> *You said "I love you."*
> *I said "Wait."*
> *I was about to say "Take me."*
> *You said, "Go."*

What's of interest here is the ambivalence associated with the opening that will be the foundation for the entire film. The "*you*," presumably, is a male. It could be either Jules or Jim; it really doesn't matter because they are both in love with her. When she says she was "about" to say "Take me" (which is completely different than saying "Take me") either Jules or Jim say "Go." The implication is that, for whatever reason, the *male* doesn't want her. The film then explodes with the music and series of scenes which allude to upcoming scenes:

1 Jules and Jim opening a basket of clothes

2 A close shot of Catherine laughing

3 Jules and Jim jogging together

4 Jules and Jim conceding to each other as to whom should walk through the gate first

5 Jules walking with a woman, while Jim walks behind him with another woman

6 A young child (whom we find out is Sabine, Jules' daughter) playing darts; she throws a bulls-eye

7 Jules and Jim pretending to sword fight with brooms

8 Jules being carried by Jim who pretends he's blind and uses a cane

9 An hourglass which is about to run out of sand

10 An impressionist painting of two lovers

11 A man (whom we find out is Albert) playing a guitar

12 A character that appears to be Jim walking with Sabine

13 Jules and Jim jogging around a track

Fade to black

Of those 13 scenes, seven are with Jules and Jim; the others are of: Catherine; Albert (one of Catherine's lovers); Sabine (Catherine's daughter); the hourglass; and the impressionist painting. These are not aleatory scenes. Clearly, the hourglass running out of time is a significant part of the overall structure of the film, as is the painting, for two reasons: (1) it's an Impressionist painting (reflective of the era); and (2) it is a painting of two lovers. Whether the painting is meant to be by Picasso, I'm not sure; however, the scene with Catherine is placed in between two scenes with Jules and Jim which is hardly coincidental.

At the conclusion of these 13 scenes (and you can make of that number as you wish), the film "re-opens" with Jules and Jim playing dominoes perhaps in an apartment while *Voice Over #2* begins telling the story alluded to at the beginning.

The *Voice Over #3* continues with Jim looking through a book and Jules looking on:

The next day they saw their first real conversation. Then they met every day.

The VO continues as Jules and Jim are walking somewhere outside:

> They taught the other his language and culture until the early hours. They shared their poems and translated them together. They also shared a relative indifference to money. They chatted easily. Neither had ever had such an attentive listener.

The VO continues now with Jules and Jim and two young women in a boat with Jim rowing:

> Jules had no girls in Paris and he wanted one.

The VO continues now with Jules and Jim meeting two women:

> Jim had several.

The VO continues now with Jim and a woman talking at a café:

> He introduced Jules to a musician.

The CAMERA slides to another table with Jules sitting by himself.

> Things started out well. They were in love for about a week.

The VO continues now with Jules and Jim walking in the woods with two women whom we cannot see.

> Then a free and easy girl came along who stayed up all night in cafés.

The VO continues now with Jim shaking hands with another woman while Jules looks on.

> Next it was a pretty blond widow. The three went out together. She confused Jules whom she found nice, but clumsy.

The VO continues now with Jules and two women. "She brought him a quiet friend. Too quiet for Jim."
The VO continues with Jules entering a hotel.

> Finally, against Jim's advice Jules took up with professionals. But found no satisfaction there.

The voice over, which has gone on for 02.43 minutes, establishes most of the narrative including the back-story. What's implied from the beginning is that if Jules and Jim are inseparable friends from the start, then it's axiomatic that someone, probably a woman, will change all of that. The cliché works: two's company, three's a crowd.

Thérèse shows up, and after escaping from Merlin (odd name for an abuser) runs away with Jules and Jim. She asks for a place to spend the night. Jim says no, because he's meeting Gilberte and that information puts us on notice that he has a "steady" woman.

Thérèse goes home with Jules. Nothing happens between them, though we get the refrain of the hourglass and we see the painting in his apartment.

Jim, on the other hand, spends the night with Gilberte, his lover, but refuses to stay after dawn since that would seem like they were "married." One can see that on the wall over the bed is a painting that is clearly supposed to be a Picasso: man, woman, and child. Jim goes home.

Next day at a café, Thérèse picks up another guy and leaves Jules who accepts the rejection. His acceptance establishes a lot of things about his character; mainly, that he does not get too emotional over these rejections, but, rather, accepts them as part of life. In a way, it's a very Existentialist approach to the human condition and not an uncommon perspective given the time the film was produced. As a matter of fact, according to Existentialist thought, "an 'authentic life,' cannot be lived by following the run of any kind of 'herd' and its collective beliefs and preoccupations, but only by resolutely living out of a profoundly personal self—out of the recognized and accepted loneliness of an individuality that finds itself in a dark and meaningless universe." To that extent, both Jules and Catherine are much more in line with that kind of thinking than Jim.

As far as Thérèse is concerned, if she's there at the beginning, then she should probably show up at the end: which she does.

At the café, Jules talks about the three women in his life: Lucie, Birgitta, and Helga—all of whom he has loved and he begins to sketch one of them on the café table. As he does, there's another *Voice Over* #4:

> Jules sketched a woman's face in bold strokes on the round table. Jim wanted to buy the table, but the owner would only sell all twelve tables as a set.

What's of interest is that the sketch looks remarkably like a line drawing by Picasso of whom I'll speak later.

Jules and Jim visit a friend, Albert, who was the musician in the beginning of the film. As they take some chairs from the kitchen into the sitting room, one can see yet another Picasso (or, perhaps, Braque) hanging in the kitchen and Jules alludes to the fact that Albert knows all the French painters who will eventually be famous.

Albert shows them a few slides of some stone sculptures that he saw on a trip. Both Jules and Jim are taken by one statue in particular, that of a woman, which Jim wants to see again. *Voice Over #5*: "The tranquil smile on the crudely sculpted face mesmerized them." The voice over continues as Jules and Jim are visiting the same island:

> The statue was in an outdoor museum on an Adriatic Island. They set off immediately to see it. They both had the same white suit made. They spent an hour by the statue. It exceeded their expectations. They walked rapidly around it in silence. They didn't speak of it until the next day. Had they ever met such a smile? Never. And if they ever met it? They'd follow it.

What's of interest here is that after 09.18 minutes, Truffaut uses the technique of introducing Catherine without introducing Catherine. The fact they are both overwhelmed by the statue prepares us for something to follow. This technique, if you will, of introducing a character either by alluding to the character through dialogue or through a medium is something we also see in *The Graduate*.

The voice over continues as Jules and Jim are back in Paris: "Jules and Jim returned home full of this revelation. Paris took them gently back in."

Back in Paris, we see them boxing at the gym. During a break, Jim reads part of his novel to Jules, confessing that it is more like an autobiography based on their friendship. Although the names of his two characters are Jacques and Julien, at one point Jim refers to them as Don Quixote and Sancho Panza—although he doesn't say which is which. Jules suggests that he translates it into German and they head for the showers.

In the showers, Jules' cousin wrote him that some girls who studied with him in Munich are coming to Paris: one is from Belgium, one is from Holland, and one is from France. They are going to dine at Jules' apartment the next night.

In the next scene, three young women show up for a dinner at Jules' apartment. It is at that time, that we meet Catherine, who, not coincidentally, looks exactly like the stone statue that they were both enamored of, appears at 11.15 minutes of the film. The *Voice Over #6* says: Catherine, the French girl, had the smile of the statue on the island. Her nose, mouth, chin and forehead bore the nobility of a province she personified as a child in a religious celebration. It started like a dream."

When she reaches the bottom of the stairs, both Jules and Jim are waiting for her, while the other two women are by themselves.

Jules suggests that instead of linking arms, they put their feet on each other's feet under the table and drink. The *Voice Over #7* says:

> And thus they did. In high spirits, Jules moved his feet away. Jim's feet stayed a moment near Catherine's, who gently moved hers away first. A shy, happy smile played on Jules' lips and told the others he held them in his heart.

The VO continues with Jules and Jim getting a massage:

> He saw Catherine everyday on his own. But the two friends naturally met at the gymnasium.

Jules invites Jim to dinner that evening and right before they enter the apartment, Jules turns to Jim and says: "Pas cel-là, Jim!" ["But not this one, Jim. Okay?"]. Jim nods.

The three of them go out, but not before Catherine dresses like a man, wearing a cap and a drawn moustache. Jules calls her Thomas. Without going into any Freudian interpretations of what that might mean, what becomes patently clear is that Catherine literally comes in between Jules and Jim. She is asked by a passer-by for a light and then we hear the *Voice Over #8* say:

> Catherine was proud of her successful disguise. The men were moved, as if by a symbol they didn't understand.

In fact, that's true. They didn't understand the symbol at all. It's said that it's raining to which Catherine says, "If it's raining, let's go to the seashore. We leave tomorrow." Now there's no discussion about this. She's decided and there is no argument from either one of the men. Then she proposes a race across the bridge. Jules says one, two and she takes off before the count of three. The "race" on the bridge is significant for the main reason that SHE "cheats" by starting early, so she's capable of winning. This aspect of her character, that she is in "control" or wants to be in control of things is established very early in the film and continues throughout.

She asks Jim to help her with her bags the following morning and she leaves, which allows Jules to give us a brief back-story of her past, her parents, and including the fact she teaches Shakespeare.

We then hear the *Voice Over #9* say:

Jim considered her to be Jules' and didn't try to form a clear picture of her. Catherine once again wore that calm smile. It came naturally to her and expressed everything about her.

Jim comes the next day to carry her bags to the train station. This is an excellent scene in terms of discussing her character and motives.

1 In the previous scene it is HER idea to go to the beach.

2 SHE asks Jim, not Jules, to come help her with her bags.

3 SHE packs enough stuff for three people including a bike, a duffle bag, and a suitcase.

4 SHE is burning some papers which she refers to as "lies" and her gown catches fire. What these lies are is not clear, but, presumably, they are letters; the burning gown is open to interpretation.

5 Jim, then, sweeps up the "lies."

6 SHE plans to take a bottle of sulfuric acid with her. Jim asks why, she simply states "for men who tell lies." Jim advises against it since it will burn her clothes, although he doesn't pass judgment. She pours out the acid, since Jim says she can buy the acid anywhere; however, the "bottle" is important for some reason.

Clearly, there is a relationship here between "lies" and "men." What is emphatically not present is her motive for burning what appear to be crumpled letters and for taking the acid on vacation. Jim doesn't invade her decisions with questions, but it's patently clear that Catherine has had her failures with men and, as we discover, she's had a lot of them.

The train to the coast, at which time we hear *Voice Over #10* say:

They searched up and down the coast before finding the house of their dreams. Thought too big, it was isolated, imposing, white inside and out, and empty.

What is brilliant about the morning scene when they step out on their respective balconies is that Truffaut has presented us with this picture:

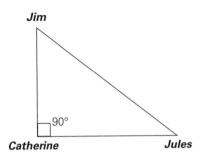

It is not merely a "triangle," but a specific kind of triangle: a *right triangle*. This was not done by accident. A right triangle (or right-angled triangle, formerly called a *rectangled triangle*) has one of its internal angles equal to 90° (a right angle). The side opposite to the right angle is the hypotenuse; it is the longest side in the right triangle. The other two sides are the *legs* or catheti (singular: cathetus) of the triangle. Right triangles obey the Pythagorean theorem: the sum of the squares of the two legs is equal to the square of the hypotenuse: $a^2 + b^2 = c^2$, where a and b are the lengths of the legs and c is the length of the hypotenuse. The distance between Catherine and both Jules and Jim is the same; the distance between Jules and Jim is longer precisely because of Catherine's position in the triangle. What's even more engaging is the fact that the word "*hypotenuse*" comes from the Greek which means "*to stretch*" and that's exactly what Catherine has done to the friends: stretched them. Please acknowledge that it is Catherine who says "let's go to the beach," thus continuing to be the person in control.

They go out for an "adventurous" walk with Jules and Jim wearing the exact same clothes except for different caps. They discover the following: a piece of tire, a bottle, old shoes, a can, matches, a postcard, a shard, presumably of a porcelain vase, a cup, and a cigarette butt, and a pack of English cigarettes. You can make of those discoveries what you will, but what they all have in common is the fact they are old and they have been used. To that end, they each have a story behind them.

Jules asks Jim if he should marry her and Jim's response is very telling: "Is she cut out to be a wife and mother? I'm afraid she'll never be happy on this earth. She's a vision for all, but not meant for any one man alone." Of course, the comment is prescient because that's exactly who she is and that's exactly what happens to the three of them. She's constantly the one who controls: she decides not to walk anymore, so they carry her; she asks them to help her with the clothes on the clothesline; as they leave to go cycling she says, "Let's go, kids."

Subsequently, they cycle to the beach at which time she begins talking about what sounds like centrifugal force, that things are pulled to the outside. Centrifugal force comes from the Latin for "center fleeing." This is in combination with the physics of centripetal force, which is the push or pull on a moving object toward the center of its curved path. In other words, Catherine believes in that the attraction pulls outside towards a solid crust in which this bubble exists. As they leave, Jules asks Catherine to marry him. Because he's had few women and she's had many men, she thinks it might work out between them. As they ride back towards the house, Catherine leads.

Dominoes. The game of dominoes appears in several scenes. This is the second time Jules and Jim play together. What's interesting here is that the game is only played by the two of them. Most domino games are *blocking games*, i.e. the objective is to empty one's hand while blocking the opponent. Each domino is a rectangular tile with a line dividing its *face* into two square *ends*. Each end is marked with a number of *spots* (also called pips) or is *blank*. In *blocking games* the scoring happens at the end of the game. After a player has emptied his hand, thereby winning the game, the score consists of the total pip count of the losing teams' hands. In some rules the pip count of the remaining stock is added. If a game is blocked because no player can move, the winner can often be determined by counting the pips in all players' hands. What's of interest here is that neither Jules nor Jim ever wins.

While they play, Catherine talks to herself. First, about a dream in which she gets pregnant by Napoleon, who leaves her. Poor Napoleon. Then she talks about the prayer, "Our father who art in heaven" but she misunderstood it and thought it was "arts" in heaven. Neither Jules nor Jim react and she gets upset with that because she's not the center of attention.

During their game, Catherine intervenes and talks about her look and why her look has always been dour until now. Truffaut brilliantly stops the film at different intervals so that her facial expressions look like photographs capturing different moods.

The next day it rains. She misses Paris so SHE decides they should return—which they do.

Jim comes to their apartment. Says he's just sold his book and he brings a painting which is clearly a Picasso and specifically from his *Blue Period* (1901–4). Picasso and Roché, who was an art critic, were friends and the latter was responsible for Picasso's coming to America. Roché did not write novels until late in his life. But the use of Picasso's work also establishes a time period which the characters never speak of. He also brings a back-scratcher for Catherine, which is a comment on what happened in a previous scene in which she asks one of them to scratch her back for her. Jim says he has three tickets for a play that night by a Swedish author. Jules tips the hourglass and says they have to get dressed when the sand runs out.

The *Voice Over #11* says:

Jim saw his friends often and enjoyed their company. The great Merovingian bed was officially inaugurated. Jules' two pillows lay side by side on the bed, and the bed smelled nice. Catherine grew more beautiful and learned to live again.

Of course, we don't know why she didn't live before, but, presumably, it had to do with a man.

The play over, Catherine claps enthusiastically. They do not. Presumably, the play is *Miss Julie* (1888) and the playwright, August Strindberg. This is a major turning point in the film. Not only is the name Julie tied with Jules, but the play itself is a comment on Catherine/Julie's character. The play was banned in Sweden and in Great Britain for a number of reasons.

"The root of contention over the play stemmed from its frank portrayal of sex. Not only does *Miss Julie* contain a sexual encounter between a lower-class servant and an upper-class aristocrat (in itself outrageous for the times), the play clearly describes the sex act as something apart from the concept of love. The idea of intercourse based completely on lust was scandalous to late-nineteenth-century thinking and enough to provoke censure. And it was nothing more than the idea of sex without love that caused the trouble: the act is only referred to in the play, not actually depicted on stage.

"Strindberg's drama focuses on the downfall of the aristocratic *Miss Julie*, a misfit in her society (the author refers to her in his preface as a "man-hating half-woman"). Julie rebels against the restrictions placed on her as a woman and as a member of the upper-class. From the beginning of the play, her behavior is shown to alienate her peer class and shock the servants. She displays a blatant disregard for class and gender conventions: at one moment claiming that class differences should not exist, and the next demanding proper treatment as a woman of aristocracy. Her antics result in her social downfall, a loss of respect from her servants, and, ultimately, her suicide."[1]

However, Catherine likes the girl because "She wants to be free. She invents her own life every moment." While Jules discusses why he didn't like the play and why fidelity for a woman is more important than fidelity for a man, Catherine walks silently in front of them.

He then quotes Baudelaire: "Woman is natural, therefore abominable," and proceeds to quote more misogynistic things about women. Catherine leaves them to their talk and walks away saying that she "protests." Living the

[1] http://www.enotes.com/miss-julie [accessed May 2013].

line she spoke earlier and wanting to live an authentic life, she jumps in the river losing her *chapeau*. Of course, the subtext of the play is a comment on Catherine herself since she'd feel an overwhelming affinity for Julie.

In *Voice Over #12* we hear:

Catherine's plunge into the river so astonished Jim that he drew it the next day, though he didn't usually draw. Admiration for Catherine welled up in him and he sent her a kiss in his mind. He was calm. He imagined himself swimming with her and holding his breath to frighten Jules.

When Jim asks why, she doesn't answer, although he calls her "crazy." The voice over continues:

Catherine's hat drifted away in the current.

In the carriage on the way home, the voice over continues:

Jules was pale, silent, less self-assured and more handsome than ever. Catherine wore her same smile, like a modest young general after his first brilliant campaign. No one spoke of her plunge.

As Jim begins to leave, SHE asks him to meet her at their café the next morning at seven to talk. As he waits, the *Voice Over #13* says:

With his usual optimism, Jim had arrived late. He was upset with himself, afraid he had missed her. Jim thought, 'A girl like that might well have left at 7.01. A woman like that could have rushed across the room never noticing me behind my newspaper, and left.' He kept repeating to himself, 'A woman like that.' But just what was she like? For the first time, he began to really think about Catherine.

The clock changes from 7.10 to 7.20 to 7.30 to 7.50, and then he leaves. It's at that point that she shows up. Once again, it reveals how SHE is in control of them. For her, time is relative. It's an arbitrary decision to make exact appointments because she lives in the moment. Clearly, Jim doesn't understand that.

Jules and Catherine are to marry in Germany, but at that point World War I begins (1914–18). In *Voice Over #14* we hear:

War broke out a few days later. Jules and Jim were called up by their respective armies and lost touch for a long time.

What follows is stock footage of World War I with the *Voice Over #15* saying:

> The war dragged on and on and men settled into it. Gradually a normal life emerged, marked by the different seasons, with its down time, routines, pauses, and even distractions. Jim received parcels from Gilberte. He almost saw her a few times, but each time his leave was canceled. Then, in spring of 1916, he spent a week in Paris.

On leave, Jim visits Gilberte and they talk of marriage. Shift back to the front lines. From the battlefield, Jules writes a love letter to Catherine, who is pregnant with their "son"; he says he's going to the Russian front which, on the face of it, doesn't sound promising. There's more stock footage of the war until the *Voice Over #16* says:

> Jules' country had lost the war. Jim's country had won. But the true victory was that both were alive. They made contact through a neutral country and resumed correspondence. Catherine and Jules lived in a chalet on the Rhine. A daughter, Sabine, was born. Jim wrote Jules, 'Should I marry and have children too?' Jules replied, 'Come and judge for yourself.' Catherine added a few words of invitation. Jim left. It was such an important event that he took his time getting there. He lingered along the Rhine, stopping in several towns. A large Paris paper was publishing his articles on postwar Germany. He wanted to revisit the places where he had fought the hardest. Some places had been bombed so heavily that the land was a mass of iron where nothing could ever grow again. They became cemeteries where Jim searched crosses for familiar names and schoolchildren were already brought to visit.

As the train approaches the station, the voice over continues:

> Catherine was waiting at the station with her daughter. Her glance shone with fantasy and daring just barely held in check.

Catherine has given birth to a girl, Sabine. Of all the names to give their daughter, Sabine is an interesting one. The name means, "being of the Sabine tribe." Legend says that the Romans abducted Sabine women to populate the newly built town: the first recorded example of alleged bride kidnapping. The resultant conflict ended only by the women throwing themselves and their children between the armies of their fathers and their husbands. Clearly, Sabine comes in between Catherine and the men. At the train station, Jim is met by a rather subdued Catherine and Sabine. What's very interesting in the film is that emotions are all underplayed especially between Catherine and her men.

Voice Over #17 continues:

Jim felt she was making a long delayed appearance for their café rendezvous and had dressed up especially for him. She took him to their chalet, surrounded by pines near a sloping meadow.

There's a kind of quiet discomfort in the chalet when they all get together for the first time since the end of the war. We find out that Jim is now a novelist and Jules is a nature writer. In showing Jim around the house we see that both Catherine and Jules have separate rooms, which clearly is an indication that things are not as good as they could be. Jim plays with Sabine.

As Jules and Jim play dominoes once again, *Voice Over #18* begins by saying:

Jules and Jim resumed their long-interrupted conversation. They talked about the war. Jules avoided talking about his family. Catherine was both kind and stern to Jules, but Jim sensed something was not going well.

Jim tells Jules that motherhood fits her. He says that Catherine is less the grasshopper and more the ant, which is clearly an allusion to *The Ant and the Grasshopper*, also known as *The Grasshopper and the Ant*, a fable attributed to Aesop, providing a moral lesson about hard work and preparation. The implication, of course, is that Catherine has "changed"—which she has not.

As Jules talks to Jim, sitting next to the hourglass, the sand of which has run out, he tells him that she's run away, has taken lovers (three that he knows of) as a kind of "retribution," and that Albert, whom we met earlier, is in love with her and wants to marry her and take Sabine. He reports these incidents with utter detachment as he always has. She has terrible mood swings (bi-polar). After that disclosure, the scene ends.

Voice over #19 from Jim's POV [point of view] of the house:

Jim could see the chalet from his bedroom window. So, Catherine was there, the radiant queen, ready to fly off. Jim wasn't surprised. He recalled Jules' mistakes with Thérèse, Lucie and all the others. He knew Catherine was terribly demanding. Jim was sad for Jules, yet he could not condemn Catherine. She jumped in men's arms like she'd jumped in the river. A threat hung over the household. The second week began. Fade to black.

Of course, one cannot entirely blame Jules for what Thérèse did since she was clearly an opportunist. Any man would work for Thérèse since she, like Catherine, lived in the moment. For some reason, Jim didn't get that.

The wine vs. beer scene is instrumental. Not only is Catherine sitting between the two of them, but she's clearly attacking Jules because he talked about German beer. She counters with French wines being the best in the world. No argument there, but Jules is talking about beer and French beer is not the finest in the world. It's yet another example of how she likes to control the situation. She goes on and on and on naming French wines until Jules decides he wants to talk to Jim about the war. At that moment, Catherine decides to "run away." In a scene that continues to expand her character as someone who must be in control, Catherine runs out of the house and Jim, not Jules, follows her. At that point, she makes a kind of confession about her life, but wants Jim to talk about his.

And we get the *Voice Over #20*:

Jim began: 'There were once two young men ...' whom he didn't name. He told of their friendship in Paris, before meeting a certain girl, the impact she made on them, and all that ensued. Even the line, 'Not this one, Jim.' There he couldn't avoid saying his own name. He described the trio's outings, their trip to the seashore. Catherine saw that Jim remembered everything about her very clearly. She argued a few points on principle, and added other details. He described the missed rendezvous at the café, and the three of them seen through his eyes. He spoke of Jules' hidden qualities and how he sensed Jules could never keep Catherine.

Jim, then, discloses his interest in her and she tells Jim about what attracted her to Jules and what distanced her from him. The fact that Jules' mother offended her (we don't know why) and she took it out on Jules by sleeping with an old lover the night before the wedding is very telling about her character, in that everything she says is very egocentric. If she does not have complete control over people and situations, she's unhappy. Jim is too much in love with her to see that. And so the *Voice Over #21*, continues:

Jim desired her, but he fought it back more than ever. She mustn't leave. To what extent was Jim about to act for Jules' sake? For his own sake? He would never know. Perhaps she was seducing him, though Jim was far from sure of it. It was impossible to tell. Catherine revealed her goals only when she'd achieved them. Fade to black.

In a subsequent scene, Albert shows up with his guitar. Sitting with Jules and Albert, Jim recounts the story of the soldier and the letter he sent to his epistolary lover which ends badly for the soldier. The story is essentially a foreshadowing of the relationship Jim will have with Catherine. Of course, Catherine overhears Jim's story and interrupts, then she asks Albert if he's finished "her" song, then tells Albert to come up to the house and work on it. In a subsequent scene, Albert plays the song, which is a recapitulation of her life and her loves.

The five of them all go cycling. It is not coincidental that she always leads. *Voice Over #22* begins:

> Catherine meant different things to each and couldn't please them all, but too bad. Jim could only admire Catherine unreservedly on her own. In the company of others, she changed in his eyes.

It's evening outside the house. Jim and Catherine think they're alone. He kisses the nape of her neck. Jules, who's standing at the top of the stairs, sees them and recites something in German, which she translates as: "Hearts yearning for each other, O God, O God the pain they cause." Presumably, this is a poem or a line of one by Heine. Jules says she added the "O God."

For some reason, Catherine asks Jules for a copy of Goethe's, *Elective Affinities* (1809). Jules says Jim has the book, but once again, we're given an intertextual reference, since in the novel, the chemical term "elective affinities" extends to human relationships, both intimate and political. Like the alkalis and acids of which Goethe's characters speak, words and images, although apparently opposed, may have a remarkable affinity for one another. At the same time, as one of the characters in the book objects, such affinities are problematic, and "are only really interesting when they bring about separations."

Jules calls Jim and asks him to return the book that night because she wants it now. He also asks him to marry Catherine, but let him see her. Jim returns to the main house with the novel. He gives it to Catherine, kisses her. The *Voice Over #23* then begins:

> She was in his arms speaking in her deep voice. It was their first kiss and it lasted all night. They didn't speak, but drew close instead. Towards dawn, they become one. Her face expressed incredible joy and curiosity. Jim was enslaved. Other women had ceased to exist for him.

The following morning, Jules is playing dominoes with Sabine. Obviously, the game has changed. Catherine tells Jules she's asked Jim to move into the main house. Jules warns Jim to "be careful." Jim moves in and *Voice Over #24* begins:

> They were known in the village as the three lunatics, but otherwise they were well liked. On hearing that, Catherine invented a game: the village idiot. The village was the table. They took turns as the idiot. Sabine especially set them roaring with laughter.

The voice over continues:

> Catherine had said, 'One only truly loves for a moment,' but for her that moment came back again and again. Life was one long holiday. Jules and Jim had never handled such large dominoes. Time passed. Happiness isn't easy to record and wears out without anyone noticing. One Sunday Catherine decided to seduce Jules. While Jim reads downstairs she took Jules into her room. Jules kept saying no, but Catherine kept saying yes.

The laughter upstairs began to annoy Jim. The voice over continues:

> Though Jim told himself he had no right to be jealous, he was anyway. Catherine noticed this and never repeated the experiment.

The French uses the word "experience" and not "experiment." Fade to black. The voice over continues:

> One day, the four walked around a lake hidden in the mist of a lush, humid valley. There was complete harmony between them. Catherine had a brief headache, Jim had worse from fatigue. He thought, 'If we had children, they'd be tall and thin and have headaches too.' On the shore of the lake they played with pebbles. She made him throw them endlessly. She and Jules learned to make them skip. The sky seemed so near. Jim was needed in Paris. His paper was calling him. Leaving would have been agony but for the certainty they'd be together again soon, intact. The details of their perfect month together were carved in their memories. They waved gently for a long time as he left. Jules gave them a sort of blessing and promised Jim he'd take care of her, for they wanted to marry and have children.

Jim tells Gilberte that Jules will file for a quick divorce and he's going to marry Catherine. She leaves. Presumably, that's the end of their affair, but we discover it isn't. Soon after that, Jim accidentally runs into Thérèse at their café. She goes into elaborate detail about all of her sexploits even though he's obviously not interested in hearing about any of it. The irony is that Thérèse is more like Catherine than Catherine, since she truly lives with anyone for the moment. Acquaintances ask Jim how Jules is, etc., and one of them introduces Jim to a girl he's involved with, stating that their relationship is entirely predicated on sex, nothing else. Fade to black.

Voice Over #25 begins:

> Catherine spent the winter at home before the fireplace. She was Jim's fiancée entrusted to Jules. Every day she asked Jules, 'Do you think Jim loves me?' Jules doesn't answer.

Jim is in bed with Gilberte. Jim can't leave Gilberte in the same way Jules cannot leave Catherine. Gilberte wants him to stay a week longer. *Voice Over #26* begins:

> Jim could no more leave Gilberte than Catherine could leave Jules. They couldn't hurt Jules or Gilberte, who both counterbalanced each other as fruit of the past.

Back at the chalet, Catherine is reading a letter to Jules. When she finishes, she asks Jules, "Do you think Jim loves me?" Fade to black.

Jim returns to the cabin, but is met by Jules not Catherine. When they arrive at the chalet Catherine is not there. Jules admits that she left the day before, but he thought she'd be back by then. Jules then talks about her whims and her previous sexual encounters, and Jim decides to return to Paris when, coincidentally, she shows up. Timing is everything.

In bed, she talks of her past lovers and that she had to finish with them by having sex, so they can't make love since she won't know who the father is. That displeases Jim and he asks if she loves Albert. No, but she had to settle the score: Gilberte, Albert. They must start with a clean slate and the *Voice Over #27* begins:

> A clean slate, all debts paid. That was Catherine's philosophy. There they lay, trembling and chaste. Catherine fell asleep, but Jim never closed his eyes. He realized she loved him as he loved her, that some force drew them together. So they started over again, flying high like great birds of prey. They remained chaste until she was sure she wasn't carrying Albert's child. This restraint left them elated. They were always together. They never cheated. The promised land was in view.

THE PROMISED LAND ABRUPTLY RECEDED.

When they were ready for a child Catherine did not become pregnant. They saw a specialist who told them to be patient that these things took months with many couples.

But anything that isn't in Catherine's control causes her anguish, and she orders Jim to sleep in his own room. Love isn't all that counts, she counts too and she loves him less. She orders him to go back to Gilberte since she writes him daily. She even admits she's heartless. She also says that he's younger than she is and when they're older he'll leave her for a younger woman. He says he'll leave the next day for three months.

She then goes to Jules and says it's over. She says he lied to her by not breaking it off with Gilberte. Jules has heard this all before, but she confides in him as if he were a good friend. He says he'll love her forever regardless. She says she loves him as well. He says she can sleep in his room and he'll sleep downstairs. He talks of the Chinese play about the sad emperor who has two wives: wife number one and wife number two. The same. He goes downstairs and stares at the fire. At which point the *Voice Over #28* begins:

For Jules their love [Jim–Catherine] was now relative while his for Catharine was absolute. Jim left the house the next morning. Catherine wanted to take him to the station once more. A mist had settled over the meadow in the night. The rest of the hive sensed confusedly that Jim had lost favor with his queen. It was thus natural he should leave. The autumn railway schedule had just taken effect. There was no train until the next day.

They spend the night in a hotel. The voice over continues as she removes make up:

Jim thought of the children they might have had. He imagined a houseful of handsome children. He also knew that if they had none, Catherine would take up her adventures again. They didn't speak, but they made love once more in that cold, sad hotel room, not knowing why—perhaps to bring their story to a close. It was like a burial, or as if they were already dead. But the next day she took him to his train, but they didn't wave goodbye. They parted on the verge of tears, though nothing forced them to. [On the train] Jim thought to himself that it was all over.

Back in Paris, Jim is with Gilberte. Apparently he suffers from a lung ailment. Perhaps, asthma. The letter from Catherine states she *thinks* she's pregnant. He writes back that he's not interested and it's probably not his child anyway.

That begins the letter writing which is kind of a refrain from the story Jim told earlier about the soldier and his lover. The letters crisscross, making communication difficult. She writes that she's pregnant and he's the father. Given what he knows about her, he's not so sure, but eventually believes her. *Voice Over #29* begins:

They had promised never to call each other fearing to hear each other's voice when they couldn't touch. The mail took three days. Their letters crossed.

Finally, they seem to get back to some kind of agreement about things. *Voice Over #30* begins:

Jim finally received a letter from Jules.

The letter indicates that she has had a miscarriage and only wants silence between them now.
Voice Over continues:

So they had created nothing. Jim thought 'It's fine to want to rediscover the laws of human life, but how practical it must be to conform to existing ones. We played with the sources of life and lost.' Fade to black.

Sometime later, Jules and Jim meet accidentally at the gym. They have moved back to France. In the next scene, they are playing dominoes again. Jules mentions the talk about suicide. Of buying a gun. Jules finally meets Gilberte. Jules invites Jim to take a drive in "her" car.
Jim visits them. She shakes his hand. What is curious about all of this is the fact that Sabine is nowhere to be seen. Before they go for a ride in her car, Catherine wraps her sleeping gown as if it were a present.
Voice Over #31 begins:

Catherine was smiling, but she had a look of intrigue about her. She wrapped her white pajamas in a parcel just so. Jim wondered why, but then forgot about it, and they left for a drive.

They go for a drive and she decides to stop at a restaurant of her choosing. At that point, Albert shows up because he lives there. Curious, that Catherine wouldn't know that. The four of them eat together. As they're about to leave, Catherine takes the parcel that Jim has been carrying, and says she's going to spend the night with Albert. Jules and Jim leave together with Jim telling

Jules he's going to marry Gilberte. They walk back to Jules' house. Fade to black.

Jim returns to Paris. In a measure of her mental instability, she shows up at Jim's apartment, at what appears to be very early in the morning, honks the horn and drives erratically around a plaza across the street from his apartment. *Voice Over #32* begins:

> Jim recognized the rhythmic call of Catherine's car. At first he saw nothing, then he saw the car weaving among the trees on the empty square, grazing benches and trees like a riderless horse or a phantom ship.

Then, she leaves. She returns to her house, calls Jim and pleads with him to visit her which he does. She brings him into her bedroom and asks him to lie down on the bed and kiss her. Jim tells her that he's going to marry Gilberte since she can still have children. She talks about the children she wanted and he wanted. She begins to cry, then suddenly reaches beneath her pillow and pulls out a gun threatening to kill him. Jim wrestles the gun from her, leaps out the window and runs away.

SEVERAL MONTHS LATER.

Jim is in a movie house watching news clips of Nazis burning books which would make it approximately 1933. Jules and Catherine are also in the theater sitting several rows behind him. After getting Jim's attention, Jules motions Jim to join them and they leave.

The *Voice Over #33* begins:

> Jim was glad to see Jules and to find his heart no longer leapt at seeing Catherine. She didn't want to leave them alone and suggested a drive. Jim agreed. What was in store this time? Catherine toyed with the speed of her car and took almost imperceptible risks. There was an air of expectancy, like the day of their outing when they had met Albert. They stopped at an open air café by the water.

Jules and Jim talk about the Nazis and Jules talks about Jim's love for Catherine and vice versa. As a pretext of telling Jim something, Catherine coaxes Jim into the car. Given her history, it's hard to believe he'd do it, but he does.

She drives off, telling Jules to watch them carefully and smiling at Jim as if nothing is wrong, when we discover that she's chosen a particular bridge that really isn't a bridge and she drives the car into the water.

The *Voice Over #34* begins:

Jules would no longer dread, as he had from the beginning, that Catherine would cheat on him or, quite simply, die since it had happened now. Their bodies were found entangled among the reeds. Jim's coffin was even larger than life dwarfing Catherine's at its side. They left nothing of themselves, but Jules had his daughter. Had Catherine loved conflict for conflict's sake? No. But she bewildered Jules with it to the point of nausea. A sense of relief flooded over him. Jules' and Jim's friendship had no equivalent in love. They delighted together in the smallest things. They accepted their differences with tenderness. From the start, everyone called them Don Quixote and Sancho Panza.

They were both cremated and their urns were placed one on top of the other. The *Voice Over #35* begins:

The ashes were placed in urns and sealed in separate compartments. Left to himself, Jules would have mingled them. Catherine had always wanted hers scattered to the winds from a hilltop, but that was against regulations.

And so, ironically, in the end she could not control what happened to her after her death. In the end, Jules walks alone out of the cemetery.

What distinguishes *Jules & Jim* from the other films (except for *Sunset Boulevard*) is the almost exclusive reliance on voice overs. I've mentioned how voice overs in European films have always been a mainstay of the narrative precisely because of the tradition of European narratives. As in *Sunset Boulevard*, the voice overs in *Jules & Jim* carry the storyline forward *externally*, while the dialogue within the scenes advance the storyline *internally*. Although Truffaut uses many of the techniques I addressed in the introduction, he relies heavily on the voice overs to maintain scenic continuity, advance the storyline, develop character, and elicit conflict to an even greater degree than the dialogue itself. It is a tribute to Truffaut that he can carry that off and it is a tribute to European filmmaking that they still look at voice overs not as something that inhibits the effectiveness of telling a story, but as something that enhances the story.

6

Lolita (1963)

Screenplay by Vladimir Nabokov and Stanley Kubrick

I've chosen this scene since it's actually the one that initiates the entire film even though it doesn't occur until much later in the film. It is the scene that opens with Humbert meticulously painting Lolita's toenails with cotton balls carefully placed in between each toe. It, like so many of Kubrick's scenes, is very long. This is an adaptation of what Nabokov wrote on pages 152–154 of the screenplay. The entire scene in Nabokov's script is about 1½ pages long and has very little bearing on the storyline or the character, whereas Kubrick's adaptation goes on for about ten pages. It's worth repeating because we need to see what Kubrick did in terms of the dialogue that Nabokov was incapable of doing, since as extraordinarily gifted as Nabokov was with writing novels he was equally inept at writing screen dialogue.

Even though this scene is significantly shorter than the one in *The Graduate*, there are some startling similarities. We find the following topic divisions:

1   Dialogue about tardiness

2   Dialogue about boys

3   Dialogue about dates

4   Reprise about tardiness

5   Dialogue about Michelle

6   Dialogue about their relationship

 7   Dialogue about fun

 8   Dialogue about pride

 9   Dialogue about the play

 10 Reprise about boys

 11 Dialogue about love

Since there is no "shooting script" extant (not even from Nabokov's son), I've written out the entire dialogue for the scene below and we can look at what Kubrick has done in detail, especially in relation to how he uses the dialogue links. I have deconstructed the scene in such a way as to allow someone to see how the scene itself is really masterfully written not only in terms of the way Kubrick constructed it, but in the way he writes dialogue to make the scene work.

> HUMBERT
> Why were you so late coming
> home from school yesterday
> afternoon?

> LOLITA
> Yesterday, yesterday. What was yesterday?

> HUMBERT
> Yesterday was Thursday.

> LOLITA
> Oh, was I late?

> HUMBERT
> Yes, you were. You finished
> school at 3 o'clock. You weren't home until 6 o'clock.

> LOLITA
> That's right. That's right. Michelle and I stayed late
> to watch football practice.

> HUMBERT
> In the Frigid Queen.

LOLITA
What do you mean in the Frigid Queen?

HUMBERT
I was driving around and I thought I saw you through
the window.

LOLITA
Oh, yeah, well we stopped there for a malt afterward.
What difference does it make?

HUMBERT
You were sitting at a table with two boys.

LOLITA
Yeah, Roy and Rex just happened to sit down with us.

HUMBERT
Roy and Rex.

LOLITA
The co-captains of the football team.

HUMBERT
I thought we understood. No dates.

LOLITA
What do you mean, no dates? They just sat down at our
table.

HUMBERT
I don't want you around them. They're nasty minded boys.

LOLITA
You're a fine one to talk about someone else's mind.

HUMBERT
Don't avoid the issue. I told you no dates.

LOLITA
It wasn't a date.

                    HUMBERT
                 It was a date.

                    LOLITA
               It wasn't a date.

                    HUMBERT
               It was a date, Lolita.

                    LOLITA
               It wasn't a date.

                    HUMBERT
                 It was a date.

                    LOLITA
               It wasn't a date.

                    HUMBERT
Whatever it was you had yesterday afternoon I don't want
  you to have it again. And while we're on the subject
  how was it you were so late on Saturday afternoon?

                    LOLITA
          Saturday I went to my piano lesson.

                    HUMBERT
   Your piano lesson? I thought that was on Wednesday.

                    LOLITA
No, it was changed to Saturday remember? Between 2 and
 4, Miss Starch, piano. Well ask Michelle, she was with
                      me.

                    HUMBERT
Ask Michelle, that's what you always say to me. Now for
 a change I'm going to ask you something about Michelle.

                    LOLITA
    You can't have her. She belongs to a Marine.

HUMBERT

I'll ignore that idiotic joke. Why does she give me
those searching looks when she comes to the house?

LOLITA

How should I know?

HUMBERT

Have you told her anything about us?

LOLITA

No. Have you?

HUMBERT

You told her nothing?

LOLITA

You think I'm crazy?

HUMBERT

You spend too much time with that girl. I don't want
you to see her so often.

LOLITA

Oh, come on! She's the only friend I've got in this
stinkin' world. You never let me have any fun.

HUMBERT

No fun. You have all the fun in the world. We have fun
together, don't we? Whenever you want something I buy
it for you automatically. I take you to concerts, to
museums, to movie. I do all the housework. Who does the
tidying up? I do. Who does the cooking? I do. You and I
have lots of fun. Don't we, Lolita?

LOLITA
Come here.

LOLITA
Still love me?

HUMBERT
Completely, you know that.

LOLITA
You know what I want more than anything in the world?

HUMBERT
No, what do you want?

LOLITA
I want you to be proud of me.

HUMBERT
I am proud of you, Lolita.

LOLITA
No, I mean really proud of me. You see, they want me
for the lead in the school play. Isn't that fantastic?
I have to have a letter from you giving permission.

HUMBERT
Who wants you?

LOLITA
Edusa Gold, the drama teacher, Clare Quilty and Vivian
Darkbloom.

HUMBERT
And who might they be?

LOLITA
Oh, they're the authors. They're here to supervise the
production.

HUMBERT
But you've never acted before.

LOLITA
They say I have a unique and rare talent.

HUMBERT
And how do they know that?

LOLITA
We had readings and I was chosen over thirty other
girls.

HUMBERT
This is the first I've heard about it.

LOLITA
I know. I wanted to surprise you.

HUMBERT
And I suppose that Roy has a part in this production.

LOLITA
Roy? What's he got to do with this?

HUMBERT
Roy and Rex, naturally I suppose they're in it, huh?

LOLITA
Well, how do I know? I only and met them yesterday.
Besides they're football players not actors.

HUMBERT
And you suddenly overnight are an actress. Well, it's
out of the question.

LOLITA
Out of the question!

HUMBERT
I don't want you in that atmosphere.

LOLITA
What atmosphere. It's just a school play.

HUMBERT
I've told you over and over again, I don't want you

mixing with those boys. It's just another excuse to make dates with them and get together close with them.

                    LOLITA
             You don't love me.

                    HUMBERT
              I do love you.

                    LOLITA
             You don't love me.

                    HUMBERT
           I do love you, Lolita.

                    LOLITA
You're driving me crazy. You won't let me do anything.
You want me to be locked up with you in this filthy
                    house.

                    HUMBERT
 Go wash your face and I'll go downstairs to start the
                    roast.

                    LOLITA
          Someday you'll be sorry.

                    HUMBERT
                  (angrily)
      Go wash your face. I'll start the roast.

                    LOLITA
          Someday you'll be sorry.

                    HUMBERT
 Yeah, yeah, yeah, yeah. And don't smash your toe nails.

We can look at how Kubrick then worked with the dialogue links to make this scene move more expeditiously. Rather than use arrows as I've previously done, I'm going to describe the Kubrick process as the dialogue proceeds.

HUMBERT
Why were you so late coming
home from school yesterday
afternoon?

Humbert opens with a question about Lolita's tardiness and she answers it
with another question by linking on the word "yesterday."

LOLITA
Yesterday, yesterday. What was yesterday?
Humbert links with on the word "yesterday."

HUMBERT
Yesterday was Thursday.

Lolita links with another question and the word "late."

LOLITA
Oh, was I late?

By using the phrase, "yes, you were [late] he links off Lolita's question.

HUMBERT
Yes, you were. You finished
school at 3 o'clock. You weren't home until 6 o'clock.
Lolita then links off the word "late" again.

LOLITA
That's right. That's right. Michelle and I stayed late
to watch football practice.

Humbert then links off the notion being late by bringing up the "Frigid Queen."

HUMBERT
In the Frigid Queen.

Lolita then links by repeating "Frigid Queen" as a question.

LOLITA
What do you mean in the Frigid Queen?

Humbert links on the Frigid Queen phrase by saying he saw her through the [Frigid Queen's] window.

> HUMBERT
> I was driving around and I thought I saw you through the window.

Lolita links off the FQ window, by saying she stopped "there" [the Frigid Queen] then follows that up with a question.

> LOLITA
> Oh, yeah, well we stopped there for a malt afterward. What difference does it make?

Humbert then shifts to the topic of "boys."

> HUMBERT
> You were sitting at a table with two boys.

Lolita links on his statement by specifying who the boys were "Roy and Rex."

> LOLITA
> Yeah, Roy and Rex just happened to sit down with us.

Humbert links by repeating their names.

> HUMBERT
> Roy and Rex.

Lolita links by stating what "they" are.

> LOLITA
> The co-captains of the football team.

Humbert links off the co-captains as "dates."

> HUMBERT
> I thought we understood. No dates.

Lolita then links off the line "no dates" as a question followed by stating that "they" (the boys) merely sat down.

LOLITA

What do you mean, no dates? They just sat down at our
table.

Humbert links off the boys, calling them "them," then added the bit about being "nasty minded."

HUMBERT

I don't want you around them. They're nasty minded boys.

She links off the word "mind."

LOLITA

You're a fine one to talk about someone else's mind.

Humbert re-focuses the dialogue back to "no dates."

HUMBERT

Don't avoid the issue. I told you no dates.

Lolita links on the word "date" and that links the next seven exchanges.

LOLITA
It wasn't a date.

HUMBERT
It was a date.

LOLITA
It wasn't a date.

HUMBERT
It was a date, Lolita.

LOLITA
It wasn't a date.

HUMBERT
It was a date.

                         LOLITA
                    It wasn't a date.

Humbert stops the back and forth arguing ending with whatever "it [the date] was" and then reprising the words "yesterday," "late," and shifting to "Saturday afternoon."

                         HUMBERT
Whatever it was you had yesterday afternoon I don't want
   you to have it again. And while we're on the subject
   how was it you were so late on Saturday afternoon?

Lolita links off the word "Saturday" and then states "piano lesson."

                         LOLITA
             Saturday I went to my piano lesson.

Humbert links off the "piano lesson" line as a question then suggests another day, "Wednesday."

                         HUMBERT
   Your piano lesson? I thought that was on Wednesday.

Lolita repeats the day, "Saturday," as a question, reprising the word "piano" and adding "ask Michelle."

                         LOLITA
   No, it was changed to Saturday remember? Between 2 and
   4, Miss Starch, piano. Well ask Michelle, she was with
                           me.

Humbert links off "ask Michelle" to ask another question.

                         HUMBERT
   Ask Michelle, that's what you always say to me. Now for
   a change I'm going to ask you something about Michelle.

Lolita links off "Michelle" by saying you can't have "her [Michelle]" because "she [Michelle]" is taken.

                    LOLITA
You can't have her. She belongs to a Marine.

Humbert links off the word "she" and asks a question pertaining to her "looks."

                   HUMBERT
I'll ignore that idiotic joke. Why does she give me those searching looks when she comes to the house?

Lolita answers his question with another question.

                    LOLITA
            How should I know?

Humbert answers her question with another question refocusing the dialogue to their relationship.

                   HUMBERT
      Have you told her anything about us?

Lolita answers his question with another question linking the phrase "have you."

                    LOLITA
            No. Have you?

Humbert links off the "Have you" by repeating the phrase as a question, "You told."

                   HUMBERT
         You told her nothing?

Lolita answers his question with another question linking on the word "you" reprising the word "her [Michelle]."

                    LOLITA
          You think I'm crazy?

Humbert links again with the word "you" reprising Michelle's name as both "girl" and "her."

> HUMBERT
>
> You spend too much time with that girl. I don't want
> you to see her so often.

Lolita then links off of the word "she" and adds the word "fun" thus redirecting the dialogue once again.

> LOLITA
>
> Oh, come on! She's the only friend I've got in this
> stinkin' world. You never let me have any fun.

Humbert links off the word "fun" repeating three times.

> HUMBERT
>
> No fun. You have all the fun in the world. We have fun
> together, don't we? Whenever you want something I buy
> it for you automatically. I take you to concerts, to
> museums, to movie. I do all the housework. Who does the
> tidying up? I do. Who does the cooking? I do. You and I
> have lots of fun. Don't we, Lolita?

It appears that Lolita has run out of options until she plays the card she knows will always work. She looks at him seductively.

> LOLITA
>
> Come here.

Humbert moves from painting her toenails to sitting next to her face. She asks the provocative question.

> LOLITA
>
> Still love me?

Humbert links off the word "love" by saying "Completely."

> HUMBERT
>
> Completely, you know that.

Lolita, believing that she's got him where she wants him, then redirects the focus of the dialogue by asking the question about "what she wants."

LOLITA
You know what I want more than anything in the world?

Humbert answers her question with a question of his own and links on the phrase "what do you want?"

HUMBERT
No, what do you want?

Lolita answers and states she wants him to be "proud" of her.

LOLITA
I want you to be proud of me.

Humbert links with the word "proud".

HUMBERT
I am proud of you, Lolita.

Lolita links by the phrase "really proud" then immediately follows that up with the point that "they want me" for the play.

LOLITA
No, I mean really proud of me. You see, they want me
for the lead in the school play. Isn't that fantastic?
I have to have a letter from you giving permission.

Humbert links on the word "they" by stating "Who."

HUMBERT
Who wants you?

Lolita links by giving them names.

LOLITA
Edusa Gold, the drama teacher, Clare Quilty and Vivian
Darkbloom.

Humbert links on their names by asking who "they" are.

> HUMBERT
> And who might they be?

Lolita links on "they" by stating "they're the authors" and "they're" there to supervise.

> LOLITA
> Oh, they're the authors. They're here to supervise the production.

Humbert then states the obvious about her lack of acting.

> HUMBERT
> But you've never acted before.

Lolita links by stating "they [the authors]" think she has a unique and rare "talent [to act["].

> LOLITA
> They say I have a unique and rare talent.

Humbert links by asking the question how do "they" know "that [her talent]."

> HUMBERT
> And how do they know that?

They know about her talent because of the "readings."

> LOLITA
> We had readings and I was chosen over thirty other girls.

Humbert links by stating it's the first time he's heard about "it [the play"].

> HUMBERT
> This is the first I've heard about it.

Lolita links by saying she wanted to surprise him (with it).

> LOLITA
> I know. I wanted to surprise you.

But Humbert's jealousy gets the best of him and he reprises Roy's name within the context of the play.

> HUMBERT
> And I suppose that Roy has a part in this production.

Once again, Lolita links on "Roy's" name and asks a question that implicitly links to "this [the play]."

> LOLITA
> Roy? What's he got to do with this?

Humbert reprises both boys' names within the context of "it [the play]."

> HUMBERT
> Roy and Rex, naturally I suppose they're in it, huh?

Lolita links with a rhetorical question, alludes to "them", reprises the word "yesterday" and adds that they're not "actors."

> LOLITA
> Well, how do I know? I only and met them yesterday.
> Besides they're football players not actors.

Humbert links on the word "actors" by stating "actress" then says "it's out of the question."

> HUMBERT
> And you suddenly overnight are an actress. Well, it's
> out of the question.

Lolita turns his command into an exclamation by stating the same phrase.

> LOLITA
> Out of the question!

Humbert proceeds to explain why by talking about the "atmosphere."

> HUMBERT
> I don't want you in that atmosphere.

Lolita repeats the word "atmosphere" within the context of it being a "play."

> LOLITA
> What atmosphere. It's just a school play.

But, for Humbert, plays include "boys," and if there are boys, then there are "dates."

> HUMBERT
> I've told you over and over again, I don't want you mixing with those boys. It's just another excuse to make dates with them and get together close with them.

Figuring she's lost the battle and the war, Lolita attacks with the last weapon in her arsenal ... love.

> LOLITA
> You don't love me.

Humbert links off the word, "love," or the lack of it, and there is the back and forth argument four times.

> HUMBERT
> I do love you.

> LOLITA
> You don't love me.

> HUMBERT
> I do love you, Lolita.

With nothing left to use, Lolita accuses him of driving her crazy by wanting to keep her locked up.

> LOLITA
> You're driving me crazy. You won't let me do anything. You want me to be locked up with you in this filthy house.

Humbert tries to defuse the truth by avoiding the issue by asserting his authority.

> HUMBERT
> Go wash your face and I'll go downstairs to start the roast.

As any teenager might do, Lolita makes a threat.

> LOLITA
> Someday you'll be sorry.

Humbert ignores the threat and links with the previous command.

> HUMBERT
> (angrily)
> Go wash your face. I'll start the roast.

Lolita then links with the repetition of the threat.

> LOLITA
> Someday you'll be sorry.

Finally, Humbert dismisses her comments altogether closing the scene with how it opened ... dealing with toes.

> HUMBERT
> Yeah, yeah, yeah, yeah. And don't smash your toe nails.

As with the dialogue in *The Graduate*, the dialogue in *Lolita* has many similarities. Besides the fact the ending is linked to the beginning, we can look at some of the same things as we will with the Henry script.

- HUMBERT asks 13 questions
- LOLITA asks 12
- HUMBERT makes 29 statements
- LOLITA makes 29 statements

As we'll see in *The Graduate*, these results are exactly as they should be since both of them have asked the same number of questions with the same number of answers. Of that total, we can then see how the dialogue links are dispersed.

Dispersal of dialogue links

Dialogue links related to yesterday	7x
Dialogue links related to being late	4x
Dialogue links related to the Frigid Queen	2x
(as "window of")	1x
(as "there")	1x
Dialogue links related to boys	3x
Dialogue links related to Roy and Rex	3x
(as "co-captains")	1x
(as "they")	1x
(as "them")	1x
Dialogue links related to dates	10x
(as "it")	1x
Dialogue links related mind(ed)	2x
Dialogue links related to Saturday(afternoon)	3x
Dialogue links related to piano (lessons)	3x
Dialogue links related to Michelle	3x
(as "her")	2x
(as "she")	5x
(as "that girl")	1x
Dialogue links related to have you (told)	3x
Dialogue links related to fun	5x
Dialogue links related to love	1x
(as "completely")	1x
Dialogue links related to what I (you) want	2x
Dialogue links related to "proud"	3x
Dialogue links related to want me/wants you	2x
Dialogue links related to the authors	1x
(as "they're")	2x
Dialogue links related to talent	1x
(as "know that")	1x
(as "readings")	1x
Dialogue links related to Roy	2x
Dialogue links related to not actors	1x
Dialogue links related to actress	1x
Dialogue links related to "Out of the question"	2x
Dialogue links related to atmosphere	2x

Dialogue links related to do love/don't love	4x
Dialogue links related to someday you'll be sorry	2x
Dialogue links related to wash your face	2x
TOTAL	93 LINKS

So, you see in a scene that is not much longer that five minutes, there are no fewer than 93 dialogue links. Not only that, but just as the beginning of the scene deals with Humbert meticulously painting Lolita's toenails, the scene concludes with Humbert addressing what he began doing at the beginning; namely, taking care of her toenails. *Lolita* is two decades on from *Citizen Kane* and yet the fundamentals used in writing the dialogue and how that dialogue relates to the construction of the scene are almost identical. It's apparent, or should be, that the manner in which Mankiewicz was writing dialogue in 1941 is almost exactly what Kubrick was writing in 1963. To that end, there are some fundamentals involved in writing screen dialogue that continue to persist.

7

Goldfinger (1964)

Screenplay by Richard Maibaum and Paul Dehn Based on the novel by Ian Fleming

In an American Film Institute [AFI] interview, Hitchcock once talked about cinematic tension and the example he used was the "bomb under the table" ploy. According to Hitchcock, if the audience does not know there's a bomb under the table and the bomb goes off, there's very little tension. If, however, the audience does know there's bomb under the table set to go off in five minutes, then that changes the entire dynamic of the scene. Clearly, when it comes to cinematic tension, Hitchcock is not the person to second guess and I'm writing about *Goldfinger* for the simple reason that it's unlike the other films that may be assumed to have more "creative merit" if not cinematic tension. In relation to such films as *Citizen Kane* or *Jules & Jim* or *North by Northwest* one might assume there's no place for *Goldfinger*, but, in terms of scenic integrity, I suggest that *Goldfinger* (which is, arguably, one of the best of all the Connery-Bond films) is significant precisely because of the integrity of many of its scenes, and the one scene I'd like to focus on is the scene in the laser room with Bond and Goldfinger with a strapped down Bond attempting to engage in a kind of repartee with Goldfinger in an attempt to save his life.

In the previous sequence of action scenes, Bond is attempting to escape from Goldfinger's henchmen by driving his Aston Martin through the streets and alleys of Goldfinger's plant. Somehow, Bond is duped into believing that he's heading for a head-on crash with an oncoming Mercedes. Avoiding the disaster, Bond drives into a wall and is knocked unconscious. Oddjob, who's first on the scene, smiles at the fact that Bond was deceived by a mirror that was set an angle to reflect the appearance of an oncoming car and, as Bond swerved to avoid it, crashed into a wall. Of course, we need to relinquish our disbelief to think that Goldfinger would have erected such a mirror at such a place in such an angle as a way to deceive potential intruders, but the sequence works nevertheless.

When Bond awakes from his semi-comatose state, he finds himself in the laser room lying on a metal table with his arms tied and legs spread. The table is in the middle of the room with a laser gun above his head. Off-screen, Goldfinger says, "Good evening, double-o-seven." Bond turns to see Goldfinger standing near the control panel with his colleagues, Ling, Kisch, and Mellinger, and several guards. Bond replies that his name is "James Bond," to which Goldfinger suggests there are few of his ilk in number. Goldfinger approaches the table and from the script we read:

> GOLDFINGER
> You have been recognized—let's say by one of
> your opposite numbers, who is also licensed to
> kill.—Oh, that interesting car of yours!

PAN on Goldfinger as he moves to the right. The laser gun comes into view. Goldfinger wipes his eye and laughs.

> GOLDFINGER
> I, too, have a new toy, but considerably more
> practical.

BOND glances up at the laser gun.

> GOLDFINGER (O.S.)
> You are looking at an industrial laser ...

BOND'S POV—THE LASER GUN

GOLDFINGER (O.S.)
... which emits an extraordinary light, not to
be found in nature.

Goldfinger looks down at him and paces back past the
table.

GOLDFINGER
It can project a spot on the moon—or, at closer
range, cut through solid metal. I will show you.

At that point, Goldfinger snaps his fingers at someone in the control room and
the barrel of the laser gun begins to move from behind Bond's head, down
his torso, stopping at a place at the end of the table between Bond's legs.
As Bond looks down at the laser beam, it begins burning through the edge
of the solid gold tabletop, inching its way towards Bond's crotch. Bond now
realizes what's in store for him as Goldfinger elaborates on how much gold
means to him.

GOLDFINGER
I welcome any enterprise which will increase my
stock, which is considerable.

The laser beam continues its unmitigated approach toward Bond's genitals to
which Bond responds:

BOND
I think you've made your point, Goldfinger.
Thank you for the demonstration.

GOLDFINGER
(studying the beam)
Choose your next witticism carefully, Mister
Bond. It may be your last.

Bond looks at it then up at Goldfinger.

GOLDFINGER
The purpose of our two previous encounters is
now very clear to me. I do not intend to be
distracted by another. Good-night, Mister Bond.

Indifferent to Bond's mild protestation, Goldfinger turns to leave as Bond continues to monitor the laser beam getting closer and closer. Presumably, this is the end for Bond who responds:

BOND

Do you expect me to talk?

GOLDFINGER

No, Mister Bond. I expect you to die!

The excellent use of intercutting juxtaposes Goldfinger's complete and utter indifference to Bond's plight with Bond's complete and utter fear—or as utterly fearful as Bond could be. Goldfinger responds that there's nothing Bond can say that Goldfinger doesn't already know. As the laser beam gets closer and closer to his crotch, Bond resorts to a potential scare tactic by stating that if he doesn't report in, then 008 will replace him. Goldfinger sarcastically quips:

GOLDFINGER

I trust he will be more successful!

With the laser beam within inches, Bond struggles for something to say that will get him out of the predicament he's in. He follows up on Goldfinger's dialogue with the fact that 008 knows what he knows, to which Goldfinger replies as a dialogue link, that Bond knows nothing. At that point, Bond plays the only "trump card" he has in his Bondish deck by mentioning the phrase:

BOND

Operation Grand Slam, for instance!

At that point, Goldfinger and Ling consult with the others as to what that knowledge might mean to their plan. With the laser almost at the point where it would kill Bond, Goldfinger says:

GOLDFINGER

Two words you may have overheard which cannot
possibly have any significance to you or anyone
in your organization.

In fact, Goldfinger is right. It was something Bond merely overheard between Goldfinger and Ling. Bond replies:

BOND
Can you afford to take that chance?

At that point, Goldfinger hesitates as the intercutting between Bond and Goldfinger continues, and as the laser moves ever closer to ending Bond's sex life forever. The ploy works and Goldfinger has the laser beam turned off.

GOLDFINGER
You are quite right, Mister Bond. You are worth more to me alive.

Just why Bond is worth more alive than dead is subject to argument. At that point, Bond feels a sense of relief, but not before Kisch approaches Bond, points a pistol at Bond and fires. Bond slumps over, presumably "dead" (although we know better) and Goldfinger looks on "with even greater smugness."

There are specific things that are at work during the scene that are important for any scene to work effectively. One of the most important things one sees in this scene is how Maibaum and Dehn use dialogue. In order for a scene to coalesce, dialogue must drive the scene to its natural conclusion. I respectfully take issue with Hitchcock's statement that "Dialogue should simply be a sound among other sounds, just something that comes out of the mouths of people whose eyes tell the story in visual terms." In certain situations, he's absolutely correct. Obviously, in the shower scene in *Psycho* one doesn't really need any dialogue, but not every scene is a scene out of *Psycho*.

As Aristotle suggests in his *Poetics*, the end (of a scene) links to the beginning with inevitable certainty. In other words, at the beginning of the scene, Bond is condemned to death; at the end of the scene, Bond is given a reprieve. But he is given a reprieve by virtue of his wits having heard the phrase "Operation Grand Slam" purely by accident in a previous scene. So, the scene is not only dependent on the potential life–death conflict throughout the scene (i.e. will he be lasered or won't he?), but by the use of dialogue and the all-important *dialogue links* that drive the scene to its natural ending. As I alluded to in the Introduction, dialogue links are "those repetitive words, phrases, synonyms, pronouns that actually link one character's dialogue with another character's dialogue and that drives the dialogue to its natural conclusion." The links essentially create a "dialogue system" that allows for a kind of free-flowing dialogue unimpeded by abrupt starts and stops.

If one deconstructs the dialogue, one can see the unique interrelationship between what Goldfinger says and what Bond says. If one eliminates the narrative, the scene is left with the following dialogue:

>   GOLDFINGER (O.S.)
>   Good evening, **double-o-seven.**
>
>   BOND
>   My name is **James Bond.**
>
>   GOLDFINGER
>   And members of **your curious
>   profession** are few in number. **You
>   have been recognized**—let's say by
>   one of your opposite numbers, who
>   is also licensed to kill.—Oh, **that
>   interesting car of yours!** I, too,
>   have a **new toy,** but considerably
>   more practical. You are looking at
>   an **industrial laser** ... which **emits
>   an extraordinary light,** not to be
>   found in nature. It can project a
>   spot on the moon—or, at closer
>   range, **cut through solid metal.** I
>   will show you. **This is gold,** Mister
>   Bond. All my life I've been in
>   love with its **colour,** its
>   brilliance, its divine heaviness. I
>   welcome **any enterprise which will
>   increase my stock,** which is
>   considerable.

Goldfinger opens by calling Bond "*double-o-seven*" and Bond links on that by using his name which links their dialogues. The name *Bond*, then links with a number of items in Goldfinger's subsequent dialogue:

1 the allusion to his (Bond's) "curious profession" and the fact he's been "recognized";

2 Goldfinger's allusion to Bond's car (an extension of Bond himself) which, allows Goldfinger to link with his allusion to the "new toy";

3 Goldfinger's allusion to the new toy, "an industrial laser," by indicating its powers (i.e. emits an extraordinary light, cuts through solid metal [e.g. gold]) the mention of which links to its color and to any enterprise that will increase his (Goldfnger's) possession of it.

At that point, Bond makes the ironic comment about the demonstration which does not go unnoticed by Goldfinger.

>   BOND
>   I think you've made your point, Goldfinger.
>   **Thank you for the demonstration.**
>
>   GOLDFINGER
>   Choose **your next witticism carefully**, Mister
>   Bond. It may be your last. The purpose of our
>   two previous encounters is now very clear to me.
>   I do not intend to be distracted by another.
>   **Good-night, Mister Bond.**

So, Bond's "demonstration" quip links with Goldfinger's "witticism" response. Goldfinger is not someone to be taken lightly, nor does he suffer fools gladly, and he lets Bond know that he's clear about their previous meetings and that they weren't serendipitous and essentially declares "you're a dead man." At that point, Bond searches for something that will extend his life which appears to be rapidly waning.

>   BOND
>   **Do you expect me to talk?**
>
>   GOLDFINGER
>   No, Mister Bond. I **expect you to die!** There is
>   **nothing you can talk to me** about that I don't
>   already know.

There's a double link here with the words "expect" and "talk" that keeps the dialogue "alive" even though it appears Bond is (or shortly will be) "dead." Bond comments on 008, to which Goldfinger links with "he" (008) will be more successful.

>   BOND
>   You're forgetting one thing! If I fail to
>   report, **double-o-eight replaces me!**
>
>   GOLDFINGER
>   **I trust he will be more successful!**

We then get a triple dialogue link with the word "know" that continues to extend the dialogue leading to Goldfinger's comment that Bond "knows nothing" to which Bond links with the name "Operation Grand Slam."

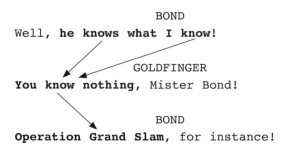

BOND
Well, **he knows what I know!**

GOLDFINGER
You know nothing, Mister Bond!

BOND
Operation Grand Slam, for instance!

GOLDFINGER
Two words you may have overheard which cannot possibly have any significance to you or anyone in your organization.

BOND
Can you afford to take that chance?

GOLDFINGER
You are quite right, Mister Bond. **You are worth more to me alive.**

The dialogic part of the scene closes with the phrase "Operation Grand Slam" linking with "two words" that links to the notion of "chance" which links to Bond's being worth more alive than dead. What is clearly noticeable is that one can distinguish several mitigating features that make a scene work regardless of the genre:

1   the use of dialogue links;

2   the use of dramatic tools (e.g. intercutting); and

3   the synergy between the opening of the scene and the ending of the scene.

What we can find in this scene is a number of tension points which could be graphed according to their significance in terms of the context of the scene beginning at the outset of the scene with Bond tied down to the table. The dramatic tension in the scene increases with each tension point within the scene, culminating with Bond saving his own life at the end of the scene.

1   The barrel of the laser gun tracing Bond's body.

2   We see the blue coils turn on as it moves downwards.

3   The barrel of the laser gun rests between Bond's legs and the laser light goes on, beaming red. Bond looks at it.

4   The laser starts cutting the outer edge of the metal table. One can assume this would increase Bond's apprehension significantly.

5   The laser continues to burn through the table.

6   The laser continues to cut through the table, inching towards Bond's crotch.

7   Bond looks at Goldfinger then at his crotch. The laser continues cutting through the table.

8   The laser continues cutting. Bond looks at it then at Goldfinger.

9   Bond looks from Goldfinger to between his legs. The laser keeps cutting toward his crotch.

10   Bond looks at Goldfinger who continues up the steps.

11   Bond looks at the laser. It continues cutting through the table. Bond tries to think of a way out.

12   Bond looks at the laser as it keeps cutting towards his crotch. He turns sideways.

13   Bond looks down at the laser again as it keeps cutting toward his crotch.

14   Bond mentions "Operation Grand Slam." Ling freezes and looks at Bond but Goldfinger barely reacts.

15   Goldfinger watches Bond as the laser is about to burn through his body.

16   Bond looks at Goldfinger as the laser keeps cutting.

17   Goldfinger consults with Ling and Kisch.

18   Bond looks again at the laser.

19   Goldfinger continues consulting.

20   Bond looks down at the laser as it inches away from his crotch. Bond looks up.

21   As Goldfinger talks, Bond hopelessly looks on at the approaching laser.

22   Goldfinger hesitates. Bond looks over at him, then back to the table. The beam keeps cutting.

23   Bond looks at Goldfinger again. Goldfinger smiles and snaps his fingers (soundlessly) at his assistants.

24   The laser suddenly goes off as Kisch walks down the from the control room.

25   Bond looks up at the laser gun then down at his legs as if to reassure himself he's safe.

26   Kisch approaches the table.

27   Bond looks at Kisch, then Goldfinger, then back to Kisch who raises a pistol and aims at Bond's chest.

28   Kisch fires the gun; it makes a thumping sound. Bond's head lowers to the tabletop.

29   Goldfinger looks on.

FADE OUT

From the time the laser beam is turned on until it is turned off there are approximately *16 shots* of the laser as it creeps its way towards Bond's crotch. Each time the laser gets closer there's an increase in the dramatic tension of the scene. In a way, the scene follows a very Aristotelian scheme of dramatic tension, as well as a kind of microcosm of Freytag's pyramid, which is primarily used in relation to the story as a whole.

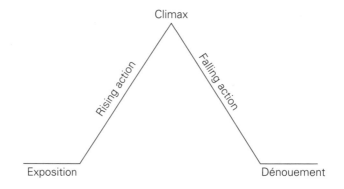

1   Exposition: setting the scene.

2   Inciting incident: shortly after the exposition, something happens to initiate the action. A single event usually signals the beginning of the main conflict. The inciting incident is sometimes called 'the complication'.

3   Rising action: the story builds with its concomitant tension.

4   Climax: the moment of greatest tension in a story.

5   Falling action: events happen as a result of the climax and we know that the scene will soon end.

6   Resolution: the character solves the main problem/conflict or someone solves it for him or her.

7   Dénouement: at this point, any remaining secrets, questions, or mysteries which remain after the resolution are solved by the characters or explained by the author.

The difference here, of course, is that even though the scene follows a line of exposition to rising action and a climax, the exposition is actually part of the rising action that climaxes when Goldfinger turns off the laser. What follows is a short period of falling action until Ling shoots Bond, at which time there's an immediate rise in action since, even though we know Bond isn't dead, there's an increase in the tension until we see him appear in the following scene somewhere in Kentucky.

Hitchcock once opined that "Dialogue should simply be a sound among other sounds, just something that comes out of the mouths of people whose eyes tell the story in visual terms." With all due respect to the master, I'm not sure I agree with that assessment, since the use of dialogue is really scene dependent. Obviously, the shower scene in *Psycho* doesn't really need any dialogue to advance the storyline, whereas the opening scenes in a film such as *The Graduate* are absolutely dependent on Buck Henry's dialogue in order to advance the storyline and develop character. What's clear, or should be, is that there are certain dialogous techniques that have been used from *Citizen Kane* to *The Graduate*, and even to *Pulp Fiction* and beyond, that work precisely because they are time-tested.

In this scene, as in many "high tension" scenes, there's a symbiotic relationship between the tension that's being created and the dialogue that is substantively a part of the tension. In agreeing with Hitchcock, one could easily have eliminated the dialogue from this scene and understood through Bond's eyes the obvious thing that was going on; however, it would not have given an audience the rather unique and often ironic relationship that relates to both Bond and Goldfinger that can only be conveyed through dialogue.

What we should be discovering at this point is that what's significant about scene structure is how it is fundamentally integrated with dialogue since it is dialogue that will maintain scenic continuity, advance the storyline, develop character, and elicit emotion.

8

The Graduate (1967)

Screenplay by Calder Willingham and Buck Henry

As I've previously alluded to, Aristotle's *Poetics* suggests that in talking about drama "the end is linked to the beginning with inevitable certainty." Although Aristotle was talking about the play as a whole, we've seen that one can apply the same rubric to the well-structured scene. For example, in Scenes 58–61 of *The Graduate*, Henry precisely choreographs the scenes in such a way that validates Aristotle's principle.

Summers can be long, hot and boring in Southern California, especially for a recent college graduate, and so Benjamin decides to take up Mrs. Robinson's sexual offer (which she proffers to him early in the film) that he can have her anytime he wants. Although reluctant at first, Benjamin's randyness and/or curiosity prompts him to call Mrs. Robinson, who meets him at the Taft Hotel. What transpires in a matter of minutes of screen time is a testament not only to what Aristotle suggested, but also to Henry's ability to make it work.

In the opening scenes, Henry has characterized Benjamin as a "track star," "an award-winning scholar," a dutiful son and, by his behavior, a kind of social geek. When Mrs. Robinson offers herself to him in the nude, Benjamin is as shocked as he is a possible virgin. To that end, the scenes are replete with ambivalence. Yet they are also "transitional scenes" in that, subsequent to them, especially Scene 61, Benjamin's entire demeanor and character changes. As we'll see, realistically one has to suspend one's belief that such an alteration can happen in such a brief period of time, but as a scene that changes Benjamin's character for the rest of the film it is both believable and effective.

In a series of formative scenes beginning with Scene 50, Benjamin's ineptness at adultery and apparent sexual incompetence is presented to us. Scenes 50–4 accent Ben's anxiety, as he sits smoking a cigarette and waiting for the arrival of Mrs. Robinson in the bar of the Taft Hotel. After she arrives, the scene augments his anxiety even more, especially when she asks him if he's reserved a room. He says, "no." She suggests it would be a good idea if he did and like a "dead man walking" he does.

In Scene 55, Ben goes to the desk clerk (who's played by Buck Henry) and, in the most inane of attempts, reserves a single room. After signing his own name then realizing he shouldn't do that, he crumples up the card and writes an alias: Mr. Gladstone. The alias will pay off in any future scenes, especially when Ben comes there in a later scene with Elaine Robinson, Mrs. Robinson's daughter. The scene with the clerk is remarkable for several reasons. First, it continues to accent his anxiety at the situation; second, it establishes the absurdity and the clearly obvious ploy that he's reserving a room for himself, since he comments to the clerk that the only luggage he has is a "tooth-brush"; and, third, it prepares the audience for the major anxiety he will have when, in fact, Mrs. Robinson enters the room in Scene 58.

Scenes 58–9 clearly establish Benjamin as someone "out of his league" with Mrs. Robinson. After Mrs. Robinson meets him at the Taft Hotel she asks if he's reserved a room. He has not. She suggests he do so which he does with all the finesse of a matador with two red capes. Once he's reserved the room, Benjamin goes to a pay phone outside the hotel and calls Mrs. Robinson as she waits for him in the bar. She's handed the phone by a waiter and the dialogue cuts between Benjamin and Mrs. Robinson as Benjamin tells her he got a room, but he thinks the clerk is suspicious. She suggests that he go up first, to which he agrees and starts to hang up.

                    MRS. ROBINSON
          Isn't there something you want to
          tell me?

                         BEN
          To tell you?

                    MRS. ROBINSON
          Yes.

                         BEN
          Well—I want you to know how much
          I appreciate this—really—

> MRS. ROBINSON

The number.

> BEN

What?

> MRS. ROBINSON

The room number, Benjamin. I think
you ought to tell me that.

> BEN

Oh? You're absolutely right. Absolutely.
It's 512.

> MRS. ROBINSON

Thank you.

> BEN

You're welcome. Well—I'll see you
later, Mrs. Robinson.

After Benjamin hangs up, he proceeds to the room and we see him walking by himself down the corridor. As soon as he enters the room, he turns the lights on, then off. He brushes his teeth, which is an act that not only plays off of an earlier line when he tells the clerk the only "luggage" he has is a toothbrush, but also accents the absurdity that he'd even bring a toothbrush with him in the first place. As soon as Mrs. Robinson enters the room she flips on the lights (which he turns off again): an act which clearly works as a metaphor for their relationship. She walks towards the bed and takes a drag off her cigarette. Before she can exhale, Benjamin walks up to her, clears his throat and gives her the "mother of all superficial kisses." When he pulls back, she finally exhales and the dialogue begins with Segment One of three precise segments with her saying she'll get dressed and Benjamin asking what he should do.

> MRS. ROBINSON

Why don't you watch?

> BEN

Oh—sure. Thank you.
She takes off her jacket.

> MRS. ROBINSON

Will you bring me a hanger?

> BEN

What?

> MRS. ROBINSON

A hanger.
Ben opens the closet door.

> BEN

Oh—yes. Wood?

> MRS. ROBINSON

What?

> BEN

Wood or wire? They have both.

> MRS. ROBINSON

Either one will be fine.

> BEN

Okay.
He brings her a hanger. She puts her jacket on
it.

> MRS. ROBINSON

Will you help me with this, please?
She turns her back and he undoes her blouse.

Each of her commands, "watch me get undressed," "get me a hanger," "help me with this," modest as they may be, comments on Benjamin's willingness to be subservient to Mrs. Robinson, and, at the same time, augments his relative inexperience in such situations. In a sense, Benjamin is entirely *reactive* until she takes off her blouse which moves to Segment Two, at which point Mrs. Robinson discovers what seems to be a blemish on it. As she tries to remove the blemish, Benjamin feels her breast to which she is totally indifferent. At that point, Benjamin begins to have second thoughts about what he's doing and that accents the conflict he has between wanting to have sex with Mrs. Robinson and feeling guilty about doing so. The second segment increases his anxiety and immediately after feeling her breast (which is at the midpoint of the scene) he walks to a wall and starts banging his head against it.

                    MRS. ROBINSON
          Would this be easier for you in the dark?

                         BEN
          Mrs. Robinson—I can't do this.

                    MRS. ROBINSON
          You what?

                         BEN
          This is all terribly wrong.

                    MRS. ROBINSON
          Benjamin—do you find me undesirable?

                         BEN
          Oh no, Mrs. Robinson. I think—
          I think you're the most attractive
          of all my parents' friends. I mean
          that. I find you desirable. For
          God's sake can you imagine my parents
          Can you imagine what they would say
          If they saw us in this room right now?

                    MRS. ROBINSON
          What would they say?

                         BEN
          I have no idea Mrs. Robinson, but for
          God's sake they brought me up, they
          made a good life for me. I think they
          deserve better than this. I think
          they deserve a little better than
          jumping into bed with the partner's
          wife.

                    MRS. ROBINSON
Are you afraid of me?

                    BEN
Oh no, you're missing the point.
Maybe we could do something
else together, Mrs. Robinson-
would you like to go to a movie?

In the film, Benjamin alludes to the fact that Mrs. Robinson's husband and Benjamin's father are partners, and that his family made a good life for him. When, as an alternative to having sex, Benjamin suggests a movie, Mrs. Robinson pauses, which leads to Segment Three.

                    MRS. ROBINSON
Benjamin, is this your first time?

                    BEN
Is this—what?

                    MRS. ROBINSON
It is, isn't it? It is your
first time.

                    BEN
That's a laugh, Mrs. Robinson.
That's really a laugh. Ha ha.

                    MRS. ROBINSON
You can admit that, can't you?

                    BEN
Are you kidding?

                    MRS. ROBINSON
It's nothing to be ashamed of—

                    BEN
Wait a minute!

                    MRS. ROBINSON
On your first time—

                    BEN
Who said it was my first time.

                    MRS. ROBINSON
That you're afraid—

                    BEN
Wait a minute.

                    MRS. ROBINSON
— of being—inadequate—I mean
just because you happen to be
inadequate in one way—

                    BEN
INADEQUATE!
LONG pause.

                    MRS. ROBINSON
(starting to dress)

                    BEN
Don't move.

He slams the bathroom door shut. The light in the room
disappears.

At that point, Mrs. Robinson answers his question with a question of her
own that *redirects* the focus of the scene, but also attacks his masculinity
as she asks: "Benjamin, is this your first time?" After all, she didn't come
to the hotel to chat nor go to the movies ... she came to have sex with a
younger man. It's here that the dialogue does such a brilliant job of eliciting
conflict by integrating a number of dialogue techniques, especially the
technique of "dialogue linkage" which links one character's dialogue with
another's.

Once again, if one deconstructs the dialogue, one can see the unique
interrelationship between what Benjamin says and what Mrs. Robinson says.
If one eliminates the narrative, the scene is left with the following dialogue:

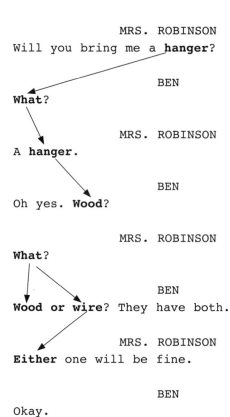

                    MRS. ROBINSON
Will you bring me a **hanger**?

                         BEN
What?

                    MRS. ROBINSON
A **hanger**.

                         BEN
Oh yes. **Wood**?

                    MRS. ROBINSON
What?

                         BEN
Wood or wire? They have both.

                    MRS. ROBINSON
Either one will be fine.

                         BEN
Okay.

                    MRS. ROBINSON
Will you help me with this, please?
She turns her back and he undoes her blouse.

Not only does their dialogue about the "hanger" move the scene forward by linking both dialogues, but it comments on Benjamin's willingness to do Mrs. Robinson's bidding. Subsequent to feeling her breast and banging his head on the wall, the dialogue links continue to work as Benjamin has second thoughts.

                    MRS. ROBINSON
Would **this** be easier for you in the dark?

                         BEN
Mrs. Robinson—I can't do **this**.

                    MRS. ROBINSON
You **what**?

                         BEN
This is all terribly wrong.

                    MRS. ROBINSON
Benjamin—do you find me **undesirable**?

                         BEN
Oh no, Mrs. Robinson. I think –
I think you're the most **attractive**
of all my parents' friends. I mean
that. I find you **desirable**. For
God's sake can you imagine my parents
Can you imagine **what they would say**
if they saw us in this room right now?

                    MRS. ROBINSON
What **would they say**?

                         BEN
I have no idea Mrs. Robinson, but for
God's sake **they brought** me up, they
made a good life for me. I think **they**
deserve better than this. I think
they deserve a little better than
jumping into bed with the partner's
wife.

                    MRS. ROBINSON
Are you **afraid** of me?

                         BEN
Oh no, you're missing the point.

>   Maybe we could do something
>   else together, Mrs. Robinson—
>   would you like to go to a movie?

Benjamin is now in a quandary: does he have sex with her or not? But the comment about going to a movie prompts Mrs. Robinson to get annoyed, and her annoyance becomes the focal point of the last segment of the scene when she asks if it's his first time.

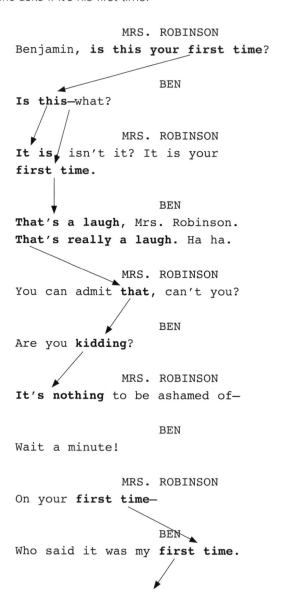

                    MRS. ROBINSON
          Benjamin, **is this your first time?**

                              BEN
          Is this—what?

                    MRS. ROBINSON
          It is, isn't it? It is your
          first time.

                              BEN
          That's a laugh, Mrs. Robinson.
          That's really a laugh. Ha ha.

                    MRS. ROBINSON
          You can admit **that,** can't you?

                              BEN
          Are you **kidding?**

                    MRS. ROBINSON
          It's nothing to be ashamed of—

                              BEN
          Wait a minute!

                    MRS. ROBINSON
          On your **first time**—

                              BEN
          Who said it was my **first time.**

MRS. ROBINSON

That you're **afraid**—

BEN

Wait a minute.

MRS. ROBINSON

—of **being inadequate**—I mean
just because you happen to be
inadequate in one way—

BEN

INADEQUATE!

BEN

Don't move.

Beginning on page 53 of the script she asks Benjamin if it's his "first time."
He answers with a question "Is this what?" the "this" linking to "first time."
To which she replies with a question: "It is isn't it?" and then answers the
question herself "It is your first time," emphasizing the word "is." So, she
emphasizes the notion of it being his "first time" and the interchange of
dialogue stresses that fact. He responds that it's really a laugh, but she
continues on the attack by asking yet another question that: "You can admit
that, can't you?" "that" related to his being a virgin.

From that point on the dialogue is really *parallel monologue* in which Mrs.
Robinson essentially ignores Benjamin's protests as he attempts to defend
himself. She continues on the attack by emphasizing that if it's his "first time"
it's nothing to get upset about. The dialogue links "first time" and "afraid,"
which eventually links to the word "inadequate" which is the clinching and
winning argument for her, since by emphasizing that he's "inadequate"
(which she repeats twice almost in passing and he screams the word as if
it were the ultimate insult) her pause allows her to feign getting dressed to
which Ben yells: "Don't move!" a command which runs exactly counter to
how the dialogue in the scene began with Mrs. Robinson giving the orders.

So, we see how even the scene itself is very self-contained. It moves from
Benjamin's acquiescent role to an active role all mediated by Mrs. Robinson's
provocations. The dialogue, then, reflects that direction. His actions, coupled
with his dialogue, direct the scene to its natural conclusion and continue to
develop character and story, to initiate conflict and to maintain continuity.

It should be clear at this point how the efficacy of a scene is directly related to the dialogue. Not only does the efficacy of the dialogue expand the nature of the characters, but it adds dimension to the storyline. But even more important than those two aspects is the fact the scene is flawlessly integrated. Benjamin's character at the end is clearly linked to Benjamin's character in the beginning. The dialogue, coupled with his behavior, arcs through the scene, balancing the end with the beginning. Although these are very brief scenes, and the dialogue itself rarely goes over six lines by either character, they expand on the previous scenes that have led up to the most critical scene between them and establishes the subsequent direction of the storyline.

As a frame sequence beginning with Scene 50 and ending with Scene 61, one can see how the beginning of that sequence arcs and coincides with ending of that sequence. Not only that, one can see, especially in Scene 61, how the scene is actually a microcosm of the sequence of scenes begun in Scene 50. To that end, one must keep in mind how that the integrity of the scene is paramount and how the dialogue must complement that scenic integrity.

9

Midnight Cowboy (1969)

Screenplay by Waldo Salt
Based on the novel by James
Leo Herlihy

Waldo Salt was, in many ways, the penultimate screenwriter. Some writers are capable of writing one master script. Few screenwriters are capable of writing more than one. Waldo Salt was one of those writers. *Serpico*, *Day of the Locust*, *Coming Home*, *Midnight Cowboy*. The last two of which garnered Academy Awards, a distinction unheard of for most screenwriters. Salt joined the Communist Party in 1938, which eventually got him ostracized from Hollywood and blacklisted from working in Hollywood 15 years. Who knows how many more Oscars he could have garnered if not for that decision? Call him the Muhammad Ali of screenwriters. Hollywood legend has it that Ernst Lubitsch was called the "master of dialogue" and scene construction. Although they were working in Hollywood at the same time, I don't know if Salt were indebted to Lubitsch in any way, but what I do know is that he was a master, himself, at dialogue and scene construction.

That said I'm using two scenes from *Midnight Cowboy* from two different portions of the film to highlight how Salt masterfully utilizes dialogue in creating a unified scene. The first scene is early on in the film, in Everett's Bar after Joe Buck has arrived in New York and, by chance, meets up with Ratso Rizzo. What's integral to this scene is the subtext that goes on with the "ancillary dialogue." In other words, not only is the "primary dialogue" between Ratso and Joe important, but Jackie's ancillary dialogue and the ancillary dialogue that is going on simultaneously on the television are also equally important. As Joe stares at his image in the mirror, Ratso begins the dialogue.

> RATSO'S VOICE
> Excuse me, I'm just admiring that
colossal shirt ...

> RATSO
> That is one hell of a shirt. I bet
you paid a pretty price for it, am
I right?

> JOE
> Oh, it ain't cheap. I mean, yeah,
I'd say this was an all right
shirt. Don't like to, uh, you know,
have a lot of cheap stuff on my
back.

> JOE
> Shee-it ...
(shakes his head)
Kee-rist, you really know the
ropes. Wish to hell I bumped into
you before. I'm Joe Buck from Texas
and I'm gonna buy you a drink, what
do you say to that?

> RATSO
> Enrico Rizzo from the Bronx. Don't
mind if I do.

> JOE
> (slaps bar)
Same all around! For my friend,
too!

                    JOE
... you see what I'm getting at
here? She got a penthouse up there
   with color TV and more goddam
diamonds than an archbishop and she
   busts out bawling when I ask for
                   money!

                   RATSO
               For what?

                    JOE
             For money.

                   RATSO
          For money for what?

                    JOE
I'm a hustler, hell, didn't you
            know that?

                   RATSO
How would I know? You gotta tell a
      person these things
          (shakes his head)
A hustler? Picking up trade on the
street like that—baby, believe
    me—you need management.

                    JOE
I think you just put your finger on
            it, I do.

                   RATSO
My friend O'Daniel. That's who you
need. Operates the biggest stable
   in town. In the whole goddam
metropolitan area. A stud like you
   —paying!—not that I blame you—
  a dame starts crying, I cut my
        heart for her ...

                    JACKIE'S VOICE
          I'd call that a very minor
                    operation

Ratso grabs the neck of a bottle, sliding back in the
                         booth.
Joe scowls as Jackie appears with the tall farm boy.

                       JACKIE
          ... in fact, you just sit comfy and
          I'll cut it out with my fingernail
            file. You won't even need Blue
                    Cross, Ratso.

                       RATSO
               The name is Rizzo.

                       JACKIE
             That's what I said, Ratso.

                        JOE
                    (suddenly)
             Hey now, you heard him.
On the TV screen—the Date Girl announces:

                    TV DATE GIRL
          I pick Number Two! He's cool!

                       RATSO
          That's okay, Joe. I'm used to these
             types that like to pick on
          cripples. Sewers're full of 'em.

                       JACKIE
          May I ask one thing, cowboy? If you
            sit there and he sits way over
          there, how's he gonna get his hand
            into your pocket? But I'm sure he
              has that all figured out ...
                    (to Ratso)
             Good night, sweets.

> TV HOST
> May I present your chosen mate!

> RATSO'S VOICE
> Excuse me, I'm just admiring that
> colossal shirt ...

Of course, Ratso is sizing up the obvious "tourist" as an easy mark since no New Yorker would wear such a shirt. His attempt at ingratiating himself with Joe is just the beginning of an exercise in trying to manipulate him.

> RATSO
> That is one hell of a shirt. I bet
> you paid a pretty price for it, am
> I right?

> JOE
> Oh, it ain't cheap. I mean, yeah,
> I'd say this was an all right
> shirt. Don't like to, uh, you know,
> have a lot of cheap stuff on my
> back.

At that point, Jackie (a transvestite) asks Joe, the cowboy, for a cigarette. Beneath his breath, Ratso alludes to the fact that Jackie is a "faggot." It's Ratso's dialogue that somehow "enlightens" Joe about the pervasively prurient culture he's just discovering. After all, Joe thinks of himself as a stud even though he's coming from the tumbleweeds of Texas.

> JOE
> Shee-it...
> (shakes his head)
> Kee-rist, you really know the
> ropes. Wish to hell I bumped into
> you before. I'm Joe Buck from Texas
> and I'm gonna buy you a drink, what
> do you say to that?

> RATSO
> Enrico Rizzo from the Bronx. Don't
> mind if I do.

>   JOE
>   (slaps bar)
>   Same all around! For my friend,
>   too!

One of the truly brilliant things that Salt does in this scene is the way he incorporates the television program and its ancillary dialogue as a subtext to the scene. What's playing on the television is a "mating game" program. Patterned after the *Dating Game*, there are three young men, visible only from the shoulders up, from whom a young woman must choose for a date. As the program continues in the background, Joe and Ratso continue their dialogue with Joe telling Ratso how annoyed he is with the fact that he's not being paid for his "studly" services.

>   JOE
>   ... you see what I'm getting at
>   here? She got a penthouse up there
>   with color TV and more goddam
>   diamonds than an archbishop and she
>   busts out bawling when I ask for
>   money!

>   RATSO
>   For what?

>   JOE
>   For money.

>   RATSO
>   For money for what?

The mention of the word "money" moves the scene in the direction Ratso wants it to move in. The issue of money links with the fact that Joe considers himself a "hustler."

>   JOE
>   I'm a hustler, hell, didn't you
>   know that?

>   RATSO
>   How would I know? You gotta tell a

> person these things
> (shakes his head)
> A hustler? Picking up trade on the
> street like that—baby, believe
> me—you need management.

> JOE
> I think you just put your finger on
> it, I do.

Being a "hustler" links to the notion of "management" which links to O'Daniel who, presumably, manages all the major New York studs.

> RATSO
> My friend O'Daniel. That's who you
> need. Operates the biggest stable
> in town. In the whole goddam
> metropolitan area. A stud like you
> —paying!—not that I blame you—a dame starts crying, I
> cut my
> heart for her ...

> JACKIE'S VOICE
> I'd call that a very minor
> operation ...

Ratso grabs the neck of a bottle, sliding back in the
booth.
Joe scowls as Jackie appears with the tall farm boy.

> JACKIE
> ... in fact, you just sit comfy and
> I'll cut it out with my fingernail
> file. You won't even need Blue
> Cross, Ratso.

The comment about his "heart" is a marvelous link to Jackie's comments which apparently go over Joe's head.

> RATSO
> The name is Rizzo.

                        JACKIE
              That's what I said, Ratso.

                         JOE
                      (suddenly)
                Hey now, you heard him.
       On the TV screen—the Date Girl announces:

                      TV DATE GIRL
                I pick Number Two! He's cool!

                        RATSO
             That's okay, Joe. I'm used to these
                types that like to pick on
             cripples. Sewers're full of 'em.

                        JACKIE
             May I ask one thing, cowboy? If you
                sit there and he sits way over
             there, how's he gonna get his hand
             into your pocket? But I'm sure he
                has that all figured out ...
                       (to Ratso)
                Good night, sweets.

As Joe comes to Ratso's defense, his dialogue is paralleled with the ancillary
television dialogue and Jackie's ancillary dialogue which continues to develop
Ratso's character, plus Ratso's comment about defending himself because
he's handicapped (i.e. a cripple).

                        TV HOST
                May I present your chosen mate!

When the host reveals who the lucky guy is, we see that he's a dwarf. If we
look closely at how Salt utilizes the links in the scene, you'll see there's very
little room for error.

INT. EVERETT'S BAR—DAY

> **RATSO'S VOICE**
> Excuse me, I'm just admiring that
> **colossal shirt** ...

> **RATSO**
> That is one hell of a **shirt**. I bet
> you paid a **pretty price** for it, am
> I right?

> **JOE**
> Oh, it **ain't cheap**. I mean, yeah,
> I'd say this was an all right
> **shirt.** Don't like to, uh, you know,
> have a lot of cheap stuff on my
> back.

> **JACKIE**
> Got a cigarette, cowboy?

> **RATSO**
> More goddam faggots in this town.

Reaching for a cigarette, Joe glances at Jackie, startled
as Jackie twitches his pink Levis angrily and turns away.

> **JOE**
> Shee-it ...
> Kee-rist, you really know the
> ropes. Wish to hell I bumped into
> you before. I'm **Joe Buck from Texas
> and I'm gonna buy you a drink, what
> do you say to** that?

> RATSO
> **Enrico Rizzo from the Bronx. Don't
> mind if I do.**

> **JOE**
> **Same all around!** For my friend,
> too!

TV HOST

... and for the losers, who don't
get the girl, we'll give as
consolation prices—a six month
supply of underarm deodorant ...

JOE

... you see what I'm getting at
here? She got a penthouse up there
with color TV and more goddam
diamonds than an archbishop and she
busts out bawling when **I ask for
money!**

RATSO

For what?

JOE

For money.

RATSO

For money for what?

JOE

I'm a **hustler,** hell, didn't you
know that?

RATSO

How would I know? You gotta tell a
person these things
A **hustler?** Picking up trade on the
street like that—baby, believe
me—**you need management.**

JOE

I think you just put your finger on
it, I do.

RATSO

My friend O'Daniel. That's who you
need. Operates the **biggest stable**

in town. In the whole goddam
metropolitan area. A **stud** like you
—paying!—not that I blame you—a dame starts
crying, **I cut my
heart for her** ...

                    JACKIE'S VOICE
I'd call that a very **minor
operation** ...

                    JACKIE
... in fact, you just sit comfy and
**I'll cut it out with my fingernail
file.** You won't even need Blue
Cross, **Ratso.**

                    RATSO
The **name is Rizzo.**

                    JACKIE
That's what I said, **Ratso.**

                    JOE
Hey now, **you heard him.**

                    TV DATE GIRL
I pick Number Two! He's cool!

                    RATSO
That's okay, Joe. **I'm used to these
types that like to pick on
cripples.** Sewers're full of 'em.

                    JACKIE
May I ask one thing, cowboy? If you
sit there and he sits way over
there, how's he gonna get his hand
into your pocket? But I'm sure he
has that all figured out...
          (to Ratso)
Good night, sweets.

TV HOST
May I present your chosen mate!

Not only do these links propel the scene forward, but they're constantly making comments on the characters and the direction of the story. The TV line "May I present your chosen mate!" works brilliantly on both the ancillary level and, of course, on the primary level between Joe and Ratso since they are chosen mates. Unfortunately, the film version leaves out the ancillary TV dialogue which, in a fundamental way, undermines the irony in the scene. Although the ancillary dialogue with Jackie remains intact, as does the majority of the dialogue, there is something lost with the omission of the TV dialogue; however, the scene has been revised to eliminate certain longer portions of the dialogue that increase the tempo of the scene. As I indicated in *The Graduate*, sometimes economical dialogue is preferable to extensive dialogue depending on the context of the scene. Once again we need to look at how the scene is unified and how the dialogue contributes to that unification.

In this instance, the scene opens in the bar and closes in the bar. The difference is that there is no relationship between Joe and Ratso at the beginning and there is a relationship between Joe and Ratso at the end augmented by the "mates" line. Not only does the dialogue maintain scenic integrity, but it also advances the storyline and develops character. What accents the unity of the scene is what Salt does with the ancillary television dialogue. He closes the scene with the television host stating to the young woman that "here is your chosen mate." When the host pulls side the screen we discover that the chosen mate is a dwarf, which causes the young woman no little consternation. The dialogue, if not the content of the television show, is a subtextual comment on the relationship between Joe and Ratso in that Joe can be considered "normal" and Ratso "abnormal" by virtue of his handicap in the same way the young woman can be considered "normal" and the dwarf "abnormal." Those labels are, of course, arbitrary ones, but in the context of the scene, if not the film, that ancillary dialogue contributes to the scene.

What was marginal, lost by omission of the ancillary TV dialogue in the bar scene, is more than made up for in the apartment scene. In the script, the scene begins with Joe returning to their squatter's apartment. Ratso is shivering and sweating. He's obviously ill. Joe is concerned by Ratso's condition, but turns his attention to the soup warming on the Sterno stove.

                    JOE

See what you think of that crap.
I'll pour your soup. Got some of
that junk you like to swill, too.
Mentholatum. Aspirin. All that shee
it ... They wrong?

                   RATSO

No. But while you was buying the
underwear, I could have lifted the
socks.

                    JOE

You couldn't lift fly specks from a
sugar bowl. Can you hold this?

                   RATSO

But thanks.
            (hesitates, then)
Hey, Joe, don't get sore about this
or anything. You promise?

                    JOE

Yeah.

                   RATSO

Well, I don't think I can walk.
            (embarrassed)
I mean, I been falling down a lot
and, uh ...

                    JOE

And what?

                   RATSO

I'm scared.

                    JOE

What of?

>   RATSO
> What'll happen. I mean what they do
> to, you know, do with you—if you
> can't—ah, Christ!

>   JOE
> Who?

>   RATSO
> I don't know. Cops. Or the—how
> should I know?

>   JOE
> Okay. Here it is. You gonna go see
> the doctor. I got nine bucks and
> twenty more Thursday and I gonna be
> riding high before you know it. So
> you gonna get you the best goddam
> doctor in this town and get
> yourself straightened out, that's
> what.

>   RATSO
> No doctors. No, sir. Not me.
> Doctors are like goddam auto
> mechanics. Fix one-thing, unplug
> another. Operate for piles and
> while they're there, they unscrew
> your liver. My old man, for God's
> sake, wasn't any sicker'n I am when
> he went to the doctor.

>   JOE
> Well, just exactly what the hell
> you think you're gonna do? Die on
>   me?

>   RATSO
> I'm going to Florida, that's my
> only chance.

                              JOE

You know what's wrong with you? You
got fevers. You kinky as a bedbug.
How you gonna get to Florida?

                             RATSO

I'll find the money. If you just
get me on the bus, that's all I
ask.

                              JOE

Just when everything's going my
way, you gotta pull a stunt like
this.

                             RATSO

I don't even want you to go.
Whaddya think of that? I got other
plans for my life than dragging
around some dumb cowboy that thinks
he's God's gift to women. One
twenty-buck trick and he's already
the biggest stud in New York City.
It's laughable.

Joe sets his Stetson on his head.

                              JOE

When I put you on that bus down to
Florida tonight, that'll be the
happiest day of my life!

In certain portions of the final draft dialogue, Salt clearly overwrote the
dialogue (e.g. the exchange about doctors, Ratso's diatribe about Joe's
studliness). The focus of the scene needed to be Ratso's illness since that's
what drives the scene to its natural conclusion. Salt remedied that in the
shooting script in a manner not unlike what Buck Henry revised in scene 81.
Salt has made the scene dramatically more effective by reducing the dialogue
to get to the critical essence of it.

   As the scene opens, we see Ratso sitting on the bed coughing. Joe comes
into the room carrying a brown paper bag.

>   JOE
>   Hey boy look. Look right in there
>   and what do you see? Look in there
>   boy. Got some of that stuff you like
>   to swill, too. **Aspirin. Mentholatum.**
>   All that crap. Whatsa' matter?

>   RATSO
>   A okay, but why'd you buy 'em. You were
>   gettin' me aspirin. I could've lifted
>   this?

He then looks at the soup.

>   Is that **hot**?

>   JOE
>   Yeah. You want some **soup**?

>   RATSO
>   Yeah.

>   JOE
>   I'll get you some **soup** then.
>   We ain't gonna have to steal no
>   more is what I'm trying to tell ya.
>   I got eight dollars in my pockets
>   twenty more to come Thursday. Boy
>   we're gonna be ridin' high soon.

>   RATSO
>   Gimme some **soup**

>   JOE
>   What do ya' think I'm getting for
>   ya'. I'm getting you some **soup.**

                    RATSO
How was **she**?

                    JOE
She was crazy if you wanna know
the damn truth of it. Turned into
a damn alley cat.

                    RATSO
Thanks for the stuff.

                    JOE
Don't mention it.

                    RATSO
Hey, don't get sore about this
or anything. **I don't think I can
walk anymore.** I mean, I been **fallin'
down** a lot. (beat) **I'm scared.**

                    JOE
What are you scared of?

                    RATSO
You know what they do to you
when you can't, when they find
out you **can't walk.** Oh Christ! (beat)
I gotta **lay down.** I gotta **lay
down.**

                    JOE
Okay, **lay down.** Take it easy. **I'll
lay you down.** Put this thing over
you. Now you stay.

                    RATSO
Where you goin'!

                        JOE
I gotta get **a doctor.**

                        RATSO
What!

                        JOE
I gotta get a **doctor.**

                        RATSO
You ain't getting' **no doctor!**

                        JOE
You're sick boy. You need a damn
doctor.

                        RATSO
Hey! No **doctors.** No cops. Don't be
stupid.

                        JOE
Well **what in the hell do you want
me to do!**

                        RATSO
Florida. You get me to **Florida.**

                        JOE
I can't go to **Florida** now.

                        RATSO
Just put me on a bus. Just put me
on a bus. I don't need you.

                        JOE
You got a damn fever. How you gonna
get to Florida.

RATSO
Just put me on a bus. You're not
sending me to Bellevue. What you doin'.
What are you doin'. **It's hot.**

JOE
Sick.

RATSP
I'm **too hot** now. **Dumb.** You're really
dumb. I don't need you.

JOE
Shut up! Just shut up!

RATSO
Dumb cowboy.

JOE
Shut up! Shut up! Just when things
go right for me you gotta pull a damn
stunt like this.

Likewise, this second scene tends to validate the first. By this time, Joe and Ratso have become friends and Joe has become a kind of provider, a guardian if you will of Ratso's physical health. The scene itself is self-contained. In other words, the scene opens with Joe arriving and closes with Joe leaving. He arrives with medicine for Ratso and he leaves to find a doctor for Ratso. The opening of the scene links to the ending since the focus of the scene is on Ratso's illness. Regardless of how "put out" Joe may appear to be at the end of the scene, ultimately he is bonded to Ratso and that is clearly established by his concern for him. Medicine, soup, doctors, Florida, they all revolve around Ratso's medical needs and how well Joe fulfills those needs.

When one looks at the film as a whole, it obeys Aristotelian notions of unity. At the beginning of the film Joe is self-serving and egocentric. At the end of the film, he has become a guardian who has relinquished his self-serving needs for the benefit of someone else. As I indicated earlier, the "microscript" mirrors what's going on in the "macroscript" and clearly in the case of *Midnight Cowboy* that parallel has been achieved.

10

Chinatown (1974)
Screenplay by Robert Towne

In the November 5, 2009 interview by Alex Simon and Terry Keefe in *The Hollywood Interview*, Towne was asked about writing the Gittes part for Jack Nicholson. Towne responded, "Well with Jack, yes, I wrote the part for him, in his voice, so to speak. We'd been close friends for a long time. But with the part of Evelyn, there were several actresses at the top of the list, and Jane was one of them. But Jack was Gittes. I could not have written that character without knowing Jack. We had been roommates, and we'd studied acting with Jeff Corey for years, so he was, in a very real sense, a collaborator." What's so engaging about that comment is that without ever seeing the film and only reading the script, Gittes would be Nicholson since there's that flavor to Gittes' character that could only have been pulled off by Nicholson. There's something clearly in the tone of the dialogue that seems to be native to Nicholson and that's because of Towne's unique abilities as a writer.

In the book *Roman Polanski: Interviews*, edited by Paul Cronin (2005), there's a revealing bit of dialogue between Cronin and Polanski. Cronin asks the question: "Is it true you argued with the author of the screenplay over the ending?" (Cronin, 2005, p. 63). Polanski replied, that "he" (the author) wanted Cross to die and Polanski wanted Dunaway to die since it was more tragic that way. To me that bit of dialogue tells all that needs to be told about how the writer is thought of in Hollywood. It's not as if Towne were a novice and *Chinatown* was his first script, but rather than call the author Towne, Cronin essentially refused to privilege him as the screenwriter and Polanski did likewise by addressing him as "he." It reminds me of something I read somewhere when Ernst Lubitsch (the famous German American actor, screenwriter, producer, and film director whose films were promoted as having "the Lubitsch touch") was giving a writer such a hard time that the writer returned the following day with a 120 blank pages, threw them at Lubitsch and said as he left, "Give that your Lubitsch touch." I hope I didn't make that up, but if it weren't said it should have been. Actually, it seems the only time Polanski recognized Towne, as Towne was in addressing him as a "script doctor."

Regardless of what Cronin or Polanski thought of Towne, the screenplay, and especially the dialogue, is masterfully written and utilizes dialogue links in the most compelling of ways as the script can attest in the following scene.

EXT. VERANDA—MULWRAY HOME—NIGHT

Gittes stands on the veranda, smoking a cigarette, staring off into the night.

Evelyn comes out to the veranda, carrying a tray with whiskey and an ice bucket on it. She sets it down—Gittes turns.

                    GITTES
            (watching her pour)
        Maid's night off?

                    EVELYN
        Why?

                    GITTES
            (a little surprised,
            he laughs)
        What do you mean, 'why?' Nobody's
        here, that's all.

                    EVELYN
            (handing Gittes his
            drink)
        —I gave everybody the night off—

                    GITTES
        —Easy, It's an innocent question.

EVELYN

No question from you is innocent,
Mr. Gittes.

GITTES

(laughing)
I guess not—to you, Mrs. Mulwray.
Frankly you really saved my a—
my neck tonight.

EVELYN

Tell me something—does this
usually happen to you, Mr. Gittes?

GITTES

What's that, Mrs. Mulwray?

EVELYN

—Well, I'm only judging on the
basis of one afternoon and an evening,
but if that's how you go about your
work, I'd say you're lucky to get
through a whole day.

GITTES

(pouring himself
another drink)
—Actually this hasn't happened
to me in some time.

EVELYN

—When was the last time?

GITTES

Why?

EVELYN

Just—I don't know why.
I'm asking.

                    GITTES
It was in Chinatown.

                    EVELYN
What were you doing there?

                    GITTES
          (taking a long drink)
—Working for the District Attorney.

                    EVELYN
Doing what?

                    GITTES
As little as possible.

                    EVELYN
The District Attorney gives his
men advice like that?

                    GITTES
They do in Chinatown.

                    EVELYN
Bothers you to talk about it,
doesn't it?

                    GITTES
No—I wonder—could I—do
you have any peroxide or something?

                    EVELYN
Oh sure. C'mon.

She takes his hand and leads him back into the house.

We can take a look at the dialogue links in detail.

EXT. VERANDA—MULWRAY HOME—NIGHT

Gittes stands on the veranda, smoking a cigarette, staring off into the night.

Evelyn comes out to the veranda, carrying a tray with whiskey and an ice bucket on it. She sets it down—Gittes turns.

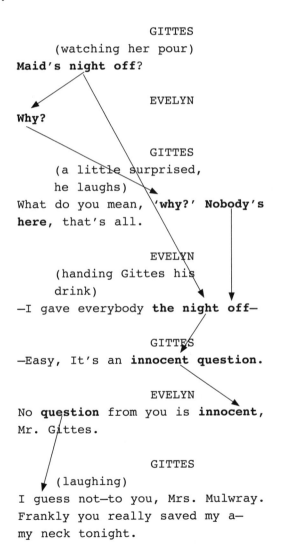

GITTES
(watching her pour)
Maid's night off?

EVELYN
Why?

GITTES
(a little surprised,
he laughs)
What do you mean, **'why?' Nobody's here**, that's all.

EVELYN
(handing Gittes his
drink)
—I gave everybody **the night off**—

GITTES
—Easy, It's an **innocent question.**

EVELYN
No **question** from you is **innocent**,
Mr. Gittes.

GITTES
(laughing)
I guess not—to you, Mrs. Mulwray.
Frankly you really saved my a—
my neck tonight.

Towne engages immediately. Gittes' question about the maid having the "night off" prompts Evelyn to ask "Why?" and Gittes links by repeating the word "Why?" and adding because "Nobody's here." Evelyn links with the phrase "night off" as Gittes replies with it being an "innocent question" and Evelyn rephrases his comment and links with "No question from you is innocent," which Gittes continues by saying "guess not."

They drink.

EVELYN
Tell me something—**does this**
usually happen to you, Mr. Gittes?

GITTES
What's that, Mrs. Mulwray?

EVELYN
—Well, I'm only judging on the
basis of one afternoon and an evening,
but if that's how you go about your
work, I'd say **you're lucky to get**
through a whole day.

GITTES
(pouring himself
another drink)
—Actually **this hasn't happened**
to me in some time.

EVELYN
—**When was the last time?**

GITTES
Why?

EVELYN
Just—**I don't know why.**
I'm asking.

Gittes touches his nose, winces a little.

Evelyn's question about "this happening" links with Gittes' question "what's that?" She plays off that line about how he's lucky to "get through the whole day," which allows Gittes to link with "this hasn't happened ... some time." Her question "when was the last time" links on the word "time," and to Gittes' question "why" she responds in kind by linking that she doesn't know "why" just asking, which prompts Gittes to tell her when it happened.

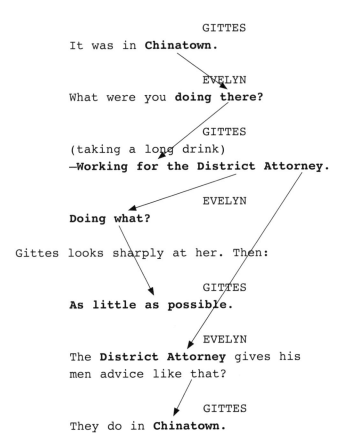

```
                        GITTES
            It was in Chinatown.

                        EVELYN
            What were you doing there?

                            GITTES
            (taking a long drink)
            —Working for the District Attorney.

                        EVELYN
            Doing what?

Gittes looks sharply at her. Then:

                            GITTES
            As little as possible.

                        EVELYN
            The District Attorney gives his
            men advice like that?

                        GITTES
            They do in Chinatown.
```

She looks at him. Gittes stares off into the night. Evelyn has poured herself another drink.

>   EVELYN
>   **Bothers** you to talk **about** it,
>   doesn't it?

Gittes gets up.

>   GITTES
>   **No**—I wonder—could I—do
>   you have any peroxide or something?

He touches his nose lightly.

>   EVELYN
>   Oh sure. C'mon.

She takes his hand and leads him back into the house.

It should go without saying at this point, now over three decades since *Citizen Kane*, that the dialogic methods used by these screenwriters have withstood the "test of cinematic time." The art of creating viable dialogue is not only linked to a thorough understanding of the methods involved, but also to the ability of these writers to "listen." We can look at another, more extensive, example of that ability.

EXT. POND—CROSS AND GITTES

>   CROSS
>   (after a long moment)
>   —no, Mr. Gittes. That's what
>   I am doing with the Valley. The
>   bond issue passes Tuesday—
>   there'll be ten million to build
>   an aqueduct and reservoir. I'm
>   doing it.

>   GITTES
>   There's going to be some irate
>   citizens when they find out they're
>   paying for water they're not getting.

                    CROSS
That's all taken care of. You see,
Mr. Gittes. Either you bring the
water to L.A.—or you bring L.A.
to the water.

                    GITTES
How do you do that?

                    CROSS
—just incorporate the Valley into
the city so the water goes to L.A.
after all. It's very simple.

Gittes nods.

                    GITTES
        (then)
How much are you worth?

                    CROSS
        (shrugs, then)
I have no idea. How much do you
want?

                    GITTES
I want to know what you're worth—
over ten million?

                    CROSS
Oh, my, yes.

                    GITTES
Then why are you doing it? How
much better can you eat? What can
you buy that you can't already
afford?

                          CROSS
                    (a long moment,
                    then:)
          The future, Mr. Gittes—the
          future. Now where's the girl? ...
          I want the only daughter I have
          left ... as you found out, Evelyn
          was lost to me a long time ago.

                          GITTES
                    (with sarcasm)
          Who do you blame for that? Her?

Cross makes a funny little cock of his head.

                          CROSS
          I don't blame myself. You see,
          Mr. Gittes, most people never
          have to face the fact that at
          the right time and right place,
          they're capable of anything. Take
          those glasses from him, will you,
          Claude?

Mulvihill moves INTO VIEW. Extends his hand for the
glasses. Gittes doesn't move.

                          CROSS
                    (continuing)
          It's not worth it, Mr. Gittes.
          It's really not worth it.

Gittes hands over the glasses.

                          CROSS
                    (continuing)
          Take us to the girl. Either
          Evelyn allows me to see her, or
          I'm not averse to seeing Evelyn
          in jail—if I have to buy the
          jail—Hollis and Evelyn kept

her from me for fifteen years—
it's been too long, I'm too old.

As with the previous example, we can see how Towne writes his dialogue to
express the individual character's voice while utilizing the things we've been
talking about relative to linking the dialogue segments effectively.

EXT. POND—CROSS AND GITTES

                    CROSS
          (after a long moment)
     -- no, Mr. Gittes. That's what
     I am doing with the Valley. The
     bond issue passes Tuesday—
     there'll be ten million to build
     an **aqueduct and reservoir.** I'm
     doing it.

                    GITTES
     There's going to be some irate
     citizens when they find out **they're**
     paying for water they're not getting.

                    CROSS
     That's all taken care of. You see,
     Mr. Gittes. Either you **bring the**
     water to L.A.—or you bring L.A.
     to the water.

                    GITTES
     How do you do that?

                    CROSS
     —just incorporate the Valley into
     the city so the water goes to L.A.
     after all. It's very simple.

These are examples of linking with analogues as well as repeating words.
Cross begins by alluding to the construction of an "aqueduct and reservoir,"
which prompts Gittes to comment on citizens paying for "water" they're not
getting. Cross then links with the phrase "that's all taken care of" (namely,

paying for water they're not getting), then links on the word "water" (twice) by alluding to bring L.A. to the "water." That would naturally inspire Gittes to ask the obvious question to which Cross simply answers and links to make the Valley part of L.A. so the "water" goes there.

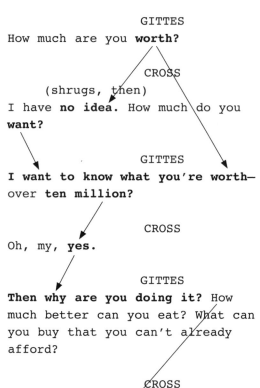

<pre>
                        GITTES
        How much are you **worth?**

                            CROSS
                (shrugs, then)
        I have **no idea.** How much do you
        want?

                        GITTES
        I want to know what you're worth—
        over **ten million?**

                            CROSS
        Oh, my, **yes.**

                        GITTES
        Then why are you doing it? How
        much better can you eat? What can
        you buy that you can't already
        afford?

                        CROSS
                (a long moment,
                then:)
        The future, Mr. Gittes—the
        future. Now where's the **girl?**
        I want the only **daughter** I have
        left ...as you found out, **Evelyn**
        was lost to me a long time ago.

                        GITTES
                (with sarcasm)
        Who do you blame for that? Her?
        Cross makes a funny little cock of his head.
</pre>

> CROSS
>
> **I don't blame myself.** You see,
> Mr. Gittes, most people never
> have to face the fact that at
> the right time and right place,
> they're capable of anything. Take
> those glasses from him, will you,
> Claude?

Mulvihill moves INTO VIEW. Extends his hand for the glasses. Gittes doesn't move.

> CROSS
> (continuing)
> It's not **worth it**, Mr. Gittes.
> It's really not **worth it.**

Gittes hands over the glasses.

> CROSS
> (continuing)
> Take us to the **girl.** Either
> **Evelyn** allows me to see her, or
> I'm not averse to seeing **Evelyn**
> in jail—if I have to buy the
> jail—Hollis and **Evelyn** kept
> **her** from me for fifteen years—
> it's been too long, I'm too old.

Towne does an extraordinary job in linking these dialogue segments and in establishing a key focus of the scene; namely, the notion of "worth." To Gittes' question about how much he's "worth," Cross replies "no idea [how much I'm worth]." To the question "How much do you want?" Gittes double links by asking that he "wants" to know how much Cross is "worth." At the suggestion of "ten million," Cross answers "Oh, my, yes" which presumes he's "worth" much more. Gittes asks why he's doing it since he doesn't need the money, to which Cross answers that it's about the "future" (twice) then shifts the focus to the "girl" and to "Evelyn," and to why the latter was "lost" to him. Gittes, of course, relates the notion of being "lost" to notions of "blame" and asks Cross if he "blames" her (i.e. Evelyn), and that allows Cross to link on denying any responsibility for "blame" and proceeds to try to justify that to himself. Cross then concludes the scene by once again bringing up the word "worth" (twice) which acts as a reprise from the opening of the scene even though it's somewhat antithetic to the opening. Cross then moves on to talk again about the "girl" and "Evelyn" using multiple internal links as he does so.

In a rather sophisticated way, Towne has linked Gittes' dialogue and Cross's dialogue by using both repetitive links and analogues which not only establish their individual voices, but also contribute to the advancement of the storyline.

11

Annie Hall (1977)
Screenplay by Woody Allen and Marshall Brickman

The theater lobby scene in Annie Hall is really a *tour de force* in imaginative screenwriting. Alvy, Allen's character, refuses to watch a film after it begins, so he and Annie have to wait until there's another showing. They leave, return, and wait in line. The scene opens with the rather pedantic dialogue of the Man in Line (MIL) who stands behind Alvy pontificating to his date, who's mute throughout the scene, about the apparent failings of one of Fellini's films. What happens throughout the scene is the dialogic exchange between and among the MIL, Alvy, and Annie. There is the brilliant use of *overlapping dialogue* (i.e. parallel dialogue, with both characters talking at the same time) throughout the scene, but the prevailing theme of "indulgence" is immediately established with the MIL's opening lines about how disappointed he was with Fellini's most recent (and unnamed) film.

                    MAN IN LINE
        Like all that Juliet of the Spirits or
        Satyricon, I found it incredibly ...
        indulgent. You know, he really is. He's
        one of the most indulgent film makers. He
        really is—

                        ALVY
            (Overlapping)
        Key word here is "indulgent."

                    MAN IN LINE
          (Overlapping)
          —without getting ... well, let's put it
          this way ...

                    ALVY
          (To Annie, who is still reading,
          overlapping the man in line who is
          still talking)
          What are you depressed about?

Alvy changes the focus of the scene from "indulgence," by asking Annie what she's depressed about. Annie says it's because she missed her therapy because she overslept. Alvy links on the word "overslept" to alter the focus of the dialogue.

                    ANNIE
          I missed my therapy. I overslept.

                    ALVY
          How can you possibly oversleep?

                    ANNIE
          The alarm clock.

                    ALVY
          (Gasping)
          You know what a hostile gesture that is
          to me?

                    ANNIE
          I know-because of our sexual problem,
          right?

                    ALVY
          Hey, you ... everybody in line at the
          New Yorker has to know our rate of
          intercourse?

Interestingly enough, the focus of the scene has moved from Fellini's presumed indulgence to their sexual relationship, which, in fact, is another form of indulgence. The brilliance of the scene relates to "communication," and the fact that "intercourse" is also another word for communication is vital to the scene. The lack of communication between Alvy and Annie is paralleled by the lack of communication between Alvy and the MIL and that lack of communication is augmented by what the MIL says next.

                    MAN IN LINE
        —It's like Samuel Beckett, you know—
        I admire the technique but he doesn't ...
        he doesn't hit me on a gut level.

                        ALVY
                  (To Annie)
        I'd like to hit this guy on a gut level.

The MIL continues his speech all the while Alvy and Annie talk, although Annie gets annoyed by Alvy's preoccupation with what the MIL says, and she tells him to stop. Alvy replies that he (the MIL) is spitting on his neck. Annie then refocuses the dialogue back to her therapy by saying that Alvy is so egocentric (i.e. self-indulgent) that if she misses *her* therapy session Alvy can only think of it as it pertains to him. At the same time, the MIL continues blabbing and, instead of listening to Annie, Alvy continues to be preoccupied with the blather coming from the MIL, which only corroborates what Annie has been contending all along about their lack of communication. Alvy continues to comment on the MIL's dialogue when, almost as an afterthought, he returns to their sexual problems.

                        ALVY
        Probably met by answering an ad in the
        New York Review of Books. "Thirtyish
        academic wishes to meet woman who's
        interested in Mozart, James Joyce and
        sodomy."
             (He sighs; then to Annie)
        Whatta you mean, our sexual problem?

                        ANNIE
        Oh!

                        ALVY
        I-I-I mean, I'm comparatively normal
        for a guy raised in Brooklyn.

                    ANNIE
        Okay, I'm very sorry. My sexual problem!
        Okay, my sexual problem! Huh?

                    ALVY
        I never read that. That was-that was
        Henry James, right? Novel, uh, the
        sequel to Turn of the Screw? My sexual …

Finally, in an even louder voice than before, the MIL says something about Marshall McLuhan. At that point, Alvy, who's had enough of the MIL's pedantry, steps forward, waving his hands in frustration, and stands facing the camera and asks the audience what does one do when stuck in a line with a pedant like that, to which the MIL steps out of line to defend himself as they both address the camera. The MIL says that he can give his opinion since it's a free country, to which Alvy replies about his apparent pontificating and the fact he knows nothing about McLuhan's work. The MIL contends he teaches a media and culture course at Columbia.

                    MAN IN LINE
             (Overlapping)
        Wait a minute! Really? Really? I happen to
        teach a class at Columbia called "TV Media
        and Culture"! So I think that my insights
        into Mr. McLuhan-well, have a great deal of
        validity.

                    ALVY
        Oh, do yuh?

                    MAN IN LINE
        Yes.

                    ALVY
        Well, that's funny, because I happen to
        have Mr. McLuhan right here. So ... so,
        here, just let me-I mean, all right. Come
        over here ... a second.

At that point, Alvy moves over to a large stand-up movie poster and pulls Marshall McLuhan from behind it, then tells McLuhan to tell the MIL he doesn't know what he's talking about.

                    MAN IN LINE
Oh.

                    ALVY
          (To McLuhan)
Tell him.

                    McLUHAN
          (To the man in line)
I hear-I heard what you were saying.
You-you know nothing of my work. You
mean my whole fallacy is wrong. How you
ever got to teach a course in anything is
totally amazing.

                    ALVY
          (To the camera)
Boy, if life were only like this!

Ironically, McLuhan's most well-known work, *The Medium is the **Massage***, which was meant to explain his philosophy of the media and communication has, over the decades since its publication in 1967, been erroneously referred to as *The Medium is the **Message**.* That fact alone underscores how the lack of communication has become a preeminent issue in contemporary society and how that lack of communication, intercourse if you will, is clearly the focal point of the entire scene. For example, if we look at the dialogue links and how those links comment on both the scene, but also on the characters we get the following.

                    MAN IN LINE
          Like all that Juliet of the Spirits or
          Satyricon, I found it incredibly ...
          indulgent. You know, he really is. He's
          one of the most **indulgent** film makers. He
          really is-

                    ALVY
          (Overlapping)
          Key word here is "**indulgent.**"

As the MIL continues to pontificate to his mute date, Alvy presumably changes the focus of the scene from the MIL's indulgent comment about Fellini and Alvy's *indulgent* comment about the MIL, to Annie's apparent depression. The irony here is that both the MIL and Alvy are fairly indulgent. Annie refocuses the scene from Alvy's annoyance with the MIL to what concerns her.

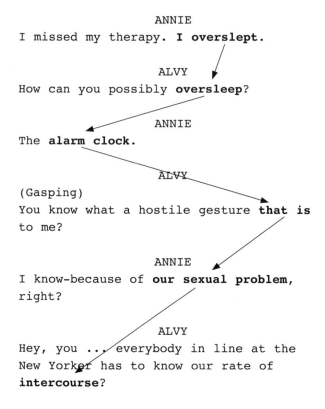

```
                        ANNIE
        I missed my therapy. I overslept.

                        ALVY
        How can you possibly oversleep?

                        ANNIE
        The alarm clock.

                        ALVY
        (Gasping)
        You know what a hostile gesture that is
        to me?

                        ANNIE
        I know-because of our sexual problem,
        right?

                        ALVY
        Hey, you ... everybody in line at the
        New Yorker has to know our rate of
        intercourse?
```

The dialogue links here work on several levels. Her apparent depression is linked to the fact she overslept and by virtue of oversleeping missed her therapy appointment. Alvy takes a fairly self-indulgent approach here by correlating her oversleeping with the sexual problems they're having, hence his allusion, albeit somewhat paranoid, that her missing the appointment is somehow related to the fact she overslept, and the fact she overslept related to the alarm clock, and that somehow relates to Alvy. In the meantime, the overlapping dialogue continues with the MIL now re-focusing his diatribe from Fellini to Beckett.

> MAN IN LINE
> —It's like **Samuel Beckett,** you know—
> I admire the technique but he doesn't ...
> he doesn't hit me on a **gut level.**

> ALVY
> (To Annie)
> I'd like to hit this guy on a **gut level.**

What's brilliant about the fact the MIL brings up Beckett's name is that it is yet another ironic comment on the notion of lack of communication. Beckett's masterpiece, *Waiting for Godot*, clearly embraces the notion that mankind's attempts at any kind of meaningful communication are bound to fail. Given that, the fact Allen inserts an allusion to the absurdist Beckett rather than another playwright is integral to the scene and to the characters in it. After making yet another comment on the MIL's comment, he sighs, then returns to Annie and re-directs the focus back to sexuality.

> ALVY
> Probably met by answering an ad in the
> New York Review of Books. "Thirtyish
> academic wishes to meet woman who's
> interested in Mozart, James Joyce and
> sodomy."
>   (He sighs; then to Annie)
> Whatta you mean, our **sexual problem**?

> ANNIE
> Oh!

> ALVY
> I-I-I mean, I'm **comparatively normal**
> for a guy raised in Brooklyn.

> ANNIE
> Okay, I'm very sorry. My **sexual problem!**
> Okay, my **sexual problem!** Huh?

> ALVY
> I never read that. That was—that was
> Henry James, right? Novel, uh, the
> sequel to Turn of the Screw? **My Sexual ...**

So, the apparent sexual dysfunction Alvy accuses "them" of having is a primary consideration in the entire scene, even though it's apparent the dysfunction is not a mutually agreed upon problem. Annie's response "Oh" is a clear indication that Alvy isn't taking agency for the problem, but attempts to share the dysfunction. In fact, the problem appears to be solely Alvy's, as he confesses his "comparative normality" for a kid from Brooklyn is, in fact, a kind of left-handed admission of his sexual dysfunction.

At the conclusion of the scene, the notion of indulgence comes full circle with both the MIL and Alvy finally "communicating" directly about the philosophy of Marshall McLuhan. After the MIL brings up McLuhan's name, Alvy has had about all he can take.

```
                    MAN IN LINE
                (Overlapping)
        Wait a minute! Really? Really? I happen to
        teach a class at Columbia called "TV Media
        and Culture"! So I think that my insights
        into Mr. McLuhan-well, have a great deal of
        validity.


                       ALVY

    Oh, do yuh?


                    MAN IN LINE

    Yes.


                       ALVY
        Well, that's funny, because I happen to
        have Mr. McLuhan right here. So ... so,
        here, just let me-I mean, all right. Come
        over here ... a second.
```

Of course, Alvy pulls out McLuhan from behind a movie poster and McLuhan then addresses the MIL directly, which is about the most dramatic form of dialogue linking one can imagine.

```
                     MCLUHAN
                (To the man in line)
        I hear-I heard what you were saying.
        You-you know nothing of my work. You
        mean my whole fallacy is wrong. How you
```

ever got to teach a course in anything is
totally amazing.

                    ALVY
          (To the camera)
     Boy, if life were only like this!

How then does the beginning of the scene integrate with the ending of the scene? The beginning of the scene focuses on Fellini's apparent "indulgence." As the MIL uses it in relation to Fellini, it would appear that Fellini is gratifying his desires in some particular way, indulging in them. The comment is ironic in that the MIL is indulging in somewhat the same manner in which he accuses Fellini, and although Alvy calls that to our attention Alvy is guilty of the same self-indulgence throughout the scene. As a matter of fact, all three of the characters, Alvy, Annie, and the MIL, are guilty of that. The scene itself acts a microcosm of indulgences, especially on Alvy's part, and the conclusion of the scene with Alvy pulling out McLuhan from behind a movie poster only to prove his point seems to be the ultimate of indulgences. So, there's a very succinct relationship between the indulgence Alvy accuses the MIL of having and the indulgence that Alvy doesn't recognize in himself. These indulgences are all mediated by the dialogue that Allen has written, that links all these apparent indulgences together.

As we've seen in other scenes, it's becoming more and more apparent that there is a kind of unified structure in the well-written scenes that incorporate how the dialogue functions and how the focus of the scene not only sets a tone for the scene, but also works to comment on the individual characters. It is this Aristotelian notion of a unified dramatic field that makes these scenes work most effectively.

12

Breaking Away (1979)
Screenplay by Steve Tesich

Steve Tesich and I went to Indiana University together. He was a Phi Kappa Psi and I was a Sigma Alpha Mu, and we lived across the street from each other. He graduated in 1965, I some four years later. We actually didn't begin to correspond with each other until many years later, many years after he graduated from Columbia (1967) with an MA in Russian Literature, and his success with such Broadway plays as *Division Street* (1987) and *Speed of Darkness* (1989). After the success of *Breaking Away* (1979), for which he won an Academy Award, he had critical success with such films as *Eyewitness* (1981), *Four Friends* (1981), *The World According to Garp* (1982), *American Flyers* (1985), and *Eleni* (1985).

In 1994, we reconnected and I invited him to spend a week as a Screenwriter-in-Residence at Chapman University, conducting a Master's course in screenwriting, after which time he admitted that it was so stressful he could never do that again. I understood what he meant. But one of the things he told his students was that they should think seriously about writing plays, since that's how he got started, and, by virtue of writing plays, one can improve one's sense of "listening," and how that act of listening aids in how one writes dialogue of which he was clearly a master. Steve also told his students that "I became a writer to survive as a human being," and that, "I write out of necessity, not compulsion. I do it so I can be decent to everybody else, including my family. It really keeps me together and happy."

Breaking Away is a *minor ensemble film*; that is, a film that would deal with no fewer than three or more than four main characters in relation to a *major ensemble film* that may have six or more. What brings the four adolescents together is that they are all "cutters," a nickname given to those people who are native to Bloomington, Indiana. The word comes from the fact that the largest employer in the town, Indiana University, was essentially built by men who cut limestone. The term is a pejorative term, generally applied to the locals by the university students who are merely temporary residents. But each character has individuality that surfaces in relation to the others and their individuality tends to contrast them. I use selected scenes from *Breaking Away* in my own classes precisely because the writing is not only laconic, but also the dialogue is absolutely flawless, as this opening quarry scene testifies.

The main characters are: Cyril, the comic/self-deprecator; Mike, the rebellious leader; Moocher, the angry little man; and Dave the romantic Italophile. Although the film is really Dave's film (since we specifically follow his quest) each character shares something in common in that they are in the process of growing away from each other, "breaking away" if you will, from the past. What happens with the characters during the course of the film is that each one comes to terms with his own individuality, and that often results in conflict, since they are all at a point in their lives where doing everything together as they once did is not altogether appealing.

Cyril begins as someone without direction; he ends by taking the SAT (Scholastic Aptitude Test). Mike begins as a somewhat embittered young man envious of the college boys, but taking pride in the fact he's the leader of the group; he ends by being somewhat less embittered, but no longer leader of the pack. Moocher begins as one of the guys and ends up by being the first to get married. Dave begins without an interest in higher education and enamored of things Italian, but soon gets trapped in his own delusions; he ends by realizing the "error of his ways," finally goes off to college, and ends by becoming a Francophile and gimmick that clearly relates to the opening of the film in which he's an Italophile. Probably the best example of this "division" occurs as early as page one of the script with the four of them walking towards the quarry.

> MIKE
>
> I sent away for this stuff from Wyoming. It'll tell you everything. Since you don't believe me maybe you'll believe it when you see it.

> CYRIL
>
> And we'd work on the same ranch and sleep in the bunkhouse together, eh?

                    MOOCHER
That's the whole point.

                    CYRIL
I always miss the whole point.

                    MOOCHER
It'd be nice to have a paying job again, that's
for sure.

                    DAVE
Niente lavorare. Niente mangiare.

                    MIKE
What's that mean?

                    DAVE
You don't work. You don't eat.

                    CYRIL
That's a terrible thing to say. Are you really
going to shave your legs?

                    DAVE
Certo. All the Italians do it.

                    MIKE
That's some country. The women don't shave
theirs.

                    CYRIL
STOP!
        (pauses as if thunderstruck;
        hand on heart)
It was somewhere along here that I lost all
interest in life. Ah, right over there. I
saw Dolores Reineke and fat Marvin. Why? Why
Dolores?

                    MOOCHER
They're married now.

                    MIKE
You see what I saved you from, Cyril. Had I not
told you about the two of them you never would
have followed them out here.

                    CYRIL
Thank you, Mike. You made me lose all interest
in life and I'm grateful.

                    MIKE
My brother says he saw you and Nancy. Moocher.

                    MOOCHER
When?

                    MIKE
Last Friday?

                    MOOCHER
Wasn't me. I'm not seeing her anymore.

                    MIKE
I sent away for this stuff from Wyoming. **It'll
tell you everything.** Since you don't believe me
maybe you'll believe it when you see it.

                    CYRIL
**And we'd work on the same ranch and sleep in the
bunkhouse together,** eh?

                    MOOCHER
That's the **whole point.**

                    CYRIL
I always miss the **whole point.**

MOOCHER

It'd be nice to have a **paying job again,** that's for sure.

DAVE

Niente lavorare. Niente mangiare.

MIKE

What's that mean?

DAVE

You don't work. You don't eat.

CYRIL

That's a terrible thing to say. **Are you really going to shave your legs?**

DAVE

Certo. All the Italians do it.

MIKE

That's some country. **The women don't shave theirs.**

CYRIL

STOP!
    (pauses as if thunderstuck;
    hand on heart)
It was somewhere along here that **I lost all interest in life. Ah, right over there. I saw Dolores Reineke and fat Marvin. Why? Why Dolores?**

MOOCHER

They're married now.

MIKE

You see what I saved you from, Cyril. Had I not told you about the two of them **you never would have followed them** out here.

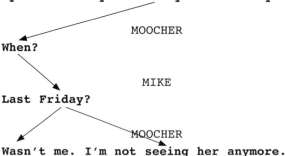

It's clear from the dialogue that the characters are not only becoming individualized, but each of them is on a kind of individual quest (this is a film that coalesces comedy, romance, and quest), which is ultimately satisfied by the end of the film. Mike takes the lead in almost everything—he wrote to Wyoming about the ranch, he informed Cyril about Dolores, he has a comment about Dave's legs, he tells Moocher about Nancy; Dave responds to almost everything with an Italian accent; Moocher, who says he's not seeing Nancy, actually is; and Cyril is the group clown. But in terms of character arc we find one overriding arc, Dave's, and three minor arcs that intersect with the major arc with each one of the four characters learning something about himself by the end of the film. But one can see how ingeniously Tesich has interwoven the dialogues.

There are as many excellent repartees in *Breaking Away* as you might find in a Woody Allen film.

> DAVE
> Did you ever go to confession?

> MOOCHER
> Twice.

> DAVE
> Did it make you feel better?

> MOOCHER
>
> Once.

Or...

> DAVE
>
> You mean we might be a father?

> RAYMOND
>
> No. I might be a father. And your mom might be
> a mother. And YOU might be a brother. See, that
> way I keep it all in the family.

> MOOCHER
>
> Wow! Hey, I didn't think people your age ...

> RAYMOND
>
> The next word may be your last, kid!

Not only does the dialogue engage, but it links effectively. One of my favorite scenes in *Breaking Away* is the scene with Dave's mother and father as she prepares dinner.

> DAD
>
> What is **this**?

> MOM
>
> It's sautéed zucchini.

> DAD
>
> It's I-tey food. I don't want no I-tey food.

> MOM
>
> It's not. I got it at the A&P. It's like ...
> **squash.**

> DAD
>
> **I know I-tey** food when I hear it! It's all them
> "eenie" foods ... **zucchini** ... and linguine
> ... and fettuccine. I want some American food,
> dammit! I want French fries!

> MOM
> [to the cat, who has jumped up onto the table]
> Oh, get off the table, **Fellini!**

> DAD
> Hey, that's 'my' cat! His name's not **Fellini,**
> it's **Jake!** I won't have any "eenie" in this
> house!
> [to the cat]
> Your name's **Jake, you hear?**

What separates Tesich from a lot of writers is his keen ability to say a lot in very few words. One can see that in Henry's script of *The Graduate* as well and, given Henry's background in writing for television, one can see remarkable similarities in how they write precise dialogue.

> DAD
> What is **this?**

> MOM
> **It's sautéed zucchini.**

> DAD
> **It's I-tey food. I don't want no I-tey food.**

> MOM
> It's not. I got it at the A&P. It's like ...
> squash.

> DAD
> **I know I-tey** food when I hear it! It's all them
> "eenie" foods ... **zucchini** ... and linguine
> ... and fettuccine. I want some American food,
> dammit! I want French fries!

MOM
[to the cat, who has jumped up onto the table]
Oh, get off the table, **Fellini!**

DAD
Hey, that's 'my' cat! His name's not **Fellini,**
it's **Jake!** I won't have any "eenie" in this
house!
 [to the cat]
Your name's **Jake, you hear?**

To the question what is "this," mom replies "sautéed zucchini," to which dad links with it being "I-tey" food (twice). Mom counters with it being "like ... squash," which, in fact, it is, but dad re-links by using "I-tey" and "zucchini" in the same dialogue segment and then demands that he wants some "American food"; namely, "French fries." Off that classic bit of Tesich irony, mom calls the cat "Fellini," to which dad links by repeating the name "not Fellini," but "Jake," to which he internally links by letting the cat know his name is "Jake."

What genuinely distinguishes a lot of Tesich's work from other screenwriters is his ability to handle multiple voices. In great measure, that's a testament to his ability as a writer, but also to his ability as a listener. Given the fact he began his screenwriting career as a playwright, that ability to listen and to distinguish various voices has contributed to his masterly approach to dialogue writing. One can only speculate on what he would have accomplished had he not died so young.

13

When Harry Met Sally (1988) Screenplay by Nora Ephron

A lot of these dialogous scenes are fairly lengthy, but some are pointedly brief. One of these is the classic Carnegie Katz Deli scene in *When Harry Met Sally*. The script opens with Harry and Sally "about to eat large pastrami sandwiches." Not only is this one of the most memorable scenes in the film, but it also comes almost at the midpoint (pp. 57–59) of a 122-page script. And what is the focus of the scene? SEX. Almost everything in the scene moves to a climax, no pun intended, predicated on how the dialogue is orchestrated. This is the scene:

> SALLY
>
> So what do you do with these women, you just get up out of bed and leave?
>
> HARRY
>
> Sure.
>
> SALLY
>
> Well explain to me how you do it. What do you say?
>
> HARRY
>
> You'd say you have an early meeting, early haircut or a squash game.
>
> SALLY
>
> You don't play squash.

                    HARRY
They don't know that they just met me.

                    SALLY
That's disgusting.

                    HARRY
I know, I feel terrible.

                    SALLY
You know I'm so glad I never got involved with
you. I just would've ended up being some woman
you had to get up out of bed and leave at three
o'clock in the morning and clean your andirons,
and you don't even have a fireplace. Not that I
would notice.

                    HARRY
Why are you getting so upset? This is not about
you.

                    SALLY
Yes it is. You are a human affront to all women
and I am a woman

                    HARRY
Hey I don't feel great about this but I don't
hear anyone complaining.

                    SALLY
Of course not you're out of the door too fast.

                    HARRY
I think they have an OK time.

                    SALLY
How do you know?

                    HARRY
What do you mean how do I know? I know.

                    SALLY
Because they ...

                    HARRY
Yes, because they ...

                    SALLY
And how do you know that they really ...

                    HARRY
What are you saying, that they fake orgasm?

                    SALLY
It's possible.

                    HARRY
Get outta here!

                    SALLY
Why? Most women at one time or another have
faked it.

                    HARRY
Well they haven't faked it with me.

                    SALLY
How do you know?

                    HARRY
Because I know.

                    SALLY
Oh, right, that's right, I forgot, you're a man.

                    HARRY
What is that supposed to mean?

                    SALLY
Nothing. It's just that all men are sure it
never happened to them and that most women at
one time or another have done it so you do the
math.

> HARRY

You don't think that I could tell the
difference?

> SALLY

No.

> HARRY

Get outta here.

> SALLY

Ooo ... Oh ... Ooo ...

> HARRY

Are you OK?

> SALLY

Oh ... Oh god ... Ooo Oh God ... Oh ... Oh ...
Oh ... Oh God ... Oh yeah right there. Oh! Oh
... Yes Yes Yes Yes Yes Yes ... Oh ... Oh ...
Yes Yes Yes ... Oh ... Yes Yes Yes Yes Yes Yes
... Oh ... Oh ... Oh ... Oh God Oh ... Oh ...
Huh ...

Now we can turn our attention to the dialogue links and how, after establishing the direction of the scene, the scene unfolds.

> SALLY

So what do you do with these women, you just get
up out of bed and **leave**?

> HARRY

Sure.

> SALLY

Well explain to me how you **do it**. What do you say?

In terms of the techniques being used, Sally opens with two questions related to how Harry "operates" after he's had sex with women and Harry answers. The word "leave" links with the word "Sure" since his answer is an implied "sure [I leave]." She wants him to explain how he does "it"; namely, leave and what the pretext is for his leaving.

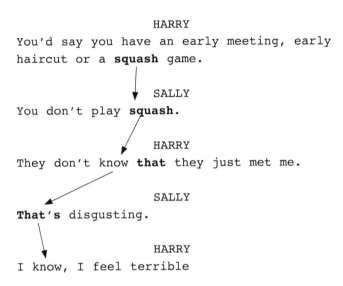

> HARRY
> You'd say you have an early meeting, early haircut or a **squash** game.
>
> SALLY
> You don't play **squash**.
>
> HARRY
> They don't know **that** they just met me.
>
> SALLY
> **That's** disgusting.
>
> HARRY
> I know, I feel terrible

She follows with a statement and a follow up question as to what Harry tells the women after having sex with them and he says that he tells them, "I have an early meeting or an early haircut or an early **squash** game." She links by saying "You don't play **squash**." "They don't know that. They just met me." The word "that" links back to the game of "squash." She says it's "disgusting" and he says he feels "terrible."

These dialogue segments contribute to the overall tenor of the scene and for what's to follow, since Sally slowly begins to get irritated with Harry's machismo and says she's glad she never got involved with him if that's what he does. That apparent "disgust" is the separating moment of the scene that moves it closer to the epiphany at the end of the scene.

> SALLY
>
> You know **I'm so glad I never got involved with you.** I just would've ended up being some woman you had to get up out of bed and leave at three o'clock in the morning and clean your **andirons,** and you don't even have a **fireplace.** Not that I would notice.
>
> HARRY
>
> Why are you **getting so upset? This is not about you.**
>
> SALLY
>
> **Yes it is.** You are a human affront to all women and I am a woman.

Sally continues the dialogue that was established earlier by alluding to her previous question about what Harry "says" when he "leaves." So, getting involved and getting out of bed and "leaving" at three in the morning to do something like clean andirons (which he doesn't have) precipitates his asking the question, "Why are you getting so upset? This isn't about **you**." But it is. He's an affront to all **"women"** and "I'm a **woman**." In an attempt to regain some kind of "macho" control, Harry goes on the offensive.

> HARRY
>
> Hey I don't feel great about this but I don't **hear anyone complaining.**
>
> SALLY
>
> Of course not you're **out of the door** too fast.

Of course Harry doesn't hear anyone "complaining" because he leaves "too fast" which links back to Sally's previous statement.

HARRY

I think they have an **OK time**.

SALLY

How do you know?

HARRY

What do you mean **how do I know? I know.**

SALLY

Because they ...

HARRY

Yes, **because they** ...

SALLY

And how do you know that they really ...

HARRY

What are you saying, that they **fake orgasm?**

SALLY

It's possible.

HARRY

Get outta here!

SALLY

Why? Most women at one time or another have **faked it.**

HARRY

Well they haven't **faked it** with me.

SALLY

How do you know?

HARRY

Because I know.

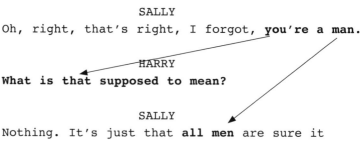

> SALLY
> Oh, right, that's right, I forgot, **you're a man.**

> HARRY
> **What is that supposed to mean?**

> SALLY
> Nothing. It's just that **all men** are sure it never happened to them and that most women at one time or another have done it so you do the math.

> HARRY
> **You don't think that I could tell the difference?**

At this point, the links are moving the entire scene in Sally's direction and towards the culmination that was established early on. "An OK time" links with her question about how he "knows," which continues with his internal double link. When she alludes to "orgasm" by saying "because they" and gestures, that's an implicit link back to an "OK time." Harry links with the same "because they" phrase because they're both using hand gestures to get the point across. When she repeats the line "how do you know" they orgasm, it acts as a refrain from the first time she asked it and continues the flow of the dialogue. Of course, such a suggestion goes against Harry's macho grain, which prompts him to ask the question about them "faking orgasm." Sally's response that "it's possible" is an implied link back to the "orgasm" suggestion and, regardless of Harry's protestations, Sally suggests that most women have "faked it," and he links with the fact they haven't "faked it" with him. This statement once again precipitates the question about "knowing," which Harry links on by saying "because I know."

She suggests that it's because he's a "man" and the implied arrogance that all men know it never happens to them even though women have "faked" it at one time or another. That statement is, in a way, "throwing down the gauntlet" since his hubris rises to the top by suggesting there's no way he couldn't tell the difference. Her statement provokes Harry to ask, "You don't think I can tell the difference?" And Sally replies unequivocally:

> SALLY
>
> No.

> HARRY
>
> Get outta here.

> SALLY
>
> Ooo ... Oh ... Ooo ...

> HARRY
>
> Are you OK?

> SALLY
>
> Oh ... Oh god ... Ooo Oh God ... Oh ... Oh ...
> Oh ... Oh God ...Oh yeah right there. Oh! Oh ...
> Yes Yes Yes Yes Yes Yes ... Oh ... Oh ... Yes
> Yes Yes ... Oh ... Yes Yes Yes Yes Yes Yes ...
> Oh ... Oh ... Oh ... Oh God Oh ... Oh ... Huh
> ...

Her response clearly indicates where the direction of the scene is going and after she finishes her "faked orgasm" accompanied by pounding on the table, she takes another bite of the sandwich as Harry looks on in disbelief and an older woman customer (Crystal's mother, I believe) closes the scene by saying "I'll have what she's having."

The scene opens with them eating and closes with her eating, and the entire scene is beautifully arranged in terms of structure and rhythm. If we break down the scene into its dialogous components we have approximately 11 questions that are composed mainly of questions and answers. But there are number of important links as well:

Early	3x
Squash	2x
They/they're	4x
This isn't/it is	2x
Women/woman	2x
How do I/they know	6x
Because they	2x
Fake/faked/orgasm/it	5x
Man/men	2x
TOTAL	28 Links

But, as you can see, the links are not necessarily repetitions of the same word or phrase. What's important is how she uses the phrases that imply the same thing. To constantly repeat the same word or phrase would not only become monotonous, but undermine the rhythm of the dialogue and retard the movement to the ultimate destination of the scene. As brief scenes go, this particular scene is a "classic" in terms of how effective dialogue is meant to be written.

14

The Fisher King (1991)
Screenplay by Richard LaGravenese

*T*he *Fisher King* is a rather remarkable script for a number of reasons. In a way, it's very prescient in that what LaGravenese was writing about 20 years ago, in many ways, has come to fruition today. That is, how media talk show hosts, especially radio talk show hosts, can influence their listeners to the extent that some may, in fact, take the law into their own hands. This was the basis for the script in that a self-serving, egocentric, arrogant, and opinionated person like Jack Lucas could, through a thoughtless and flippant comment, influence someone to take deadly action, which is exactly what Edwin does. Subsequent to Edwin's mass murder, Lucas gets fired, becomes depressed and alcoholic, and is only rescued by Parry, who was at Babbitt's the night of the murders, before Lucas himself is nearly murdered.

The remainder of the film explores how Lucas redeems himself through Parry's mentorship; the latter of whom has become homeless and psychologically unstable. What clearly establishes the flow of the entire film is the opening scene, which is brilliantly written not only for the way it establishes Jack Lucas's character, but in the way it incorporates all the individual aspects of dialogue writing that I've mentioned above. The focus of the scene is meant to characterize Lucas and his desultory behavior, and to establish a point of departure for the entire scene if not the entire film. To that end, as you'll see, the myriad number of cuts in the final draft doesn't really focus on Lucas himself, and by virtue of cutting from one person to another instead of keying on Lucas tends to undermine the point of the scene.

What LaGravenese has done in the shooting script is to remove those cuts and direct his attention exclusively on Lucas's character *vis à vis* his dialogue. The final draft is markedly different than the film version, which opens with Lucas in the studio with studio people listening to what Lucas is saying on air. We can compare the scenes to see what, in fact, LaGravenese did to improve the script. Not unlike what was done in *The Graduate*, LaGravenese reduced an eight-page scene to a three-page scene, and at the same time increased the dramatic potential of the scene and accented Lucas's rather abhorrent behavior. As we've seen in other scripts, (notably in *The Graduate*) the need for scenic economy is critical. You can see what LaGravenese has done with this scene.

> LUCAS
> Hey, it's Monday morning,
> and I'm Jack Lucas.

> CALLER #1
> Hi. This is about my husband.

> LUCAS
> —Yes?

> CALLER#1
> —Well, he drives me crazy.
> I'll be talking and he'll never
> let me finish a sentence.
> He's always finishing ...

> LUCAS
> He's always finishing your thoughts.
> That's awful.

> CALLER#1
> It absolutely drives ...

> LUCAS
> It drives you crazy, doesn't it?
> He's a scoundrel!

> CALLER#1
> Jack, you've hit the nail ...

LUCAS
Hit the nail on the head. Yeah,
somebody ought to hit you on the head.

LUCAS
Tell us, how long have you and
Senator Payton been having this ...
... this sleazy affair?

CALLER #2
Oh, great.
This is great.
This is disgusting.
I'm so tired of the public ...
... invading a person's
private life.

LUCAS
You had sex with a U.S. Senator
in the parking lot of Sea World.
And you're a private person?
No, you're our ...
Spotlight Celebrity!
We want to hear about
the back seats of limos ...
... about the ruined lives
of people we want to be.
Exotic uses for champagne corks.

CALLER #2
Listen, I have been humiliated
enough already, okay?

LUCAS
Well, no, perhaps not.
We need those details.

CALLER TWO
You're a pig, Jack.

                    LUCAS
          You're on the air, caller.

                    EDWIN
          Hello, Jack. It's Edwin.

                    LUCAS
              It's Edwin!
      Haven't heard you in, what, a day?
              I've missed you.

                    EDWIN
            I've missed you too.

                    LUCAS
            It's confession time.
              What've you got?

                    EDWIN
        I went to this bar, this very,
      you know, hard-to-get-into place ...
            ... called Babbitt's.

                    LUCAS
            Yeah, it's one of those
        chic, yuppie watering holes.

                    EDWIN
          I met this beautiful woman.

                    LUCAS
          Come on, Ed. If you start
      telling me you're in love again ...
            ... I'm gonna remind you
        of the time we made you propose ...
      ... to that checkout girl at Thrifty's.
        Do you remember her reaction?

                    EDWIN
            She was just a girl.
        This is a beautiful woman.

                    LUCAS
    And Pinocchio is a true story.
    You'll never get this tart
       to your dessert plate.

                    LUCAS
        This is different.
          She likes me.

                    LUCAS
               Edwin!
    I told you about these people.
  They only mate with their own kind.
       It's yuppie inbreeding.
     That's why they're retarded
     and wear the same clothes.
         They don't feel love.
    They only negotiate love moments.
        They're evil, Edwin.
   They're repulsed by imperfection,
       horrified by the banal ...
          ... everything that
          America stands for!
     They must be stopped before
   it's too late. It's us or them.

                    EDWIN
             Okay, Jack.

                    LUCAS
             All right.
  Well, it's been a thrill, as always.
        Have a perfect day.
       Everyone here at the
    Jack Lucas Show says "bye."
       This is Jack Lucas.
       So long. Arrivederci.
   I'll send you a thought today
   as I lie in my stretch limo ...
          ... having sex with
       the teenager of my choice.

And that thought will be:
"Thank God I'm me."

The reduction in length has made the opening scene significantly more dramatic by focusing on those elements that are so critical to scene construction: namely, emphasizing Lucas's egocentricity, and his ability to alienate and influence his listeners, and by virtue of that arrogance has become highly successful. Not only that, but it alludes to Pinocchio who will manifest as a subplot that either directly or indirectly plays out in more than one scene throughout the film. In terms of an arc, the scene opens with Lucas in his studio and closes with Lucas in his studio. It opens with Lucas being arrogant and condescending and closes with Lucas being arrogant and condescending. But, more important, it establishes a point of departure for his character, and by establishing that point of departure also establishes a point of destination. In other words, if Lucas starts out as an arrogant, condescending, egocentric human being then, by virtue of something that happens outside of his control, his character must change by the end of the film. And so it does. But how does the dialogue assist in that? What does LaGravenese do with the dialogue to maintain scenic continuity, advance the storyline, develop character, and elicit conflict? We can see how he utilizes many of the techniques I've previously described in the shooting script dialogue.

> LUCAS
> Hey, it's Monday morning,
> and I'm **Jack Lucas.**

> CALLER #1
> *Hi. This is about **my husband.***

> LUCAS
> —Yes?

> CALLER #1
> *—**Well, he drives me crazy.**
> I'll be talking and **he'll never
> let me finish a sentence.**
> **He's always finishing** ...*

> LUCAS
> **He's always finishing** your thoughts.
> That's awful.

```
                    CALLER#1
              It absolutely drives ...

                     LUCAS
         It drives you crazy, doesn't it?
                He's a scoundrel!

                    CALLER#1
           Jack, you've hit the nail ...

                     LUCAS
         Hit the nail on the head. Yeah,
      somebody ought to hit you on the head.
```

LaGravenese immediately establishes the "who." Jack Lucas. But who is Jack Lucas? We get a notion of who he is by virtue of the way he condescends to his caller. But it's not only the *manner* of his condescension that's at work, but *how* his condescension is at work. Namely, how Lucas links on her dialogue with the same or similar dialogue in such a way that it not only advances the scene, but comments on his character. The same thing happens with the second caller.

```
                     LUCAS
         Tell us, how long have you and
      Senator Payton been having this ...
              ... this sleazy affair?

                   CALLER #2
                   Oh, great.
                 This is great.
               This is disgusting.
         I'm so tired of the public ...
             ... invading a person's
                  private life.

                     LUCAS
        You had sex with a U.S. Senator
        in the parking lot of Sea World.
          And you're a private person?
                No, you're our ...
              Spotlight Celebrity!
```

> We want to hear about
> the back seats of limos ...
> ... about the ruined lives
> of people we want to be.
> Exotic uses for champagne corks.

>   CALLER #2
> *Listen, I have been* **humiliated**
>   **enough already,** *okay?*

>   LUCAS
>   Well, no, **perhaps not.**
>   We need those details.

>   CALLER TWO
>   *You're a pig, Jack.*

She says she's been humiliated enough which prompts Lucas to say "perhaps not," alluding to the possibility of further humiliation by him or someone else. When she declares that he's a "pig" he may very well be, since he has very little respect for anyone other than himself. By virtue of his position as a "media celebrity," Lucas has been given free rein to say anything on the air, and his dialogue continues to reflect that license. The links are all embedded in such a way that we have no other impression of Lucas other than the one that's been established. That's patently clear when we hear from his third caller, Edwin.

>   LUCAS
>   You're on the air, **caller.**

>   EDWIN
>   *Hello, Jack. It's* **Edwin.**

>   LUCAS
>   It's **Edwin!**
> Haven't heard you in, what, a day?
>   **I've missed you.**

>   EDWIN
>   *I've missed you too.*

> LUCAS
> It's **confession time.**
> **What've you got?**

> EDWIN
> *I went to this bar, this very,*
> *you know, hard-to-get-into place ...*
> *... called Babbitt's.*

> LUCAS
> Yeah, **it's one of those**
> **chic, yuppie watering holes.**

> EDWIN
> *I met this beautiful woman.*

> LUCAS
> Come on, Ed. If you start
> telling me you're **in love again ...**
> ... I'm gonna remind you
> of the time we made you propose ...
> ... to that **checkout girl** at Thrifty's.
> Do you remember her reaction?

> EDWIN
> *She was just a girl.*
> *This is a beautiful woman.*

> LUCAS
> And *Pinocchio* is a true story.
> You'll never get **this tart**
> to your dessert plate.

> LUCAS
> *This is different.*
> *She likes me.*

> LUCAS
> Edwin!
> I told you about **these people.**
> **They** only mate with their own kind.

It's **yuppie inbreeding.**
That's why **they're retarded**
and wear the same clothes.
They don't feel love.
They only negotiate love moments.
They're evil, Edwin.
They're repulsed by imperfection,
horrified by the banal ...
... everything that
America stands for!
They must be stopped before
it's too late. It's us or them.

                    EDWIN
             Okay, Jack.

                    LUCAS
             All right.
  Well, it's been a thrill, as always.
           Have a perfect day.
        Everyone here at the
    Jack Lucas Show says *"bye."*
This is Jack Lucas. So long. *Arrivederci.*
     I'll send you a thought today
   as I lie in **my stretch limo ...**
        ... having sex with
      the teenager of my choice.
      And that thought will be:
        "Thank God I'm me."

So, the flippant comment goes relatively unnoticed by Lucas, since he's in the habit of making flippant comments, but the dialogue is absolutely flawless in the manner in which LaGravenese has not only augmented Lucas's character and his hubris, but how that hubris will not only eventuate in mass murder, but in Lucas's downfall. In this scene, one not only finds scenic continuity, but character development, storyline development, and dramatic conflict all neatly coalesced in how Lucas speaks.

Four scenes later, while watching television, Lucas discovers that Edwin murdered dozens of people at Babbitt's and that begins Lucas's tragedy. So, in a sequence of five scenes we see how Lucas has gone from the top of his profession to having no profession at all. In terms of a point of departure and a point of destination, Lucas has to suffer for what he's done if he's going to be redeemed. What's unique about this sequence of scenes is that not only does each scene have an arc to it in which the end is linked to the beginning, but also the entire sequence is linked. In scene one, Lucas is at the top of his game—financially successful, arrogant, a womanizer. At the end of scene five, he realizes that his professional career is finished and that realization propels him in a downward spiral that results in his near death, saved only by Parry. LaGravenese has presented a kind of primer not only for how to construct a flawless sequence of scenes, but how to incorporate dialogue in such a manner as to accent that flawlessness.

15

Thelma & Louise (1991)
Screenplay by Callie Khouri

Perhaps it's something in the Hollywood drinking water. In his book, *Ridley Scott: Interviews* edited by Laurence Knapp and Andrea Kulas (2005), there's a 1991 interview conducted by Maitland McDonagh for *Film Journal* in which McDonagh asks the question: "How did this project [*Thelma & Louise*] develop?" to which Scott replied, "Scripts that are written on spec fly around Hollywood like confetti and most of them aren't that good. But we [Scott and producer Mimi Polk, etc.] came across this piece of material from a first-time writer, read it, thought it was interesting and that's where it started" (Knapp and Kulas, 2005, p. 72). To give Scott some leeway, since the interview was held in 1991 and Khouri won the Academy Award for the film in1992, one still has to wonder why directors seem to have such a hard time calling writers (first time or otherwise) by their names, especially when Khouri got a producer's credit as well. And although she's only written four more scripts since *Thelma & Louise*, the latter is clearly her best work especially in relation to her dialogue.

INT. THELMA'S KITCHEN—MORNING

                  THELMA
Well, wait now. I still have to ask Darryl if I
can go.

               LOUISE (V.O.)
You mean you haven't asked him yet? For Christ
sake, Thelma, is he your husband or your father?
It's just two days. For God's sake, Thelma.

Don't be a child. Just tell him you're goin'
with me, for cryin' out loud. Tell him I'm
havin' a nervous breakdown.

>   THELMA
He already thinks you're out of your mind,
Louise, that don't carry much weight with
Darryl. Are you at work?
LOUISE (V.O.)
No, I'm callin' from the Playboy
Mansion.

>   THELMA
I'll call you right back.

>   THELMA
Darryl! Honey, you'd better hurry
up.

>   DARRYL
Damnit, Thelma, don't holler like
that! Haven't I told you I can't
stand it when you holler in the
morning.

>   THELMA
I'm sorry, Doll, I just didn't want you to be
late.

>   THELMA
Hon.

>   DARRYL
What.

>   THELMA
(she decides not to
tell him)
Have a good day at work today.

                    DARRYL

Uh-huh.

                    THELMA

Hon?

                    DARRYL

What?!

                    THELMA

You want anything special for
dinner?

                    DARRYL

No, Thelma, I don't give a shit
what we have for dinner. I may not even make it
home for dinner. You know how Fridays are.

                    THELMA

Funny how so many people wanna buy
carpet on a Friday night. You'd
almost think they's want to forget
about it for the weekend.

                    DARRYL

Well then, it's a good thing you're not regional
manager and I am.

                    THELMA

'Bye, honey. I won't wait up.

                    DARRYL

See ya.

                    THELMA

He's gonna shit.

Thelma laughs to herself. She goes back into the kitchen
and picks up the phone and dials it.

INT. THELMA'S KITCHEN—MORNING

>   THELMA
> Well, wait now. I still have to **ask Darryl** if I
> can go.

>   LOUISE (V.O.)
> You mean **you haven't asked him** yet? For Christ
> sake, Thelma, is **he your husband** or your father?
> It's just two days. For God's sake, Thelma.
> Don't be a child. Just **tell him** you're goin'
> with me, for cryin' out loud. **Tell him** I'm
> havin' a **nervous breakdown.**

>   THELMA
> **He** already thinks you're **out of your mind,**
> Louise, that don't carry much weight with
> Darryl. **Are you at work?**

>   LOUISE (V.O.)
> **No, I'm callin' from the Playboy**
> **Mansion.**

>   THELMA
> I'll **call** you right back.

The dialogue creates voice and character immediately. By virtue of their individual dialogue segments one can immediately understand who these characters are; namely, Louise, the active one and Thelma, the passive one. Not only is this established early on, but it will also maintain itself throughout the script. To the fact that Thelma has to "ask Darryl" Louise turns the statement into a linking question: "You haven't asked him [Darryl] yet?" Then, after repeating the pronoun (an internal link to Darryl) she repeats the phrase "tell him" (twice) and alludes to her having a "nervous breakdown." Louise links on the nervous breakdown by establishing that "he" (Darryl) already thinks Louise is "out of her mind." Thelma then asks Louise if she's "at work," to which Louise ironically responds "no, I'm callin' from the Playboy Mansion," which allows Thelma to link again with "I'll call" you back.

                    THELMA
Darryl! Honey, you'd better **hurry
up.**

                    DARRYL
Damnit, Thelma, **don't holler** like
that! Haven't I told you I can't
stand it when you **holler** in the
morning.

                    THELMA
I'm sorry, Doll, I just didn't want you to be
late.

                    THELMA
Hon.

                    DARRYL
What?

                    THELMA
(she decides not to
tell him)
Have a good day at work today.

                    DARRYL
Uh-huh.

                    THELMA
Hon?

                    DARRYL
What?!

                    THELMA
You want **anything special for
dinner?**

                    DARRYL
No, Thelma, I don't give a shit
what we have for dinner. I may not even make it
home **for dinner.** You know **how Fridays are.**

                    THELMA
Funny how so many people wanna **buy
carpet** on a **Friday night.** You'd
almost think they's want to forget
about it for the weekend.

                    DARRYL
Well then, it's a good thing **you're not regional
manager** and I am.

                    THELMA
'Bye, honey. I won't wait up.

                    DARRYL
See ya.

                    THELMA
He's gonna shit.

Thelma laughs to herself. She goes back into the kitchen
and picks up the phone and dials it.

Khouri isn't doing anything unique in terms of the dialogue, but she does
adhere to the principles I set out earlier, especially the one related to
dialogue linkage; however, even this brief exchange characterizes who these
characters are and how they react to certain situations. That characterization
is exhibited to an even greater extent in the following scene.

INT. SILVER BULLET—NIGHT

                    LOUISE
I haven't seen a place like this since I left
Texas.

                    THELMA
Isn't this fun?

                    WAITRESS
Y'all wanna drink?

                    LOUISE
No thanks.

                    THELMA
I'll have Wild Turkey straight up and a Coke
back, please.

                    LOUISE
Thelma!

                    THELMA
Tell me somethin'. Is this my vacation or isn't
it? I mean, God, you're as bad as Darryl.

                    LOUISE
I just haven't seen you like this in a while.
I'm used to seeing you more sedate.

                    THELMA
Well, I've had it up to my ass with sedate! You
said you and me was gonna get outta town and,
for once,
just really let our hair down. Well, darlin,'
look out 'cause my hair is comin' down!

                    LOUISE
                    (laughing)
Alright ...
(to Waitress) I changed my mind. I'll have a

margarita with and a shot Cuervo on the side,
please.

                    THELMA
         Yeah!

As the Waitress leaves, a MAN comes over with a chair
which he pulls up to the table and straddles backwards.
He is in his late-40's, heavyset, his face is shiny in
the neon light.

                    MAN
         Now what are a couple of Kewpie dolls like you
         doin' in a place like this?

LOUISE   THELMA
Mindin' our own   Well, we left town for
business, why   the weekend 'cause we
don't you try it.   wanted to try and have a
                               good time. And because
                               Louise here is mad
                               because her boyfriend
                               won't call her while
                               he's out on
                               the road ...

Louise kicks Thelma under the table.

                    THELMA
                   (quieter)
         We just wanted to get somethin' to eat.

                    MAN
         Well, you come to the right place. You like
         chili? They got good chili.

The Waitress returns with Louise's drink.

                    WAITRESS
         Harlan, are you botherin' these poor girls?

                         HARLAN (MAN)
Hell, no. I was just bein'
friendly.

                         WAITRESS
(making eye contact
with Louise)
It's a good thing they're not all as friendly as
you.

Louise understands.

                         THELMA
Your name's Harlan? I got an uncle named Harlan!

                         HARLAN
You do? Is he a funny uncle?
'Cause if he is, then he and I got somethin' in
common.

Harlan laughs. Thelma laughs, too, but doesn't really get
the joke. Louise does not laugh.

                         LOUISE
                    (to Harlan)
I don't mean to be rude, but I've got something
I need to talk to my friend about. In private.

                         HARLAN
Aw, I understand. I didn't mean to bother ya.
It's just hard not to notice two such pretty
ladies as yourselves.
                    (standing, to
                    Thelma)
You better dance with me before you leave, or
I'll never forgive you.

                         THELMA
Oh, sure. That'd be fun. Jeez, Louise, that
wasn't very nice.

                         LOUISE
         Can't you tell when somebody's hittin' on you?

                         THELMA
         So what if he was? It's all your years of
         waitin' tables has made you jaded, that's all.

                         LOUISE
         Maybe.

                         THELMA
         Well, just relax, will ya. You're makin' me
         nervous.

Thelma knocks back her shot of Wild Turkey and holds up
her glass to the Waitress to bring her another one. The
Waitress sees her and nods. She turns back to face her
friend.

                         THELMA
         So, Jimmy still hasn't called yet?

                         LOUISE
         Givin' him a taste of his own medicine. Asshole.

                         THELMA
         I'm sorry, Louise. I know you're all upset. It's
         just I'm so excited to be out of the house, I
         guess.
         (pause)
         I wonder if Darryl's home yet.

                         LOUISE
         I wonder if Jimmy's gotten back.

                         THELMA
         Why don't you tell him to just to get lost once
         and for all?

                         LOUISE
         Why don't you ditch that loser husband of yours?

They both drift off momentarily, contemplating their domestic problems, until the Waitress comes over:

> WAITRESS
> (rolling her eyes)
> This one's on Harlan.

Thelma looks over at the bar where Harlan is grinning at her, making dancing motions. She smiles and waves at him. Her face becomes serious again as she turns back to Louise.

> THELMA
> Jimmy'll come in off the road, you won't be
> there, he'll freak out and call you a hundred
> thousand times,
> and Sunday night you'll call him back and, by
> Monday. He'll be kissin' the ground you walk on.

Thelma's mind goes too fast for her mouth, and the speed at which she speaks can be staggering. Louise is used to it. Louise smiles wistfully at Thelma's assessment of the situation.

> LOUISE
> Exactly.

> THELMA
> In the meantime, you said we were gonna have
> some fun. So let's have some!

She again drinks her whole shot of Wild Turkey and holds up her glass, as the BAND strikes up a lively tune. Practically the whole place "whoops" and heads for the dance floor. Louise drinks her shot of tequila and holds up her glass, too.

INT. SILVER BULLET—NIGHT

> LOUISE
> I haven't seen a **place** like this since I left
> Texas.

> THELMA
> Isn't **this** fun?

> WAITRESS
> Y'all wanna **drink**?

> LOUISE
> **No thanks.**

> THELMA
> I'll have **Wild Turkey** straight up and a Coke
> back, please.

> LOUISE
> **Thelma!**

> THELMA
> Tell me somethin'. Is this my **vacation** or isn't
> it? I mean, God, you're **as bad as Darryl.**

> LOUISE
> I just haven't **seen you like this** in a while.
> I'm used to seeing you more **sedate.**

> THELMA
> Well, I've had it up to my ass with **sedate!** You
> said you and me was gonna get outta town and,
> for once, just really let our **hair down.** Well,
> darlin,' look out 'cause my **hair is comin' down!**

This scene continues to shape their individual characters and clearly places
the burden of responsibility on Louise. It's apparent from the beginning that
there is a contrast between these two characters as well there should be,
since to have them mimic each other would only undermine the storyline.
The links are apparent even though they may appear not to be. The bar

reminds Louise of one she had been in in Texas, but as she's driving she's the one responsible for not drinking. At the same time, Thelma has no reservations about drinking, hence her order for "Wild Turkey," which is not only a comment on the drink but also a comment on how she feels. It's not as if she asks for sherry. To the order of Wild Turkey, Louise reacts in a somewhat astonished fashion and Thelma links with the fact it's her "vacation" and that she accuses Louise of being a lot like "Darryl." Louise responds with the comment that she hasn't seen her like that in "a while" and accents that with the notion of her being "sedate." Thelma not only links on that word, but also uses the additional phrase "hair down" (twice) as a way of reinforcing the fact that she's NOT going to be sedate any longer.

> LOUISE
> (laughing)
> Alright ...(to Waitress) I changed my mind. I'll have a **margarita** and a shot **Cuervo** on the side, please.
>
> THELMA
> **Yeah!**

> MAN
> **Now what are a couple of Kewpie dolls like you doin' in a place like this?**

LOUISE	THELMA
Mindin' our own business, why don't you try it.	Well, we left town for the weekend 'cause we wanted to try and have a good time. And because Louise here is mad because her boyfriend won't call her while he's out on the road ...

> THELMA
> (quieter)
> We just wanted to **get somethin' to eat.**

                    MAN
Well, you come to the **right place. You like
chili? They got good chili.**

                  WAITRESS
Harlan, are you **botherin' these poor girls?**

                HARLAN (MAN)
Hell, no. I was just **bein'
friendly.**

                  WAITRESS
          (making eye contact
          with Louise)
It's a good thing they're not all as **friendly** as
you.

                  THELMA
Your name's **Harlan?** I got an **uncle named Harlan!**

                  HARLAN
You do? Is he a **funny uncle?**
'Cause if he is, then he and I got somethin' in
common.

Once again, the dialogue develops character. Louise joins Thelma in ordering a drink before Harlan shows up. Of course, he uses the time-worn line that one might expect in a bar like that. What's of interest is how the two women respond to the same question at the same time. Louise, who's been "around the block" more than once, realizes it's a come on, while Thelma doesn't. Their responses reflect their characters, as Louise essentially tells him to "bug off," but the naïve Thelma takes the question quite literally.

After Louise kicks her under the table, Thelma "comes to her senses" and merely responds that they're there to get something to eat. Harlan links the "eat" with the "chili" before the waitress interrupts and does two things: (1) calls him by his name; and (2) alludes to the fact that he might be "bothering" the girls. Of course, Harlan links on the "bothering" with "being friendly," which allows the waitress to link on "friendly" in the most ironic of ways that Louise gets, but Thelma doesn't. But the mention of the name Harlan allows Thelma to link on the word about her "uncle" having the same name and that allows Harlan to link on the same word. At that point, Louise needs to give Thelma a lesson.

> LOUISE
> (to Harlan)
> I don't mean to be rude, but I've got something I need **to talk to my friend** about. **In private.**
>
> HARLAN
> Aw, **I understand.** I didn't mean to **bother ya.** It's just hard not to notice two such pretty ladies as yourselves.
> (standing, to
> Thelma)
> You better **dance with me before you leave,** or I'll never forgive you.
>
> THELMA
> Oh, sure. **That'd be fun.** Jeez, Louise, that **wasn't very nice.**
>
> LOUISE
> Can't you tell when somebody's **hittin' on you?**
>
> THELMA
> **So what if he was?** It's all your years of waitin' tables has **made you jaded,** that's all.
>
> LOUISE
> **Maybe.**
>
> THELMA
> Well, **just relax,** will ya. You're makin' me nervous.

This is an interesting turn in the dialogue in terms of character. To the request that Harlan leave them alone to talk "in private," Harlan says he "understands" and then links on the word "bother" that was stated earlier. Before he leaves, he drops yet another cliché about "dancing" to which Thelma, the literalist, replies it would be "fun," which prompts Louise to link with the notion of getting "hit on." Thelma links by stating "so what if he was? [hitting on me]" and then adds the fact that she thinks Louise has been "jaded" by waitressing too long and Louise really corroborates that. The "Maybe" really links with Thelma's suggestion that she "relax" which re-focuses the direction of the dialogue to their respective partners.

THELMA
So, **Jimmy** still **hasn't called** yet?

LOUISE
Givin' **him** a taste of his own **medicine. Asshole.**

THELMA
I'm sorry, Louise. I know you're **all upset.** It's just I'm so excited to be out of the house, I guess. (pause) I wonder if **Darryl's** home yet.

LOUISE
I wonder if **Jimmy's** gotten back.

THELMA
Why don't you tell **him** to just to **get lost** once and for all?

LOUISE
Why don't you **ditch** that **loser husband of yours?**

WAITRESS
(rolling her eyes)
This one's on **Harlan.**

                    THELMA

Jimmy'll come in off the road, you won't be
there, **he'll** freak out and call you a hundred
thousand times, and Sunday night you'll call him
back and, by Monday. **He'll** be **kissin' the ground
you walk on.**

                    LOUISE
Exactly.

                    THELMA
In the meantime, you said we were gonna have
some **fun. So let's have some!**

Thelma is perceptive enough to understand that Louise is preoccupied with
Jimmy and asks as much to which Louise links "hasn't called" with "a taste
of his own medicine." Thelma reconfirms Louise being "upset" with Jimmy
and, at the same time, reconfirms her concern about "Darryl," which links
again to "Jimmy" and Thelma's suggestion that Louise dump him, which
prompts Louise to tell Thelma to do the same thing with Darryl. This part of
the scene ends, with Harlan buying them drinks and Thelma trying to raise
Louise's spirits about "Jimmy" and about having "fun" which is a reprise link
from the beginning of the scene.

   Not only does the dialogue maintain the integrity of the scene, but it also
develops their characters as individuals and, more important, as friends.

16

Toy Story (1995)

Screenplay by Joss Whedon, Andrew Stanton, John Lasseter, Pete Docter, Joe Ranft, and Alec Sokolow

What makes *Toy Story* so different from the other films in this collection, beyond its animation status, is that it was written "by committee." No fewer than six people collaborated on the script which in itself makes it rather unique. Some scripts by committee come immediately to mind—*Casablanca* had three; *The Name of the Rose* had four; and *Il Postino* had five—but whether the writers in the previous films worked together harmoniously or not at all is open for discussion; however, the fact that six Disney writers were able to collaborate not only on the story, but also on the dialogue is a tribute to their flexibility.

What the writers have done is incorporate the same dialogue techniques one might find in any of the other scripts we've been discussing. One of the best scenes to show this is the scene in which Buzz Lightyear makes his appearance in Andy's room, and introduces himself to all the other toys there, including Woody.

                    MR. POTATO HEAD
          Oh, really? I'm from Playskool.

                         REX
          And I'm from Mattel. Well, I'm not
          actually from Mattel, I'm actually
          from a smaller company that was
          purchased in a leveraged buy-out.
          Well, I don't really understand the
          financials, but ...

Woody walks over to Bo Peep.

                        WOODY
          You'd think they've never seen a
          new toy before.

                       BO PEEP
          Well sure, look at him. He's got
          more gadgets on him than a Swiss
          army knife.

Slinky presses the button on Buzz's arm, activating his
laser light. Buzz quickly pulls his arm away.

                        BUZZ
          Ah, ah, ah, please be careful! You
          don't want to be in the way when my
          laser goes off.

                    MR. POTATO HEAD
          Hey, a laser! How come you don't
          have a laser, Woody?

                        WOODY
          It's not a laser! It's a little
          light bulb that blinks!

                        HAMM
          What's with him?

MR. POTATO HEAD
Laser-envy.

WOODY
All right, that's enough. Look,
we're all very impressed with
Andy's new toy—

BUZZ
Toy?

WOODY
T-O-Y. Toy.

BUZZ
Excuse me, I think the word you're
searching for is Space Ranger.

WOODY
The word I'm searching for I can't
say because there's pre-school toys
present.

MR. POTATO HEAD
Gettin' kind of tense, aren't you?

REX
Oh, uh, Mr. Lightyear? Now I'm
curious. What does a Space Ranger
actually do?

WOODY
He's not a Space Ranger! He
doesn't fight evil or shoot lasers
or fly—

BUZZ
Excuse me.

Buzz calmly hits a button and wings pop out.

Again the toys GASP IN AWE.

                    HAMM
          Oh, impressive wingspan. Very good!

                    WOODY
          Oh, what?! ... What?! These are
          plastic. He can't fly!

                    BUZZ
          They are a terillium-carbonic alloy
          and I CAN fly.

                    WOODY
          No, you can't.

                    BUZZ
          Yes, I can.

                    WOODY
          You can't!

                    BUZZ
          Can!

                    WOODY
          Can't! Can't! Can't!

                    BUZZ
          I tell you, I could fly around this
          room with my eyes closed!

                    WOODY
          Okay then, Mr. Lightbeer! Prove it.

                    BUZZ
          All right, then, I will.
               (to toys)
          Stand back everyone!

                    BUZZ
          To infinity and beyond!!

Whether it's Benjamin Braddock or Rick Blaine or Jake Gittes or even Buzz Lightyear who's doing the talking, some things remain constant relative to how the dialogue reflects voice and we can see that at work in *Toy Story* as well.

There is a cartoon drawing of Buzz giving the exact, word-for-word spiel that Buzz is now giving.

> MR. POTATO HEAD
> Oh, really? **I'm from Playskool.**

> REX
> **And I'm from Mattel.** Well, I'm not actually from Mattel, I'm actually from a smaller company that was purchased in a leveraged buy-out. Well, I don't really understand the financials, but ...

> WOODY
> You'd think they've never seen a **new toy** before.

> BO PEEP
> Well sure, look at him. He's got **more gadgets** on him than a Swiss army knife.

> BUZZ
> Ah, ah, ah, please be careful! You don't want to be in the way when my **laser goes off.**

> MR. POTATO HEAD
> Hey, a **laser**! How come you don't have a **laser**, Woody?

> WOODY
> It's not a **laser**! It's a little **lightbulb** that blinks!

                    HAMM
What's with him?

                         MR. POTATO HEAD
Laser-envy.

                    WOODY
All right, that's enough. Look,
we're all very impressed with
Andy's **new toy—**

                         BUZZ
Toy?

                         WOODY
T-O-Y. Toy.

Once again there's a focus to the scene; namely, toys. Mr. Potato Head says he's from "Playskool" which naturally links with "Mattel," which allows Woody to link off the names of those two toy manufacturers by mentioning "new toy" in relation to Buzz. Bo Peep links to "new toy" with the number of "gadgets" Buzz has, and that naturally links with Buzz's mention of the word "laser." The next three–four dialogue segments play off the "laser" link until Woody comes back with the "new toy" refrain, to which Buzz takes umbrage by linking with the question "Toy?" and Woody, wanting to clarify the word spells it for him. That sets up the remainder of the dialogue.

                    BUZZ
Excuse me, I think **the word you're**
searching for is **Space Ranger.**

                    WOODY
The word I'm searching for I can't
say because there's pre-school toys
present.

                    MR. POTATO HEAD
Gettin' kind of tense, aren't you?

                    REX
Oh, uh, Mr. Lightyear? Now I'm
curious. What does a **Space Ranger**
actually do?

> WOODY
>
> He's **not a Space Ranger**! He
> doesn't fight evil or shoot **lasers**
> **or fly—**

To establish his identity, Buzz says "The word you're searching for is Space Ranger," and Woody links beautifully by repeating the same phrase with a twist. Mr. Potato Head comments on Woody's apparent unease when Rex links with the "Space Ranger" phrase, only to have Woody adamantly deny that he is a "Space Ranger" and that he has no "lasers" nor can he "fly." Of course, Buzz takes umbrage with that comment, as it being an insult to his relative stature as a "Space Ranger."

> BUZZ
>
> Excuse me.

Buzz calmly hits a button and wings pop out. Again the toys GASP IN AWE.

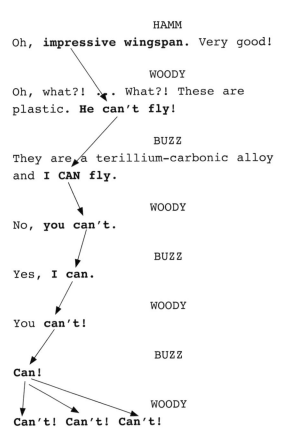

> HAMM
>
> Oh, **impressive wingspan.** Very good!

> WOODY
>
> Oh, what?! .. What?! These are
> plastic. **He can't fly!**

> BUZZ
>
> They are a terillium-carbonic alloy
> and **I CAN fly.**

> WOODY
>
> No, **you can't.**

> BUZZ
>
> Yes, **I can.**

> WOODY
>
> You **can't!**

> BUZZ
>
> **Can!**

> WOODY
>
> **Can't! Can't! Can't!**

                    BUZZ
I tell you, I could **fly** around this
room with my eyes closed!

                    WOODY
Okay then, Mr. Lightbeer! **Prove it.**

                    BUZZ
All right, then, I will.
(to toys)
Stand back everyone!

                    BUZZ
To infinity and beyond!!

Buzz thinks he knows who he is and opens up his "wings." Although the other toys are impressed with his "wingspan," Woody is not. What ensues is an exchange between Buzz and Woody predicated on the fact he can "fly," and when Woody says "prove it" it, re-enforces who Buzz thinks he is and establishes the phrase "To infinity and beyond!" which will act as a kind of leitmotif throughout Buzz's dialogue and which we see at the conclusion of the film as well.

One of the better dialogue scenes in the film is the one between Buzz and Woody in the evil Sid's bedroom. What's truly engaging about the scene is that it's the major scene in the film that unifies their friendship in a way that hadn't been done before. It also reinforces the notion set in Joseph Campbell's *The Hero With a Thousand Faces* (2008) that, in the hero's journey, s/he must not be the same character at the end of the journey that s/he was at the beginning. This aspect of a character's arc is evinced particularly well in this scene.

INT. SID'S ROOM

                    WOODY
Ps-s-s-s-t! Psst! Hey, Buzz!

                    WOODY
Hey! Get over here and see if you can get this
tool box off me.

                    WOODY

Oh, come on, Buzz. I ... Buzz, I can't do this
without you. I need your help.

                    BUZZ

I can't help. I can't help anyone.

                    WOODY

Why, sure you can, Buzz. You can get me out of
here and then I'll get that rocket off you, and
we'll make a break for Andy's house.

                    BUZZ

Andy's house. Sid's house. What's the
difference.

                    WOODY

Oh, Buzz, you've had a big fall. You must not be
thinking clearly.

                    BUZZ

No, Woody, for the first time I am thinking
clearly.
    (looking at himself)
You were right all along. I'm not a Space
Ranger. I'm just a toy. A stupid little insig-
nificant toy.

                    WOODY

Whoa, hey—wait a minute. Being a toy is a lot
better than being a Space Ranger.

                    BUZZ

Yeah, right.

                    WOODY

No, it is. Look, over in that house is a kid
who thinks you are the greatest, and it's not
because you're a Space Ranger, pal, it's
because you're a TOY! You are HIS toy.

                         BUZZ
But why would Andy want me?

                        WOODY
Why would Andy want you?! Look at you! You're a
Buzz Lightyear. Any other toy would give up his
moving parts just to be you. You've got wings,
you glow in the dark, you talk, your helmet does
that—that whoosh thing—you are a COOL toy.

                        WOODY
              (continued; depressed)
As a matter of fact you're too cool. I mean—I
mean what chance does a toy like me have against
a Buzz Lightyear action figure? All I can do is
...
          (Woody pulls his own pull-string)

                  WOODY (VOICE BOX)
There's a snake in my boots!

Woody bows his head.

                        WOODY
Why would Andy ever want to play with me, when
he's got you? (pause) I'm the one that should be
strapped to that rocket.

                        WOODY
Listen Buzz, forget about me. You should get out
of here while you can.

He is on top of the milk crate, trying to push the tool
box off.

                        WOODY
Buzz!! What are you doing? I thought you were—

                         BUZZ
Come on, Sheriff. There's a kid over in that

house who needs us. Now let's get you out of
this thing.

                  WOODY
Yes Sir!

Both Buzz and Woody push the milk crate and together, they
finally get it to move but it's slow progress.

                  WOODY
(strained)
Come on, Buzz! We can do it!

The scene has a significant arc to it. It begins with Buzz having a rather self-pitying moment only to be supported by Woody. At around the middle of the scene, it then becomes Woody's turn to have a rather self-pitying moment only to be supported by Buzz. The scene's arc begins with a kind of "defeat" or "failure" and ends with "victory" and "success." In that sense, the writers were keenly focused on how the arc of the scene should progress specifically through the dialogue of each character.

INT. SID'S ROOM

                  WOODY
Hey! Get over here and see if you can get this
tool box off me. Oh, come on, Buzz. I ... Buzz,
I can't do this without you. **I need your help.**

                  BUZZ
I can't help. I can't help anyone.

                  WOODY
Why, **sure you can**, Buzz. You **can** get me out of
here and then I'll get that rocket off you, and
we'll make a break for **Andy's house.**

                  BUZZ
Andy's house. Sid's house. **What's the
difference.**

                  WOODY

Oh, Buzz, you've had a big fall. You must **not be thinking clearly.**

                  BUZZ

No, Woody, for the first time **I am thinking clearly.**
    (looking at himself)
You were right all along. I'm not a **Space Ranger.** I'm **just a toy.** A stupid little insig-nificant toy.

Woody declares that he needs Buzz's "help" to which Buzz links by saying he's incapable of "help." Woody links off that comment by saying that "sure you can" (help, that is) and follows it up with an allusion to "Andy's house." Buzz links on "Andy's house" by declaring what's the difference between Andy's house or Sid's house. Woody suggests that he must have had a big fall because he's not "thinking clearly," to which Buzz links with he is "thinking clearly" and he reprises the "Space Ranger" line that was set up at the beginning of the script, acknowledging that he's "just a toy."

                  WOODY

Whoa, hey—wait a minute. Being a **toy** is a lot better than being a **Space Ranger.**

                  BUZZ

Yeah, right.

                  WOODY

No, it is. Look, over in that house is a kid who thinks you are the greatest, and it's not because you're a **Space Ranger, pal,** it's because you're a **TOY!** You are HIS **toy.**

                  BUZZ

But why would Andy want me?

                  WOODY

Why would Andy want you?! Look at you! You're a **Buzz Lightyear.** Any other **toy** would give up his moving parts just to be you. You've got wings,

you glow in the dark, you talk, your helmet does
that—that whoosh thing—you **are a COOL toy.**
    (continued; depressed)
As a matter of fact you're **too cool.** I mean—I
mean what chance does a **toy** like me have against
a **Buzz Lightyear** action figure? All I can do is
...
    (Woody pulls his own pull-string)

            WOODY (VOICE BOX)
There's a snake in my boots!
Woody bows his head.

            WOODY
**Why would Andy ever want to play with me, when
he's got you?** (pause) I'm the one that should be
strapped to that rocket.

Woody follows up the links with "toy" and "Space Ranger" twice before Buzz
asks the question "Why would Andy want me?" In a beautiful play off that
line, Woody links with the same sentence, but with exclamation and then
clarifies why Andy would want him highlighting that he's a "Buzz Lightyear"
(twice) and that he's a "cool" toy (twice) before denigrating himself taking
Buzz's line and turning it against himself in "Why would Andy ever want to
play with me ..."

            WOODY
Listen Buzz, **forget about me.** You should get out
of here while you can.
He is on top of the milk crate, trying to push
the tool box off.

            WOODY
Buzz!! **What are you doing?** I thought you were—

            BUZZ
Come on, Sheriff. There's a kid over in that
house who needs us. **Now let's get you out of
this thing.**

                              WOODY
          Yes Sir!

Both Buzz and Woody push the milk crate and together, they
finally get it to move but it's slow progress.

So, while the scene begins in "defeat" it ends in "victory," all mediated by
their dialogue and the significant way the writing team uses dialogue links to
carry the scene to its natural conclusion. One could conclude here that there
isn't much of a difference between what Mankiewicz was doing in *Citizen
Kane* in 1941 and what the *Toy Story* team was doing a half-century later in
1995 in terms of using dialogue techniques that clearly have withstood the
"test of time," regardless of the era in which the dialogue was written.

17

Good Will Hunting (1997)

Screenplay by Matt Damon and Ben Affleck

Ordinary People (1980)

Screenplay by Alvin Sargent Based on the novel by Judith Guest

As I've written before, presumably, the screenplay of *Good Will Hunting* (1997) was written by both Matt Damon and Ben Affleck, although the credits don't say "Screenplay by," but "Written by," which is not the same thing. There has been a lot of controversy about the script. In the February, 1998 issue of *Written By*, Damon says: "We met with a lot of studios and they were basically saying, 'This is what we'd want to do with it.' And we went with the place that we thought was the smartest place for that movie. And there was a lot of development. There was a lot of rewriting that went on once we went to Castle Rock, and when we went to Miramax. There were a lot of really good meetings—we met a lot of really good writers, from Terrence Malick to William Goldman to Ed Zwick. There were a lot of people who were friends of the court who came in and threw in their two cents for us, which was great. It was really helpful." Add to that what Goldman himself has written in *Which Lie Did I Tell?* (2001) that "I think the reason the world was so anxious to believe Matt Damon and Ben Affleck didn't write their script as simple jealousy. They were young and cute and famous; kill the fuckers," and "When I read it, and spent a day with the writers, all I said was this: Rob's [Reiner] dead right [i.e. in corroborating that they wrote the script]. Period. Total contribution. Zero" (Goldman, 2001, p. 333) and it would appear the jury is no longer out.

Regardless of who wrote and/or doctored it, what's clear about the film is that it neatly adheres to what I've been talking about *vis-à-vis* dialogue techniques. The film is an extremely dialogue-driven script with a significant number of scenes taking place between two people. Not unlike Alvin Sargent's brilliant script, *Ordinary People* (1980), (which, as we'll see, *Good Will Hunting* holds significant measure), a majority of scenes take place between the therapist, Sean, and Will himself with one particular scene actually being Sean's extensive monologue as Will sits and listens, in which case there are no external links to deal with; however, there are several key scenes in the script that not only utilize the techniques that I've been talking about, but also elicit a significant amount of conflict which is of paramount importance in writing dialogue. This is the first meeting between Sean and Will, and it is significant not only for the fact that it establishes conflict but also the manner in which the dialogue functions. Because of some legal troubles Will has gotten into, he can either do time or seek therapy. It's at that point that Will meets Sean, who will become his primary therapist.

> SEAN
> Where you from in Southie?

> WILL
> Did you buy all these books retail,
> or do you send away for like a "shrink
> kit" that comes with all these volumes
> included?

> SEAN
> Have you read all these books, Will?

> WILL
> Probably not.

                    SEAN
(indicating a shelf)
How about the ones on that shelf?

                    WILL
Yeah, I read those.

                    SEAN
What did you think?

                    WILL
I'm not here for a fuckin' book
report. They're your books, why
don't you read 'em?

                    SEAN
I did.

                    WILL
That must have taken you a long time.

                    SEAN
Yeah, it did take me a long time.

                    WILL
(looking at book)
"A History of the United States,
Volume I." If you want to read a
real history book, read Howard Zinn's
"A People's History of the United
States." That book will knock you on
your ass.

                    SEAN
How about Noam Chomsky's
"Manufacturing Consent?"

                    WILL
You people baffle me. You spend all
this money on beautiful, fancy books—
and they're the wrong fuckin' books.

                         SEAN
You think so?

                         WILL
Whatever blows your hair back.

                         SEAN
(indicating cigarette)
Guy your age shouldn't smoke so much.
Stunt your growth.

                         WILL
You're right. It really gets in the
way of my jazzercizing.

                         WILL
Do you lift?

                         SEAN
Yes, I do.

                         WILL
Nautilus?

                         SEAN
Free weights.

                         WILL
Oh yeah? Me too. What do you bench?

                         SEAN
285.

                         WILL
Oh.

                         WILL
You paint this?

                         SEAN
Yeah. Do you paint?

                    WILL
No.

                    SEAN
Crayons?

                    WILL
This is a real piece of shit.

                    SEAN
Tell me what you really think.

                    WILL
Poor color composition, lousy use of
space. But that shit doesn't really
concern me.

                    SEAN
What does?

                    WILL
The color here, see how dark it is?
It's interesting.

                    SEAN
What is?

                    WILL
I think you're one step away from
cutting your ear off.

                    SEAN
Oh, "Starry Night" time, huh?

                    WILL
You ever heard the saying, "any port
in a storm?"

                    SEAN
Sure, how 'bout "still waters run
deep"—

                        WILL
—Well, maybe that means you.

                        SEAN
—In what way?

                        WILL
Maybe you were in the middle of a
storm, a big fuckin' storm—the
waves were crashing over the bow,
the Goddamned mast was about to snap,
and you were crying for the harbor.
So you did what you had to do, to
get out. Maybe you became a
psychologist.

                        SEAN
Maybe you should be a patient and
sit down.

                        WILL
Maybe you married the wrong woman.

                        SEAN
Watch your mouth.

                        WILL
That's it isn't it? You married the
wrong woman. She leave you? Was she
bangin' someone else?

Sean is walking slowly towards Will.

                        WILL
How are the seas now, D—

In a flash, Sean has Will by the throat. Will is
helpless.

> SEAN
> If you ever disrespect my wife
> again ... I will end you.

> WILL
> Time's up.

Now we can take a look at how they've used the dialogue links.

> SEAN
> Where you from in Southie?

> WILL
> Did you buy all **these books** retail,
> or do you send away for like a "shrink
> kit" that comes with all **these volumes**
> included?

> SEAN
> Have you read all **these books**, Will?

> WILL
> Probably not.

> SEAN
> (indicating a shelf)
> How about the **ones** on that shelf?

> WILL
> Yeah, I read **those**.

> SEAN
> What did you **think**?

> WILL
> I'm not here for a fuckin' **book**
> report. They're your **books**, why
> don't you read 'em?

> SEAN
> **I did.**

```
            WILL
That must have taken you a long time.


            SEAN
Yeah, it did take me a long time.
```

Sean opens with a question that Will answers with a question. Ostensibly, Sean is interested in where Will comes from, but the focus of the dialogue has nothing to do with anything that pedestrian, but with something more intellectual. By ignoring the question as to where he lives (which is clearly an avoidance issue throughout the script) he focuses on the "books." From the mention of that word, everything links: "books" to "reading books," to "probably not [have read all of them]," to "ones [books on the shelf]," to "read those [on the shelf]," to "thinking about [the ones he's read on the shelf]," to "book reports," to "why don't you read them [the books]," to "I did [read them]," to "took a long time [to read them]." Each dialogue segment is clearly linked to every other dialogue segment with the main focus being "books" and all that intellectually implies.

```
            WILL
        (looking at book)
"A History of the United States,
Volume I." If you want to read a
real history book, read Howard Zinn's
"A People's History of the United
States." That book will knock you on
your ass.
```

Here is an example of multiple imbedded links including the phrase "History of the United States," the link with the word "read," as well as the word "book."

```
            SEAN
How about Noam Chomsky's
"Manufacturing Consent?"


            WILL
You people baffle me. You spend all
this money on beautiful, fancy books—
and they're the wrong fuckin' books.
```

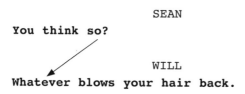

SEAN

You think so?

WILL

Whatever blows your hair back.

The book links continue from with the double internal link with "history book," to "Chomsky's [book]." to another double internal link with "fancy books— … wrong fuckin' books," to "think so [implied wrong books]," to "whatever [books you want to buy]." Once the dialogue has established that, at least intellectually, they're on a level playing field, the dialogue can continue in the direction Sean wants it to go.

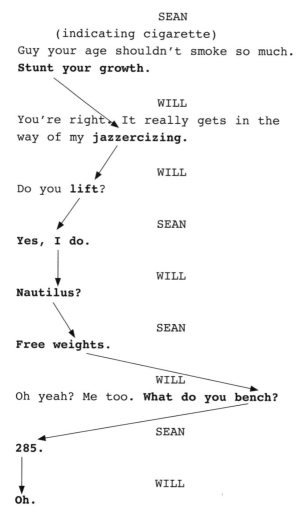

SEAN
(indicating cigarette)
Guy your age shouldn't smoke so much.
Stunt your growth.

WILL
You're right. It really gets in the
way of my **jazzercizing.**

WILL
Do you **lift**?

SEAN
Yes, I do.

WILL
Nautilus?

SEAN
Free weights.

WILL
Oh yeah? Me too. **What do you bench?**

SEAN
285.

WILL
Oh.

This is a brilliant part since it links cigarette smoking with jazzercizing (albeit an ironic statement), with lifting weights, to working out with Nautilus, to working out with Free weights, to benching, to 285, to Will's understanding that Sean isn't someone to mess with physically which pays off at the end of the scene. So, by the middle of the scene, two things have clearly been established: (1) they're both intellectuals; and (2) Sean is a physical match for Will if, in fact, it comes to that. Will then gets up and sees Sean's painting of an old sailboat caught in a storm.

                         WILL
          You **paint this**?

                         SEAN
          Yeah. Do you **paint**?

                         WILL
          No.

                         SEAN
          Crayons?

                         WILL
          This is a real **piece of shit**.

                         SEAN
          Tell me **what you really think**.

                           WILL
          Poor color composition, lousy use of
          space. But **that shit doesn't really
          concern me**.

                         SEAN
          What does?

                         WILL
          The **color here**, see how dark it is?
          It's interesting.

                         SEAN
          What is?

WILL

I think you're one step away from
cutting your ear off.

SEAN

Oh, **"Starry Night"** time, huh?

WILL

You ever heard the saying, **"any port
in a storm?"**

SEAN

Sure, how 'bout **"still waters run
deep"**—

WILL

—Well, **maybe** that **means you.**

SEAN

—**In what way?**

WILL

Maybe you were in the middle of a
storm, a big fuckin' storm—the
waves were crashing over the bow,
the Goddamned mast was about to snap,
and you were crying for the harbor.
So you did what you had to do, to
get out. **Maybe** you became a
psychologist.

SEAN

Maybe you should be a patient and
sit down.

WILL

Maybe you married the **wrong woman.**

SEAN

Watch your mouth.

>   WILL
>   That's it isn't it? **You married the
>   wrong woman.** She leave you? Was she
>   bangin' someone else?

Sean is walking slowly towards Will.

>   WILL
>   How are the **seas now,** D—

In a flash, Sean has Will by the throat. Will is helpless.

>   SEAN
>   **If you ever disrespect my wife
>   again ... I will end you.**

>   WILL
>   **Time's up.**

Once again, the links are all there. "Paint this" links to "yeah [I did]," to "Do you paint," to "No," to "crayons," to "piece of shit," to "really think [of the painting]," to "poor color composition and spacing," to what interests Will. And what interests Will is the dark color which links to Van Gogh's ear to Van Gogh's *Starry Night* to *Still Waters* (which dates back to the fifteenth century) to the word "maybe" in relation to Sean exhibiting "still waters." Sean then links off the word "maybe," and Will double links internally with the word speculating on what the painting might mean. But Sean tries to take another tact, even though he links on the same word, although Will won't give up on it and links again on the word, but this time in relation to the fact Sean may have married the "wrong woman." The wrong woman comment links to Sean's statement that Will should "watch your mouth. Instead of ending the dialogue, Will links again to the "wrong woman" line and essentially casts his fate when he implies Sean's wife was having an affair. When Will then reprises the "seas/waves" line, Sean essentially concludes the scene by grabbing Will by the throat saying that if Will ever disrespects his wife again, he will kill him, which not only prompts to ironically state "time's up," but also puts Will on notice that Sean is not someone to alienate in any fashion.

There have been a lot of comparisons between *Good Will Hunting* and the film *Ordinary People*, directed by Robert Redford, screenplay by Alvin Sargent, for which he won an Academy Award. What I find engaging is how this particular dialogue coincides with Sargent's dialogue in *Ordinary People*. In this film, written almost two decades earlier, the Conrad character (Timothy Hutton) sees his therapist Berger (Judd Hirsch) because, as we find out, he suffers from inordinate guilt over the fact that during a boating accident he survived and his brother did not. The scene opens with Conrad going to Berger's office for the first time. Berger sits at his desk and looks up Conrad's file.

> DR BERGER
> Hmm ... Jarrett. How long since
> you've been **out of the hospital**?

> CONRAD
> A month and a half.

> DR BERGER
> **Feeling depressed?**

> CONRAD
> **No.**

> DR BERGER
> On stage?

> CONRAD
> **Pardon me?**

> DR BERGER
> **People nervous ... treating you
> like you're ... a dangerous character?**

> CONRAD
> **Yeah.** I guess a little.

> DR BERGER
> **Are you?**

> CONRAD
> **I don't know.**

                DR BERGER
How long were you **in the hospital?**

                CONRAD
Four months.

                DR BERGER
What did you do?

                CONRAD
**I tried to off myself. Isn't it
down there?**

                DR BERGER
It doesn't say what your **method
was.**

                CONRAD
Double-edged Super Blue.

                DR BERGER
Oh.   DR BERGER (cont'd)
So how does it **feel being home?**
Everybody's **glad to see you?**

                CONRAD
Yeah.

                DR BERGER
Friends?

                CONRAD
Yeah.

                DR BERGER
OK?

                    CONRAD
Yeah.

                    DR BERGER
Everything...

                    CONRAD
Yeah.

                    DR BERGER
You're back in school?
Everything okay at school?
Teachers?

                    CONRAD
Yeah.

                    DR BERGER
No problems?

                    CONRAD
Uh-uh.

                    DR BERGER
So why are you here?

                    CONRAD
Uh ... I'd like to be more in
control, I guess.

                    DR BERGER
Why?

                    CONRAD
So people can **quit worrying about
me.**

                    DR BERGER
Who's **worried about you?**

                    CONRAD
My **father**, mostly. This is his
idea.

                    DR BERGER
**What about your mother? Isn't she
worried about you, too?**

                    CONRAD
I don't know, listen. You ... You're
a **friend of Doctor Crawford, so you're
probably all right, but I'll be
straight with you, I don't like
this already.**

                    DR BERGER
Well, as long as you're **straight.**

                    CONRAD
**What do you know about me? Have
you talked to Crawford?**

                    DR BERGER
Yes. **He** called me on the phone. He
told me your name and ... he told me
to look for you. And, uh ... he said
you had a brother who died. **A ...
boating accident, wasn't it? Want
to tell me about it?**

Silence

                    DR BERGER (cont'd)
Well I suppose you **talked this over
with Crawford** at the hospital.
Right?

                    CONRAD
        Right.

Conrad nods.

                    DR BERGER
How did that go?

                    CONRAD
It **didn't change anything.**

                    DR BERGER
Why do you want **to change**?

                    CONRAD
I told you, I'd like to be more in
control.

                    DR BERGER
Why?

                    CONRAD
I told you, so people can **quit
worrying about me.**

                    DR BERGER
Well. I'll tell you something. I'll
be **straight with you,** okay? **I'm not
big on control. But it's your
money.**

                    CONRAD
So to speak.

                    DR BERGER
So to speak.
Okay ...

Dr Berger picks up his diary.

                    DR BERGER (cont'd)
**How's Tuesdays ... and Fridays?
Same time.**

                    CONRAD
Twice ... a week?

> DR BERGER
> Well. **Control's a tough nut.**

> CONRAD
> I've got **swim practice** every night.

> DR BERGER
> Well. **That's a problem. How do we solve that?**

> CONRAD
> Guess **I'll have to skip practice twice a week, and come here.**

> DR BERGER
> Well. **It's up to you.**

> CONRAD
> **I don't like being here. I got to tell you I don't like being here at all.**

Dr Berger nods.

> DR BERGER
> **Mm-mmm.**

The similarities in characters and in storyline context are remarkably similar. Although we discover that Will's psychological problems stem from childhood abuse as opposed to Conrad's overwhelming guilt for surviving a boating accident while his brother died, the relationships between them and their therapists are remarkably similar. But regardless of the similarities and/or differences between the two films, the one thing that remains fairly constant is how the dialogues have been written.

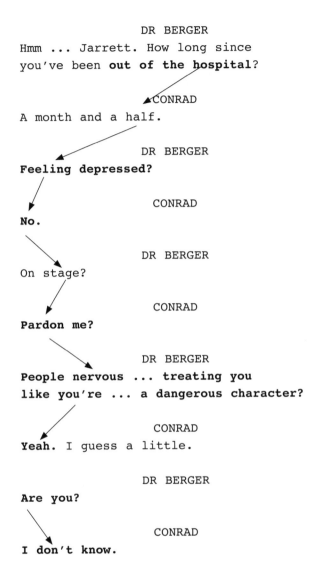

DR BERGER

Hmm ... Jarrett. How long since
you've been **out of the hospital**?

CONRAD

A month and a half.

DR BERGER

Feeling depressed?

CONRAD

No.

DR BERGER

On stage?

CONRAD

Pardon me?

DR BERGER

**People nervous ... treating you
like you're ... a dangerous character?**

CONRAD

Yeah. I guess a little.

DR BERGER

Are you?

CONRAD

I don't know.

The length of time Conrad had been out of the hospital links with "a month and a half." Berger asks a sequence of questions which are meant to create a baseline for their therapy. Conrad answers "no" to being depressed, answers with a question to Berger's question about being "on stage." Berger clarifies the question by asking if Conrad feels he's being "treated like a dangerous character." When Conrad says "Yeah," Berger links with "Are you?" to which Conrad responds "I don't know."

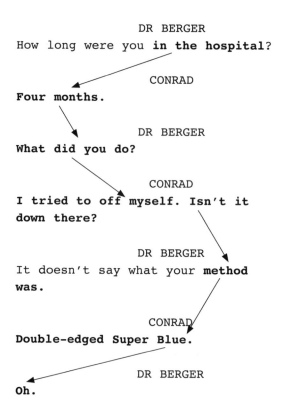

DR BERGER
How long were you **in the hospital**?

CONRAD
Four months.

DR BERGER
What did you do?

CONRAD
I tried to off myself. Isn't it down there?

DR BERGER
It doesn't say what your **method was.**

CONRAD
Double-edged Super Blue.

DR BERGER
Oh.

Berger's question about time in the hospital links with "four months," and that would naturally link with why he was in the hospital. To Berger's question "What did you do?" Conrad links with "I tried to off myself." He follows that up with a question of his own to which links "Isn't it down there?" with Berger's statement about "method" to which Conrad links with "Double-edged Super Blue."

Clearly, there are similarities in terms of character in that neither Will nor Conrad wants to be talking to a therapist. Regardless of their recalcitrance, the dialogue links establish some key things related to the M-A-D-E scheme that I alluded to in the Introduction. "Hospital" links to "month and a half," which links to Berger's question about depression, to which Conrad denies, which provokes the link "On stage," which Berger expands to "dangerous character," which Conrad links by saying "a little," which links to Berger's question "Are you?" which links to "I don't know." Berger then continues with the hospital line of questioning, and that links with "Four months," which links to why he was there, which links to the attempted suicide and its method. Through all of this interrogation, Berger is essentially uninvolved and is only interested in getting the facts in much the same way Sean was with Will.

                    DR BERGER (cont'd)
So how does it **feel being home?**
Everybody's **glad to see you?**

                         CONRAD
Yeah.

                         DR BERGER
Friends?

                         CONRAD
Yeah.

                         DR BERGER
OK?

                         CONRAD
Yeah.

                         DR BERGER
Everything...

                         CONRAD
Yeah.

                         DR BERGER
You're back in school?
Everything okay at school?
Teachers?

                         CONRAD
Yeah.

                         DR BERGER
No problems?

                         CONRAD
Uh-uh.

                         DR BERGER
So why are you here?

Everything Berger suggests to Conrad, Conrad links with something positive.
One affirmation only leads to another affirmation, which is exactly where
Berger wants to situate Conrad. If everything is fine, then why is he in
therapy? This is the point at which the dialogue focuses on the essential
problem that Conrad has and makes the importance of the dialogue linking
critical.

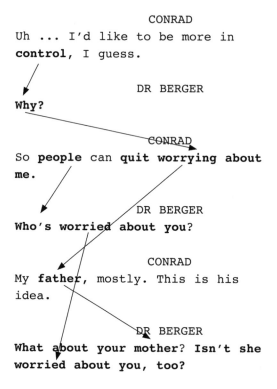

>   CONRAD
>   Uh ... I'd like to be more in
>   **control**, I guess.
>
>   DR BERGER
>   **Why?**
>
>   CONRAD
>   So **people** can **quit worrying about
>   me**.
>
>   DR BERGER
>   **Who's worried about you?**
>
>   CONRAD
>   My **father**, mostly. This is his
>   idea.
>
>   DR BERGER
>   **What about your mother? Isn't she
>   worried about you, too?**

Conrad opens with the issue of "control," which becomes the focus of the
dialogue from that point on. What Sargent does brilliantly is to weave the
dialogue in such a fashion that he gets to the real core of Conrad's problem.
To the question of why Conrad is so concerned about control, he answers
"So people can quit worrying about me." Berger double links off the word
"people" and "worrying," since Conrad follows up with "my father" (the
"people" who are apparently "worrying"). The mention of his "father"
prompts Berger to ask the obvious question about his "mother," while linking
again to the notion of "worry."

                         CONRAD
I don't know, listen. You ... You're
a **friend of Dr Crawford, so you're
probably all right, but I'll be
straight with you, I don't like
this already.**

                    DR BERGER
Well, as long as you're **straight.**

                         CONRAD
**What do you know about me? Have
you talked to Crawford?**

                    DR BERGER
Yes. **He** called me on the phone. He
told me your name and ... he told me
to look for you. And, uh ...he said
you had a brother who died. **A ...
boating accident, wasn't it? Want
to tell me about it?**
Silence

              DR BERGER (cont'd)
Well I suppose you **talked this over
with Crawford** at the hospital.
Right?

                         CONRAD
Right.

Conrad nods.

The line of questioning about his mother begins to make Conrad uncom-
fortable. To avoid those questions, Conrad retreats to a comment about "Dr
Crawford" and to the fact he wants to be "straight" about the fact he doesn't
like being there. Berger links on the word "straight," since it presupposes that
Conrad really needs to be that way. Conrad brings up "Dr Crawford" again in
the context of his history, and Berger gives us part of the backstory with the
boating accident and the death of Conrad's brother. To the question "Want
to tell me about it?" Conrad is silent and Berger, acknowledging Conrad's

avoidance of the subject, retreats to Dr. Crawford again in order to mitigate the discussion and when he asks "Right?" Conrad links with the same word.

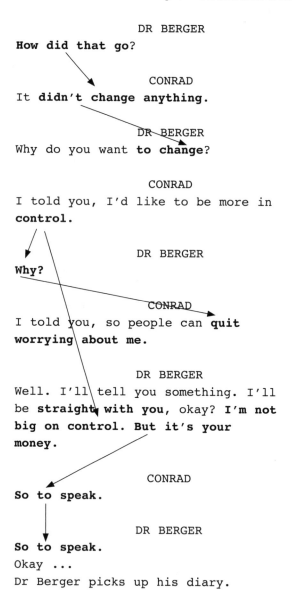

DR BERGER
How did that go?

CONRAD
It **didn't change anything.**

DR BERGER
Why do you want **to change?**

CONRAD
I told you, I'd like to be more in **control.**

DR BERGER
Why?

CONRAD
I told you, so people can **quit worrying** about me.

DR BERGER
Well. I'll tell you something. I'll be **straight with you,** okay? **I'm not big on control. But it's your money.**

CONRAD
So to speak.

DR BERGER
So to speak.
Okay ...
Dr Berger picks up his diary.

When Berger asks how things went with Dr. Crawford, Conrad states that they didn't "change anything," to which Berger links with what he wanted to "change." Conrad reprises the notion of "control," which begs the question: "Why?" Conrad links on the control issue by stating that people can quit "worrying" about him. Berger reprises the being "straight" line and then links up with the issue of "control" again. When Berger states "it's your money," Conrad replies with "So to speak" which Berger links through repeating the same phrase.

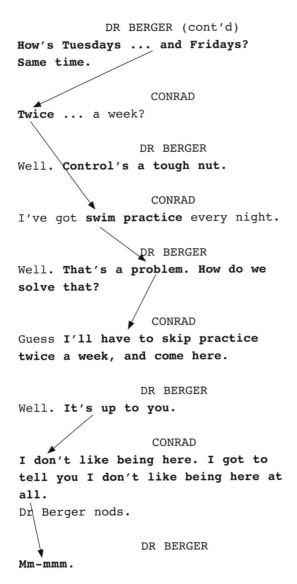

DR BERGER (cont'd)
How's Tuesdays ... and Fridays?
Same time.

                    CONRAD
Twice ... a week?

                    DR BERGER
Well. **Control's a tough nut.**

                    CONRAD
I've got **swim practice** every night.

                    DR BERGER
Well. **That's a problem. How do we**
solve that?

                    CONRAD
Guess **I'll have to skip practice**
twice a week, and come here.

                    DR BERGER
Well. **It's up to you.**

                    CONRAD
I don't like being here. I got to
tell you I don't like being here at
all.
Dr Berger nods.

                    DR BERGER
Mm-mmm.

The scene concludes not unlike it began, with Conrad's reluctance to be there. What Sargent does so well is to continue linking the dialogues throughout the scene, so to Berger's suggestion they meet "Tuesdays ...

and Fridays" Conrad links with "Twice … a week," and we get the brilliant refrain of "Control's a tough nut," which not only emphasizes the focus of the scene, but also forces Conrad to make a decision. To Conrad's statement that he has "swim practice" Berger merely asks "How do we solve that?" to which Conrad says he guesses he'll have to skip practice "twice a week," which links to his previous statement. Berger takes no responsibility for that and suggests that "It's up to you," to which Conrad closes the scene in much the same way as it opened, with him stating "I don't like being here at all," which prompts Berger merely to respond with "Mm-mmm."

Whether Sargent uses exact words/phrases or analogous words/phrases, one clearly sees how he has linked almost every segment of dialogue within the scene in a way that not only advances the scene, but also focuses on the key aspect of the scene that will play out in the rest of the film: namely, the notion of "control" or a lack of it. These two films, produced almost 20 years apart, have some significant similarities not only in form, but in content. Although Sargent's career spans almost a half-century, including the *Spider Man* films, and his garnering of his second Academy Award in 1981 about 16 years before Damon and Affleck received theirs, one discovers that if there's a science to dialogue writing then the latter have much to thank the former for.

18

American Beauty (1999)
Screenplay by Alan Ball

American Beauty has an interesting history. Of course, it opens with Lester Burnham telling his tale from the grave. Not a new idea. As a matter of fact, it's over a hundred years old if we trace it back to the writings of the Brazilian novelist, Machado de Assis, Joachim Maria and his masterpiece, *The Posthumous Memoirs of Brás Cubas* (1881). In a manner of speaking, the film could be retitled *The Posthumous Memoirs of Lester Burnham* and nothing would get lost in translation. In an interview with Amazon.com, Ball talked a lot about the first draft taking eight months, and that he and director, Sam Mendes, were in much agreement about the script. "He got it from the very minute he read it, and I knew that he picked up on it and got it. And I am so thankful that he directed this movie and not some big A-list Hollywood guy who would have missed the boat entirely. I was very impressed with how much Sam seemed to understand the script. And then I went to New York to see Sam's production of *Cabaret*. And although *Cabaret* is very different than *American Beauty*, it was really obvious to me that this was a guy who had a real strong visual sense; he really understood the whole kinetic combination of visual and music. He's also someone who can get incredible performances from actors. And I just instinctively went, 'This is the guy.'"[1] So, unlike directors such as Polanski and Scott who didn't really acknowledge the writers Towne and Khouri, Ball very clearly acknowledges Mendes, which may have a lot to say about writers.

Be that as it may, I'm not sure how long it took to write a final draft, but it's clear through the dialogue that Ball was as familiar with the techniques of dialogue writing as any other knowledgeable screenwriter and two specific

---

[1] http://www.spiritualteachers.org/alan_ball.htm [accessed May 2013].

scenes stand out for me. The first is the scene with Lester in Brad's office, at which point Lester has pretty much had it with corporate America and is seeking a way out.

INT. BRAD'S OFFICE—DAY
Brad is seated behind his desk, reading a document. Lester sits across from him, smiling.

>   BRAD
>   (reads)
>   "... my job consists of basically masking my
>   contempt for the assholes in charge, and, at
>   least once a day, retiring to the men's room so
>   I can jerk off, while I fantasize about a life
>   that doesn't so closely resemble hell."
>   (looks up at Lester)
>   Well, you obviously have no interest in saving
>   yourself.

>   LESTER
>   (laughs)
>   Brad, for fourteen years I've been a whore for
>   the advertising industry. The only way I could
>   save myself now is if I start firebombing.

>   BRAD
>   Whatever. Management wants you gone by the end
>   of the day.

>   LESTER
>   Well, just what sort of severance package is
>   "management" prepared to offer me? Considering
>   the information I have about our editorial
>   director buying pussy with company money.

A beat.

                    LESTER (cont'd)
Which I'm sure would interest the I.R.S., since
it technically constitutes fraud. And I'm sure
that some of our advertisers and rival publica-
tions might like to know about it as well. Not
to mention, Craig's wife.

Brad sighs.

                         BRAD
     What do you want?

                        LESTER
     One year's salary, with benefits.

                         BRAD
     That's not going to happen.

                        LESTER
     Well, what do you say I throw in a little sexual
     harassment charge to boot?

Brad LAUGHS.

                         BRAD
     Against who?

                        LESTER
     Against you.

Brad stops laughing.

                    LESTER (cont'd)
     Can you prove you didn't offer to save my job if
     I'd let you blow me?

Brad leans back in his chair, studying Lester.

                         BRAD
     Man. You are one twisted fuck.

> LESTER
> (standing)
> Nope. I'm just an ordinary guy with nothing to
> lose.

The brilliant part of this scene is how it arcs in a very short period of time from Brad's rather authoritative position that Lester isn't going to get anything, to his very submissive position that Lester is going to get whatever Lester wants, and the dialogue is instrumental in that.

INT. BRAD'S OFFICE—DAY
Brad is seated behind his desk, reading a document. Lester sits across from him, smiling.

> BRAD
> (reads)
> "... my job consists of basically masking my
> contempt for the assholes in charge, and, at
> least once a day, retiring to the men's room so
> I can jerk off, while I fantasize about a life
> that doesn't so closely resemble hell."
> (looks up at Lester)
>
> Well, you obviously have no interest in **saving
> yourself.**

> LESTER
> (laughs)
> Brad, for fourteen years I've been a whore for
> the advertising industry. The only way I could
> **save myself** now **is if I start firebombing.**

> BRAD
> **Whatever. Management wants you gone by the end
> of the day.**

> LESTER
> Well, just what sort of **severance package is
> "management" prepared to offer me?** Considering
> the **information I have** about our editorial
> director **buying pussy with company money.**

A beat.

> LESTER (cont'd)
> Which I'm sure would interest the I.R.S., since it technically constitutes **fraud**. And I'm sure that some of our **advertisers and rival publications** might like to know about it as well. **Not to mention, Craig's wife.**

Brad sighs.

Lester is clearly resigned to checking out the nine to five world. To Brad's line about him not being interested in "saving yourself," Lester links that after 14 years the only way he can "save myself" is if he starts "firebombing." Brad doesn't seem too concerned with the statement about "firebombing," but Lester is not to be fooled with. To Brad's comment that "management" wants Lester gone by the end of the day, Lester links by asking what kind of severance package "management" is prepared to offer. But before Brad can answer, Lester essentially brings the "firebomb" to the table by suggesting the company director used company funds to hire prostitutes which constituted "fraud" and went further in an attempt at not so subtle blackmail

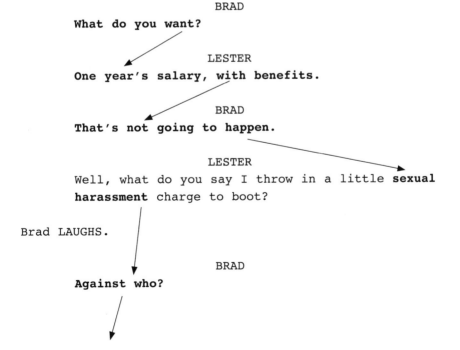

> BRAD
> **What do you want?**

> LESTER
> **One year's salary, with benefits.**

> BRAD
> **That's not going to happen.**

> LESTER
> Well, what do you say I throw in a little **sexual harassment** charge to boot?

Brad LAUGHS.

> BRAD
> **Against who?**

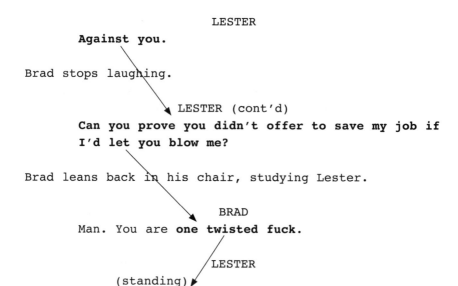

```
                    LESTER
        Against you.

Brad stops laughing.

                    LESTER (cont'd)
        Can you prove you didn't offer to save my job if
        I'd let you blow me?

Brad leans back in his chair, studying Lester.

                    BRAD
        Man. You are one twisted fuck.

                    LESTER
        (standing)
        Nope. I'm just an ordinary guy with nothing to
        lose.
```

This scene is an excellent example of how to say a lot in very little. One only needs to recall Buck Henry's *Graduate* script in which he rarely went over six lines of dialogue to make a point. Ball does the same thing here. The links are very well crafted. To Brad's question "What do you want?" Lester links with "One year's salary, with benefits." Brad, in a position of authority, states "that" (i.e. "One year's salary, with benefits") won't happen. Lester cleverly maneuvers the dialogue by dismissing Brad's statement and adding to his previous statement that he wants to "throw in" "sexual harassment." To Brad's question, "Against who?" Lester links with "Against you," following it up with the incriminating statement, "Can you prove you didn't offer to save my job if I'd let you blow me?" At that point, Brad realizes Lester isn't bluffing and states that Lester is "one twisted fuck," which Lester links with "Nope [I'm not]", just an "ordinary guy with nothing to lose."

As in the best written dialogues, these dialogue segments are linked either by using the same word/phrase or an analogue that keeps the dialogue from retarding and maintains the focus of the scene. Another scene, equally as well written, is the dining room scene with the Burnham family the day he left his job.

INT. BURNHAM HOUSE—DINING ROOM—MOMENTS LATER

                    JANE
Sorry I'm late.

                    CAROLYN
          (overly cheerful)
No, no, that's quite all right, dear. Your father
and I were just discussing his day at work.
          (to Lester)
Why don't you tell our daughter about it, honey?

                    LESTER
Janie, today I quit my job. And then I told my
boss to fuck himself, and then I blackmailed
him for almost sixty thousand dollars. Pass the
asparagus.

                    CAROLYN
Your father seems to think this kind of behavior
is something to be proud of.

                    LESTER
And your mother seems to prefer I go through
life like a fucking prisoner while she keeps my
dick in a mason jar under the sink.

                    CAROLYN
          (ashen)
How dare you speak to me that way in front of
her? And I marvel that you can be so contemptuous of me, on the same day that you lose your
job!

                    LESTER
Lose it? I didn't lose it. It's not like, "Oops,
where'd my job go?" I quit. Someone pass me the
asparagus.

                    CAROLYN
Oh! Oh! And I want to thank you for putting

me under the added pressure of being the sole
breadwinner now—

                    LESTER
I already have a job.

                    CAROLYN
                (not stopping)
No, no, don't give a second thought as to
who's going to pay the mortgage. We'll just
leave it all up to Carolyn. You mean, you're
going to take care of everything now, Carolyn?
Yes. I don't mind. I really don't. You mean,
everything? You don't mind having the sole
responsibility, your husband feels he can just
quit his job—

                    LESTER
                (overlapping)
Will someone pass me the fucking asparagus?

                    JANE
                (rises)
Okay, I'm not going to be a part of this—

                    LESTER
                (means it)
Sit down.

                    LESTER (cont'd)
I'm sick and tired of being treated like I
don't exist. You two do whatever you want to do
whenever you want to do it and I don't complain.
All I want is the same courtesy—

                    CAROLYN
                (overlapping)
Oh, you don't complain? Oh, excuse me. Excuse
me. I must be psychotic then, if you don't
complain. What is this?! Am I locked away in a
padded cell somewhere, hallucinating? That's the
only explanation I can think of—

Lester hurls the plate of asparagus against the wall with such force it SHATTERS, frightening Carolyn and Jane.

> LESTER
> (casual)
> Don't interrupt me, honey.

He goes back to eating his meal, as if nothing unusual has happened. Carolyn sits in her chair, shivering with rage. Jane just stares at the plate in front of her.

> LESTER (cont'd)
> Oh, and another thing. From now on, we're going to alternate our dinner music. Because frankly, and I don't think I'm alone here, I'm really tired of this Lawrence Welk shit.

Dealing specifically with how he handles the dialogue, based on what's been established in the previous chapters, we can see what Ball is attempting to do with the scene not only in terms of maintaining the integrity of the scene, but also in advancing the storyline, developing characters and eliciting conflict all through the use of the techniques mentioned in the Introduction.

> JANE
> **Sorry I'm late.**

> CAROLYN
> (overly cheerful)
> No, no, that's quite all right, dear. Your father and I were just discussing **his day at work.**
> (to Lester)
> Why don't you tell our daughter about **it, honey?**

> LESTER
> Janie, today **I quit my job.** And then I told my boss to fuck himself, and **then I blackmailed** him for almost sixty thousand dollars. Pass the asparagus.

CAROLYN

Your father seems to think **this kind of behavior** is something to be proud of.

LESTER

And your mother seems to prefer I go through life like a fucking **prisoner** while she keeps my dick in a mason jar under the sink.

This is choreographed quite nicely, beginning with the fact that Janie is "late." In the overall scheme of things, Janie's lateness pales in comparison to what's going to follow, which accounts for Carolyn's relative lack of concern over the tardiness. She opens the dialogue by alluding to Lester's "day at work," and then asks Lester (aka "honey") to tell "it" (i.e. the day at work) to Janie. So, there's really a double internal link that Carolyn is using linking Lester's "day" to "it." Lester easily links the "day" and "it" to "I quit my job," adds the bit about being "blackmailed," and rather indifferently asks for the "asparagus." Carolyn then links on the notions of "quitting" and "blackmailing" by stating that Lester must think that sort of "behavior" is something to be proud of. Off Carolyn's notion of what is essentially "improper" behavior, Lester links by stating that Carolyn would prefer him to be a "fucking prisoner" while withholding any sexual favors.

CAROLYN
(ashen)

How dare you speak to me that way in front of her? And I marvel that you can be so **contemptuous of me,** on the same day that you **lose your job!**

LESTER

Lose it? I didn't lose it. It's not like, "Oops, where'd my job go?" I quit. Someone pass me the **asparagus.**

CAROLYN

Oh! Oh! And I want to thank you for putting me under the added pressure of being the **sole breadwinner now—**

LESTER
I already have a job.

CAROLYN
(not stopping)
No, no, don't give a second thought as to
who's going to pay the mortgage. We'll just
leave it all up to Carolyn. **You mean,** you're
going to **take care of everything** now, Carolyn?
Yes. I don't mind. I really don't. **You mean,
everything?** You don't mind having the **sole
responsibility,** your husband feels he can just
quit his job—

LESTER
(overlapping)
Will someone pass me the fucking asparagus?

JANE
(rises)
Okay, **I'm not going to be a part of this**—

LESTER
(means it)
Sit down.

LESTER (cont'd)
**I'm sick and tired of being treated like I
don't exist.** You two do whatever you want to do
whenever you want to do it and **I don't complain.**
All I want is the same courtesy—

CAROLYN
(overlapping)
Oh, you don't complain? Oh, excuse me. Excuse
me. I must be psychotic then, **if you don't
complain.** What is this?! Am I locked away in a
padded cell somewhere, hallucinating? That's the
only explanation I can think of—

> LESTER
> (casual)
> Don't interrupt me, **honey.**

> LESTER (cont'd)
> Oh, and another thing. From now on, we're going
> to alternate our dinner **music.** Because frankly,
> and I don't think I'm alone here, I'm really
> tired of this **Lawrence Welk shit.**

The focus of the scene is, of course, Lester's lost job, since the entire scene is predicated on that. Carolyn links the notion of being "contemptuous" with the fact that he "lost" his job. Lester links on "lose your job" with "lose it" (twice) before rephrasing it in an ironic way and then, almost indifferently, asks for the "asparagus." For Carolyn, the lost job implies that she's going to have to be the "sole breadwinner," even though Lester has already alluded to the fact he has a "new" one before asking for the "asparagus" once again as a way to counterpoint the conflict over the "lost job," before he alludes to the fact he's "invisible" and that he doesn't "complain" about it, which allows Carolyn to link on "complain" (twice) and that interruption allows Lester essentially to end the scene by linking on the same word she opened the scene with, "honey," both meant ironically. The decision to change the "dinner music" is just another example of how Lester wants to "change" his life.

19

Midnight in Paris (2011)
Screenplay by Woody Allen

I think it was in the PBS documentary *American Masters* that Allen alluded to the fact that he was not "academic" in his work or that he had no predilection towards being academic in his work; however, one would be hard-pressed to find many of Allen's films in which academics don't play a role or in which academics and/or the intellectual life don't play a role and, generally, to the amusement of the main character. From the brilliant play on Dostoevsky's works in *Love and Death*, through *Deconstructing Harry*, and, lastly, to *Midnight in Paris*, Allen's literary, artistic, and intellectual sensibilities have been honed for decades and *Midnight in Paris* clearly defines that. His allusions to French painters and writers as well as expatriates (although he seems to valorize Hemingway more so than others) is apparent. Oddly enough, in Eric Lax's biography of Allen, there's very little attention paid to his intellect other than to say that "When he first attended P.S.99 he was placed in an accelerated class because of his high IQ ..." (Lax, 2000, p. 32). Whether that would account for his intellectual curiosity one can only speculate.

One of the best scenes in the film for amalgamating both the academic and the artistic, especially in terms of the dialogue, is the scene in L'Orangerie Museum.

INT. L'ORANGERIE MUSEUM—DAY

Paul, Carol, Inez and Gil in circular room with huge
Monets.

                    PAUL
        The juxtaposition of color is
        amazing. This man was the real
        father of abstract expressionism.
        I take that back, maybe Turner.

                    INEZ
        I prefer Monet. I mean I love
        Turner but this is overwhelming.

                    PAUL
        If I'm not mistaken it took him two
        years to complete this. And he
        worked out at Giverny—where he
        frequently—

                    GIL
        They say Monet used to—

                    INEZ
        Shhh. I want to hear what Paul's
        saying.

                    PAUL
        He was frequently visited by
        Caillebotte—an artist I
        personally feel was underrated.

                    CAROL
        I find Monet almost too pretty—
        like Renoir—sometimes it's
        cloying.

DISSOLVE TO:

INT. ANOTHER FLOOR OF THE MUSEUM—DAY

> PAUL
> (coming to Picasso's
> portrait of Adriana)
> Ah—now here's a superb Picasso.

> INEZ (CONT'D)
> Gil is stunned.

> PAUL (CONT'D)
> If I'm not mistaken he painted this
> marvelous portrait of his French
> mistress Madeline Brissou in the
> twenties.

> GIL
> Er—I have to differ with you on
> this one.

> PAUL
> Really?

> INEZ
> Gil pay attention and you'll learn
> something.

> GIL
> If I'm not mistaken this was a
> failed attempt to capture a young
> French girl named Adriana—from
> Bordeaux—if my art history serves me—came to
> Paris to study costume design for the theatre.
> Believe she had a brief affair with Modigliani—
> then Braque—that's where Pablo met her—er
> Picasso. You'd never know it from this portrait
> but she's quite subtly beautiful.

> INEZ
> What have you been smoking?

> GIL
> And I'd hardly call the picture
> superb. It's more of a petit
> bourgeoisie statement of how Pablo
> er Picasso sees her, saw her—he's distracted by
> the fact she was a volcano in the sack.

Of course, in this scene, Allen plays the academic for a fop, which is something he's done before. Either the academic plays the fop or the intellectual plays the fop in counterpoint to the main protagonist. The most brilliant example of this is in the movie theater scene in *Annie Hall*, but, in a way, he's done the same thing here in the museum. Without "deconstructing" Allen in this scene, one can see what he's attempting to do by virtue of looking at his dialogue.

INT. L'ORANGERIE MUSEUM—DAY

Paul, Carol, Inez and Gil in circular room with huge Monets.

> PAUL
> The juxtaposition of color is
> amazing. **This man** was the real
> father of abstract expressionism.
> I take that back, maybe **Turner.**

> INEZ
> I prefer **Monet.** I mean I love
> **Turner** but this is overwhelming.

> PAUL
> **If I'm not mistaken** it took **him** two years to
> complete this. And **he**
> worked out at Giverny—where he
> frequently—

> GIL
> They say **Monet** used to—

> INEZ
> Shhh. I want to hear **what** Paul's
> saying.

> PAUL
> **He** was frequently visited by
> Caillebotte—an artist I
> personally feel was underrated.

> CAROL
> I find **Monet** almost too pretty—
> like **Renoir**—sometimes it's
> cloying.

DISSOLVE TO:

What Allen does here is fundamentally Allen not only in terms of form, but of content as well. Gil, of course, has been meeting these famous Parisian writers and painters for some time, unbeknownst to Inez who has become a Paulian groupie. But, regardless of Allen's sensibilities to his material, the dialogue really adheres to the same fundamental processes we see as early as *Citizen Kane*. As they enter the Monet room, Paul begins his solipsistic discourse by declaring that "This man [Monet]" was the "father of abstract expressionism," then takes it back and changes it to "Turner," neither of whom could in the least be considered abstract expressionists in the manner of, say, Pollock. Inez links "Monet" with Paul's "this man" but reiterates "Turner." Paul not only has a captive audience, but one whom he believes is academically inferior to himself. It's here that he uses the somewhat disingenuous phrase "If I'm not mistaken," which is usually said by someone who's absolutely certain that he isn't, and then continues speaking about Monet by linking internally with the words "him" and "he." When Gil attempts to say something by linking again with Monet, Inez shuts him up by stating she'd rather hear "what" Paul is saying, and what Paul is saying is a continuation on Monet, but with a certain element of academic authority that Gil doesn't have. Paul continues the Monet link by stating that "he [Monet]" was visited by Caillebotte whom Paul believes was under-rated. Carol continues the Monet link, but attempts to redirect the discussion to Renoir, but it doesn't go in that direction.

The irony here is in Paul's allusion to Caillebotte, since Caillebotte is best known for his paintings of urban Paris, such as *The Bridge 'de l'Europe'* (*Le pont de l'Europe*) (1876), and, most famously, for *Paris Street; Rainy Day* (*Rue de Paris; temps de pluie, also known as La Place de l'Europe, temps de pluie*)

(1877). The irony lies in the way Allen uses the notion of Parisian streets and rain in the film for romantic purposes not associated with Paul and Inez or Gil and Inez, but for Gil and Gabrielle. The next scene finds them face-to-face with a Picasso.

```
INT. ANOTHER FLOOR OF THE MUSEUM—DAY

                    PAUL
          (coming to Picasso's
          portrait of Adriana)
          Ah—now here's a superb Picasso.

Gil is stunned.

                    PAUL (CONT'D)
          If I'm not mistaken he painted this marvelous
          portrait of his French mistress Madeline Brissou
          in the twenties.

                    GIL
          Er—I have to differ with you on
          this one.

                    PAUL
          Really?

                    INEZ
          Gil pay attention and you'll learn
          something.

                    GIL
          If I'm not mistaken this was a
          failed attempt to capture a young
          French girl named Adriana—from
          Bordeaux—if my art history serves me—came to
          Paris to study costume design for the theatre.
          Believe she had a brief affair with Modigliani—
          then Braque—that's where Pablo met her—er
          Picasso. You'd never know it from this portrait
          but she's quite subtly beautiful.
```

                              INEZ
          What have you been smoking?

                              GIL
          And I'd hardly call the picture
          superb. It's more of a petit
          bourgeoisie statement of how Pablo
          er Picasso sees her, saw her—he's distracted by
          the fact she was a volcano in the sack.

This is a brilliant example of how Allen closes the scene by drawing on the links he's already established. Paul begins by say that "here's a superb Picasso" alluding to the portrait of "Adriana," which according to Joseph Berger's May 27, 2011 *New York Times* review did not exist. "The twice-married Picasso was famous for mistresses, and in the film Marion Cotillard plays Adriana, a capricious, if melancholy stand-in for all of Picasso's lovers, models and muses. She claims to have been the lover of Modigliani and Braque as well. In actuality, Picasso's mistresses were relatively constant. Marie-Thérèse Walter, who was 17 when she met Picasso, was with him for eight years, bearing him a daughter, Maya. Dora Maar, whom he met around 1935, was his lover for at least eight years as well." This is an example of how Allen interweaves fact and fiction, not unlike what he did in *Zelig*, but without the *cinema verité*.

Regardless of the subject of the portrait, the fact of the matter is he keeps the dialogue moving by first having Paul allude to the painting in general terms, then linking with the name "Madeline Brissou" (even though there isn't a record of Picasso painting a woman with that name). Gil, who knows that it's actually a portrait of Adriana, whom he has already met, says he has to differ with Paul on "this one" which links the dialogues. His response "Really?" is almost a challenge to his artistic acumen and that is corroborated by Inez who basically tells Gil to shut up and "learn something." At this point, Gil relishes in reprising Paul's favorite line "If I'm not mistaken," and continues to elaborate on Adriana's history which is in direct response to Inez's admonition that he "learn something." After detailing much about Adriana, Inez can only assume Gil's been smoking weed, but Gil ignores the question and closes the scene by reprising the word "superb," but in a different context, and establishing that what Picasso found most engaging about Adriana was her expertise "in the sack."

One of the more engaging scenes in the film includes the intimate, revelatory dialogue between Gil and Ariana: the woman with whom he falls in love. This segment of dialogue is good because it tends to "run against the grain" in terms of dialogue writing. The reason for that is that Allen wrote and directed the film, and if you're one of those very fortunate writers who can do that than the normal rules of dialogue writing don't really apply. For example, in Henry's script for *The Graduate* directed by Mike Nichols, there aren't many dialogue segments that run longer than six lines, while Allen is not precluded from writing dialogue as long as he wants it to go. This particular scene is an example of dialogue that runs counter to the normal tenets imposed by good dialogue writing and yet works equally well. The scene takes place at the Moulin Rouge.

```
INT. MOULIN ROUGE—NIGHT

                    ADRIANA
                    (to Gil)
          Can I speak with you a minute?
          (to table)
          Permettez-moi de m'absenter un
          instant.
          (she gets him off)
          Let's never go back to the
          twenties.

                    GIL
          What are you talking about?

                    ADRIANA
          I think we should stay here—it's
          the start of the Belle Époque—
          this is the greatest, most
          beautiful era Paris has ever known.

                    GIL
          But I love the Jazz Age.

                    ADRIANA
          The twenties are full of strife and
          uncertainty. But think of it, Gil —the two of
          us—in a lovely art
          nouveau home—I'll work in the
          fashion world—I love the styles —you can write
          ... it's the age of
```

Debussy and Guimard. Maybe you can
meet Balzac.

                    GIL
But what happened to the twenties
and the Charleston and Cole Porter?

                  ADRIANA
That's the present, it's dull.

                    GIL
It's not the present for me—I'm
from 2010.

                  ADRIANA
What do you mean?

                    GIL
I dropped in on you just the way we dropped in
on the 1890's.

                  ADRIANA
You did?

                    GIL
I wanted to escape my present just
like you wanted to escape yours.
To a golden age.

                  ADRIANA
Surely you don't think the twenties
are a golden age?

                    GIL
To me they are.

                  ADRIANA
But I'm from the twenties and I'm
telling you the golden age is the
Belle Époque.

                    GIL

Yes but don't you see—to these
guys the golden age was the
Renaissance. They'd all trade the
Belle Époque to paint alongside
Michelangelo or Titian. And those
guys probably imagine life was
better when Kubla Khan was around.
I'm having an insight. A minor one
but that accounts for the anxiety
of my dream.

                  ADRIANA

What dream?

                    GIL

Last night I dreamed I ran out of
Zithromax—and then I went to the
dentist and there was no novacaine —these people
have no antibiotics

                  ADRIANA

What are you talking about?

                    GIL

And even in the twenties—no
dishwashers—no 911 if your
appendix bursts—no "movies on
demand".

                  ADRIANA

But if we love each other what does it matter
when we live?

                    GIL

Because if you stay here and this
becomes your present, sooner or
later you'll imagine another time
was really the golden time. And so
will I—I'm beginning to see why
it can't work, Adriana. The

present has a hold on you because
it's your present and while there's never any
progress in the most important things, you get
to
appreciate—what little progress
is made—the internet—Pepto—
Bismol. The present is always
going to seem unsatisfying because
life itself is unsatisfying—that's why Gauguin
goes back and
forth between Paris and Tahiti,
searching—it's my job as a writer to try and
come up with reasons why despite life being
tragic and unsatisfying, it's still worth it.

                    ADRIANA
That's the problem with writers—
you're all so full of words— but
I'm more emotional. I'm going to
stay and live in Paris' most
glorious time. You made a choice
to leave Paris once and you
regretted it.

                     GIL
Yes, that one I regretted but it
was a real choice and I made the
wrong one. This is a choice
between accepting reality or
surreal insanity.

                    ADRIANA
So finally you do love Inez more
than me.

                     GIL
No—I love you—but this way lies madness—and if
I'm ever going to write anything worthwhile I've
got to get rid of my illusions and that I'd be
happier in the past is one of them.

>   ADRIANA
>   Goodbye, Gil.

>   GIL
>   Goodbye Adriana. Good luck.

They kiss, she turns and goes to the table of artists.

We can take a look at this scene and its individual components to see what Allen is doing regardless of the length of the individual segments.

INT. MOULIN ROUGE-NIGHT

>   ADRIANA
>   (to Gil)
>   Can I speak with you a minute?
>   (to table)
>   Permettez-moi de m'absenter un
>   instant.
>   (she gets him off)
>   **Let's never go back to the
>   twenties.**

>   GIL
>   **What are you talking about?**

>   ADRIANA
>   **I think we should stay here**—it's
>   the start of the **Belle Époque**—
>   this is the **greatest, most
>   beautiful era** Paris has ever known.

>   GIL
>   But I love **the Jazz Age.**

>   ADRIANA
>   **The twenties are full of strife and uncer-
>   tainty.** But think of it, Gil—the two of us—in a
>   lovely art nouveau home—I'll work in the fashion
>   world—I love the styles -you can write ... it's

the age of Debussy and Guimard. Maybe you can
meet Balzac.

> GIL
>
> But what happened to the **twenties
> and the Charleston and Cole Porter?**

> ADRIANA
>
> **That's the present,** it's dull.

> GIL
>
> **It's not the present for me—I'm
> from 2010.**

> ADRIANA
>
> **What do you mean?**

> GIL
>
> **I dropped in on you just the way we dropped in
> on the 1890's.**

> ADRIANA
>
> **You did?**

> GIL
>
> **I wanted to escape my present** just
> like you wanted to escape yours.
> To a **golden age.**

> ADRIANA
>
> Surely you don't think **the twenties are a golden
> age?**

> GIL
>
> **To me they are.**

> ADRIANA
>
> But I'm from the **twenties and I'm**
> telling you the **golden age** is the
> **Belle Époque.**

Up to this point in the scene, the focus of the scene has been a kind of dialectic between the Adriana's perfervid interest in the Belle Époque and Gil's equally perfervid interest in the Jazz Age as the "golden age" of Parisian life. What links the dialogues is the repetition of the words "Belle Époque," "twenties" and "golden age." The simple disagreement they have as to which of the two eras represents the true "golden age" of Paris will eventually be their undoing.

> GIL
> Yes but don't you see—to these guys the **golden age** was the Renaissance. They'd all trade the **Belle Époque** to paint alongside Michelangelo or Titian. And those guys probably imagine life was better when Kubla Khan was around. I'm having an **insight. A minor one** but that accounts for the anxiety of my **dream.**

> ADRIANA
> **What dream?**

> GIL
> Last night I **dreamed** I ran out of Zithromax—and then I went to the dentist and there was no **novacaine** -these people have **no antibiotics.**

> ADRIANA
> **What are you talking about?**

> GIL
> And even in the **twenties**—no dishwashers—no 911 if your appendix bursts—no "movies on demand".

As with most of Allen's scenes, they adhere to what I mentioned early on in the book; namely, they maintain scenic integrity, advance the storyline, develop character and always elicit conflict in one manner or another. From *Annie Hall* to *Midnight in Paris*, that addiction to dialogue rarely falters.

Dialogue: A Trailer

The definition of a movie trailer is a short blank strip of film attached to the end of a reel. Of course, instead of coming at the end of a reel, we know see trailers before a film even begins. Now one might argue that the trailer should appear at the beginning of this book and not at the end, but I'm rather old school about things and so this is where it appears. But there's another reason I wanted it at the end of the book,and that is to act as a kind of summation of what's preceded it; however, I'm not going to repeat myself. What I've tried to convey in these 19 chapters from *Citizen Kane* to *Midnight in Paris*, from Mankiewicz to Allen, from 1941 to 2011, is that there are fundamental techniques that all these writers have used in order to write laconic dialogue that not only conveyed a sense of character, but that contributed to the flow of the storyline.

In Cameron Crowe's, *Conversations With Billy Wilder* (2001), Wilder included a number of screenwriting tips including, but not limited to:

Develop a clean line of action for your leading character.
Know where you're going.
	The more subtle and elegant you are in hiding your plot points, the better you are as a writer.
	If you have a problem with the third act, the real problem is in the first act.
	In doing voice-overs, be careful not to describe what the audience already sees. Add to what they're seeing.
	The event that occurs at the second act curtain triggers the end of the movie.
	The third act must build, build, build in tempo and action until the last event, and then—that's it. Don't hang around.

Curiously, he didn't say anything about dialogue, but "in terms of screenwriting, Wilder's forte is the dialogue. His dialogue propels his movies. He would cut cost and speed up the introduction of the main character(s) with an opening narration. He used voice-overs to string together the scenes. Even when he avoided voice-over, he still used dialogue with a twist—a fly in

The Spirit of St. Louis (1957), which is reminiscent of the unused cockroach speech in *Hold Back the Dawn* (1941). His dialogue is very visual and well-anchored on something material."[1] Wilder's dialogue is always precise. There are no wasted words and, I think, he links dialogue better than his mentor, Ernst Lubitsch, and his films are really a testament to his brilliance as a dialogist.

But what all these writers really have in common is an "ear" for dialogue. Perhaps, as in the case of Steve Tesich, that came from writing off-Broadway plays, or, in the cases of Buck Henry and Woody Allen, from live television. But regardless of where they learned it, they all have a keen sense of what characters sound like and what is the best way to convey that sense of character *vis-à-vis* dialogue. What I've attempted to do in this book is show how these writers have accomplished that task, with excerpts from a few of their best screenplays. My intention was that, by showing how they used the techniques at their disposal, they created vibrant and credible dialogue, and how a novice or an experienced screenwriter can employ those techniques to create or improve their dialogue. I hope I have achieved that.

Mark Axelrod
Orange, California
2013

---

[1] http://www.hinayanabawagan.com/index.php?pr=The_Dialogue_of_Billy_Wilder [accessed May 2013].

Dialogue Exercises

Dialogue exercise #1

Using the scheme below, pick three three–five minute scenes from any film of your choosing and analyze the dialogue components that we've been addressing. If you're using a screenplay, write down the name, scenes and page numbers. If you're using a film, give the name of the film and a description of the scenes. After you have done that, take three of your own scenes and do the same thing.

(SC# = Scene number; QA – Question/Answer; QSI = Question/Statement Interrupt; QSL = Question/Statement Lead; QQL = Question/Question Lead; SSL = Statement/Statement Lead; DL = Dialogue Linkage)

Film/Script

SC#	QA	QSI	QSL	QQL	SSL	DL

Script Title

SC#	QA	QSI	QSL	QQL	SSL	DL

What similarities do you find? What differences?

Dialogue exercise #2

This is a MADE assignment. Given the script as you have revised it to this point, analyze it in relation to the MADE scheme. Does the dialogue do all those things we've discussed in relation to the MADE scheme? Where are the strengths? What are the weaknesses? How can you best revise your dialogue to improve the MADE scheme.

Dialogue exercise #3

Dialogue flow chart

An example of a dialogue flow chart (DFC) for scene 61 in *The Graduate* might appear as follows.

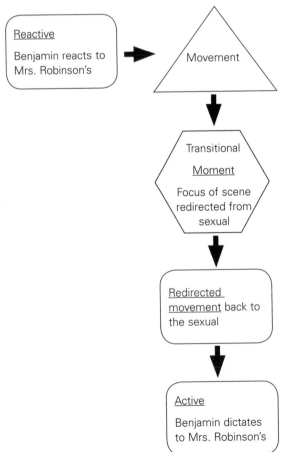

Using this DFC as a guide, create your own DFC for three of your scenes. The final event in the flow process should be the focus of the scene and one should see a kind of connection between the outset and the conclusion. What does the DFC look like for your dialogue? Is there a fluid connection? If not, rethink your DFC.

Dialogue exercise #4

Take any film of your choosing, but preferably one you don't remember well or one you've never seen. Screen a brief scene *without* the sound and attempt to *write* the dialogue for each character. Scrutinize the scene, speculating on what's happening, based on what's developed to that point then try to write the dialogue for that particular scene. After the exercise, *listen* to the dialogue to see what was actually said versus what you've written. How is the dialogue the same? How does it differ? What are the techniques being employed by the screenwriter and have you employed the same?

Dialogue exercise #5

Examine any scene from your script of between three–five pages of dialogue you have written and make the following changes:

1 Force yourself to delete at least ten to 20 words per page and/or reduce any individual piece of dialogue to a minimum of five lines.

2 Find at least three places in that scene where you will substitute physical actions for words. What does that do to the dialogue? Does that improve the flow of the scene or retard the flow of the scene?

3 Revise at least two speeches in the scene so they *do not* contain grammatically correct sentences, but instead are unfinished thoughts or phrases. What does that do to the flow of the dialogue?

4 Require at least two interruptions per page. How does that affect characterization?

5 Force yourself to increase the emotional tonality of several of the character's speeches. What does that do to the character?

Dialogue exercise #6

Write a first-person speech in which the following characteristics are revealed about the person speaking without the person being conscious of his/her own possession of those characteristics:

- poignancy

- horror

- disgust

- fear

- anger

- prejudice

- love

- friendship

- admiration

Dialogue exercise #7

Briefly relate your conversations with people outside your immediate family for one day. Develop a story and/plot from these conversations; put one of these conversations into dialogue; make an analysis of the individuals spoken to.

Dialogue exercise #8

Write a scene with two people discussing a third person—the protagonist—who will then enter and disprove what they've been saying about him/her through his/her actions and dialogue.

Dialogue exercise #9

Analyze any film you wish, looking for the following things:

- The handling of entrances and exits
- The sequences of scenes in terms of length
- The number of characters
- The distribution of speeches among the characters

How do these items relate to your own script?

Dialogue exercise #10

Write a scene in which there is dramatic conflict and in which *eating* is a functional part of the dramatic action. This scene demands the creation of an environment, usually realistic, and helps you discover the use of manners and mannerisms as methods of characterization. You may think of *American Beauty* or *The Cook, the Thief, his Wife and her Lover.*

Dialogue exercise #11

Write a dramatic scene about a screenwriting class. Stick closely to the things that do happen in the class and yet make it interesting to someone who is not a screenwriting student.

Dialogue exercise #12

We've already seen *The Cook, the Thief, his Wife and her Lover* in relation to storyline and arc. Now take a look at the script and apply everything we've been talking about to dialogue. What specific things is Greenaway emphasizing in terms of technique? What does he rely on most? Use the sample to tally your findings.

(QA = Question/Answer; QSI = Question/Statement Interrupt; QSL = Question/Question Lead; SSL = Statement/Statement Lead; DL = Dialogue Linkage)

Q A   Q S I   Q S L   Q Q L   S S L   D L

Structure exercise #1

Watch the first 10 percent of any standard feature film see how quickly the main and supporting characters are introduced and how quickly the plot is established. In what order are the characters introduced? In what way is the plot established? What elements are being used to establish the plot and how do they relate to the structure?

Structure exercise #2

Prepare two one–2 page treatments for a feature film you'd like to write. Be prepared to discuss these in tutorial.

Bibliography

Aristotle. (1971) *The Poetics*, S. H. Butcher (trans.), Francis Fergusson (Introduction), New York: Hill and Wang.

—(2001) *Which Lie Did I Tell?: More Adventures in the Screen Trade*, New York: Vintage.

Axelrod, Mark. (2001) *Aspects of the Screenplay*, Portsmouth, NH: Heinemann.

—(2004) *Character and Conflict*, Portsmouth, NH: Heinemann.

—(2006) *I Read it at the Movies*, Portsmouth, NH: Heinemann.

Berger, Joseph. (2011) Decoding Woody Allen's "Midnight in Paris," *New York Times*, May 27.

Campbell, Joseph. (2008) *The Hero With a Thousand Faces* (3rd edn), Novato, CA: New World Library (July 28, 2008).

Campbell, Joseph and Carrière, Jean-Claude. (1995) *The Secret Language of Film*, London: Faber and Faber.

Cartmell, Deborah and Whelehan, Emelda. (1999) *Adaptations: From Text to Screen, Screen to Text*, London: Routledge.

Chalvon-Demersay, Sabine. (1999) *A Thousand Screenplays*, Chicago, IL: University of Chicago Press.

Cronin, Paul (ed.). (2005) *Roman Polanski: Interviews*, Mississippi: University Press of Mississippi. (October 27, 2005).

Crowe, Cameron. (2001) *Conversations With Billy Wilder*, repr. edn, Knopf; Reprint edition (September 25, 2001).

Dardis, Tom. (2004) *Some Time in the Sun*, Montclair, NJ: Limelight Editions.

Harmetz, Aljean. (1993) *Round Up the Usual Suspects: The Making of Casablanca: Bogart, Bergman, and World War II* (1st edn), New York: Hyperion.

Hopp, Glen. (2003) *Billy Wilder: The Complete Films, The Cinema of Wit 1906–2002*, Cologne: Taschen.

Kael, Pauline. (2002) *Citizen Kane*, London, Methuen Drama.

Knapp, Laurence and Kulas, Andrea (eds). (2005) *Ridley Scott: Interviews*, Mississippi: University Press of Mississippi.

Lax, Eric. (2000) *Woody Allen: A Biography*, new edn, Boston, MA: Da Capo Press.

Machado de Assis, Joachim Maria (1881) *Memórias Póstumas de Brás Cubas* [The Posthumous Memoirs of Brás Cubas, also known in English as Epitaph for a Small Winner]. Goldman, William. (1989) *Adventures in the Screen Trade*, New York: Grand Central Publishing.

McMurtry, Larry. (2001) *Film Flam*, New York: Simon and Schuster.

Pudovkin, V. I. (2008) *Film Technique and Film Acting*, Peterborough, NH: Sims Press.

Riley, Christopher. (2009) *The Hollywood Standard: The Complete and Authoritative Guide to Script Format and Style*, Los Angeles, CA: Michael Wiese Productions.

Schiff, Stephen. (2000) *Lolita: The Book of the Film*, Montclair, NJ: Applause Theatre & Cinema Books.

Stam, Robert. (2004) *Literature Through Film*, Hoboken, NJ: Wiley-Blackwell.

Thomas, Sam. (1985) *Best American Screenplays 1*, New York: Crown Publishers.

—(ed.). (1991) *Best American Screenplays 2*, New York: Crown Publishers.

Winston, Douglas Garrett. (1973) *The Screenplay as Literature*, Madison, NJ: Fairleigh Dickinson University Press.

Written By: Magazine of the Writers' Guild of America, Los Angeles, CA (February, 1998).

Index

Page numbers in **bold** indicate screenplays in extract form.

academics 279 *see also Annie Hall*;
  Good Will Hunting; *Graduate, The*;
  Midnight in Paris
Academy Awards 133, 209, 252, 266
action scenes 109–10, 297
Affleck, Ben 241, 266
  Academy Award 266
  jealousy of 241–2
alias 122
Allen, Woody 282, 283, 285, 290, 297,
  298
  on academics 279
  length of dialogue 286
  rule breaking 286
  storyline 295, 297
American Beauty (Ball) 267–8, 272,
  276, 303
  annoyance **273**, **276**, 278
  authority **268**, **269–70**, 271, **271**,
    272, **272**, **273**, **275**, 276
  conflict 275
  death 267
  imprisonment **273**, 276, **276**
  irony **273**, **275**, 276, **276**, 278, **278**
  listening and **268**, **270**, 271
    annoyance **273–5**, **276–8**, 278
  music **275**, 278, **278**
  parallel dialogue **274**, **277**
  recognition and 267
  sexual issues **268–9**, **270–2**, 271,
    272, **273**, 276, **276**
  storyline 275
  succinctness **269**, **271–2**, 272
  time factors **273**, **275**, 276
American Film Institute 33–4
American Flyers (Tesich) 177
American Masters 279

Anatomy of Criticism (Frye) 6–7
ancillary dialogue
  awareness and
    ambivalence **141**
    limitations 139
  conflict **136**, **139–40**, **143**
  deceit **136**, **140**, **143**
  importance 133–4
  omission 144
  parallel to scene **136–7**, 138, 140,
    140, **142**, **143–4**, 144
Annie Hall (Allen and Brickman) ix, 167,
  168, 173, 295
  communication 169, **169**, **170**, 171,
    171, 173, **173**, 174, **174–5**
  conflict **168**, **172**, 282
  egocentricity 169
  indulgence and 167, **167–8**, **171**,
    171–2, 175
  parallel dialogue 167, **167–8**, 169,
    169, 170, **170**, **171**, 172, **173**,
    174
  sexual issues **168**, 168–9, **169–70**,
    172, **173**, 174
annoyance 130
  arrogance and **188–9**, 192, **192**, **193**,
    194
  faking and **189–90**, **193–4**, 194,
    195
  gestured dialogue and 194
  conflict **126–7**, **130–1**, 131, **188**,
    191, **191**, 192, **192**, **273–5**,
    276–8, 278
  parallel monologue 131
Ant and the Grasshopper, The 77
anxiety 122, 124–5, **125**, 128, **129**
  conflict **126–7**, **130–1**, 131

parallel monologue 131
Aristotle vii, 3–4, 10, 34, 113, 121, 151, 175
on tension 118
arrogance
annoyance and **188–9**, 192, **192**, **193**, 194
faking and **189–90**, **193–4**, 194, **195**
gestured dialogue and 194
authority and **280**, **281**, **282**, 283, **283**, **284**
conflict **281–2**, **284–5**, 285
egocentricity and **198**, **201–3**, 202, **206**
alienation **198–9**, 202, **203**
influence 202, 206
authority **268**, **270**
arrogance and **280**, **281**, **282**, 283, **283**, **284**
conflict **281–2**, **284–5**, 285
conflict **94**, 104, 105, **105**, 107, **268–72**, 271, 272, **273**, **275**, 276
control and see individual terms
time factors 270
autobiographical novel 69

Ball, Alan 267, 275
recognition and 267
succinctness 272
Balzac, Honoré de **287**, **291**
Baudelaire, Charles 74
beach 72–3
control 70
Beckett, Samuel **169**, 173, **173**
beginnings and endings vii–viii see also individual terms
Berger, Joseph 285
blacklisting 133
bomb under the table 109
Bond, James see Goldfinger
Braque, Georges **281**, **284**, 285
Breaking Away (Tesich) 177, 182, 183, 185
cutters 177–8
individuality and 178, **178–82**, 182
irony **183**, **184**, 185

minor ensemble film 177
succinctness 184, **184–5**
wit **182–5**
burning and lies 71

Cabaret (musical) 267
Caillebotte, Gustave **280**, 283, **283**
irony 283–4
Casablanca (Epstein, Epstein, and Koch) 11, 12, **12–13**, **15–16**, 16, **17–18**, 21, **21**, **24–5**, 25–6, 31, 231
committee of writers 227
deceit 24, **24**, **28–9**, 31
destiny 26, **26**, 27, **27–8**, 28, **29–30**
disparagement 11
irony **21**, 22, 23
letters of transit 12, **14–15**, 16, **16**, **19–21**
location **22**
constraint 11
importance 22
irony **23**
mystery 23
morality **12**, **13–14**, 16, **17**, **18–19**, **21**, **22**, 22–3, **30–1**, 31
romanticism 23, **27**, **30**, **31**
voice over 12
Castle Rock 241
Chinatown (Towne) 153, 154, **154–6**, **157**, 158, **158**, **159–60**, **162**, 163, **165**, 231, 267
changed ending 153
corruption **160–2**, **163**, 163–4, **164**, 165
evil **162**, **165**
recognition and 153, 154
sexual issues **162–3**, **164–5**, 165–6
storyline 166
time factors **155**, **158**, 159
worth and **161**, **164**, 165, 166
written for actor 153
Citizen Kane (Mankiewicz and Welles) ix, 1, 3, 107, 119, 240, 283, 297
abridgment 3–4
deductive movement 1
dissolves 1
flashbacks 10

irony 4
location 1
mystery **4–5**
   quest 4, 6, 7
   Rosebud 1, 2, 3, 4, **5–6**, 7, **7–9**, 9–10
   smash cut 6
   storyline 1–3
   points of view 2, 10
   unseen faces 3
class issues and sexual issues 74
cliff-hanger 113, 116, 118, 119
Coming Home (Salt) 133
communication 169
   breakdown **168**, 169, **169–70**, 170,
      171, **171**, 173, **173**, 174, **174–5**
   irony **169**, 173, **173**, 174
   conflict **170**
condescension **198**, **200**, **201**, 202,
   202–3, 203, **204–5**, **206**
   humiliation **199**, **203–4**
Conversations With Billy Wilder
   (Crowe) 297
Cook, the Thief, his Wife and her
   Lover, The (Greenaway) 303–4
corruption **160–2**, **163**, 163–4, **164**,
   165
Cotillard, Marion 285
Cronin, Paul 153
cutters 177–8

Damon, Matt 241, 266
   Academy Award 266
   jealousy of 241–2
Day of the Locust (Salt) 133
death 49, 83, 84–5, **85**, **111**, 115, **115**,
   117–18, **254**, **256–7**, 260, **260**,
   263, **263**, 264, **264**, 267
   avoidance **256**, **263**, 263–4
   fear and wit **112**, 115, **115**
   reprieve 113, **113**, **116**, 118
   sexual issues and **82**
   time factors **254**, 260, **260**
Debussy, Claude **286–7**, **290–1**
deceit 24, **24**, **28–9**, 31, 63, **63**, 64,
   134, **136**, 137, **137**, **140**, **141**, **143**
   conflict 58
   destiny and 28, 31
   mystery and **58–9**, **63–4**

Deconstructing Harry (Allen) 279
deductive movement 1
DeMille, Cecil B. **47**, **50**
Desmond, Norma 46, 49, 52
   irony and **52**
   wit and **46–51**
destiny 26, **26**, 27, **27–8**, **29–30**
   deceit and 28, 31
   importance 26
DFCs (dialogue flow charts) 300–1
dialogue viii, ix, 120, 160, 297, 298
   abridgment 301
   conflict 303
   course 177
   exercises 299–304
   grammar and 301
   importance vii
   interruptions 301
   links ix, 10, 113
   listening and 160
      unheard dialogue 301
   revision 301
   storyline 297
   trailer and 297
   unheard dialogue 301
   see also individual terms
dialogue flow charts (DFCs) 300–1
disguise 70, **70**
Disney 227
dissolves 1, **281**, **283**
Division Street (Tesich) 177
Dunaway, Faye 153

egocentricity
   arrogance and **198**, **201–3**, 202, **206**
      alienation **198–9**, 202, **203**
      influence 202, 206
   indulgence and 169
Elective Affinities (Goethe) 79
Eleni (Tesich) 177
emotional factors 301–2
   constraint 76–7
endings and beginnings vii–viii *see*
   also individual terms
escape
   conflict 52
   imprisonment and **94**, 104, **104**,
      273, 276, **276**

mystery and **57–8**, 62, **62–3**
evil **162**, **165**
Existentialism 68
Eyewitness (Tesich) 177

Faustian pact 49
fear **145–6**, **149–50**
    conflict **146**, **150**
    death and **112**, 115, **115**
    indifference and 112, **112**
    scare tactic and 112, **112**, 115, **115**
    trump card and 112, **112**, **113**
    wit and **111**, 115, **115**
Fellini, Federico 167, **167**, 175
Film Journal 209
film making 33
    disparagement 33–4
Fisher King, The (LaGravenese) ix, 197,
        202, 204, 206–7
    abridgment 198, 202
    arrogance **201–2**, 202, **206**
    condescension **201**, 202, **206**
    listening and 198, **198**, **200**, **202**,
        204, **205**
    alienation **200–1**, **205–6**
    arrogance **198–9**, 202, **202–3**, 206
    condescension **198**, **200**, **202–3**,
        203, **204–5**
    control 204
    influence 197, **200**, **201**, **205**, **206**
    privacy and **199**, **203–4**, 204
    multiple cuts 197
    parallel dialogue **198–9**, **202–3**
    revision 198
    storyline 197, 202, 206
    succinctness 198
flashbacks 10
Four Friends (Tesich) 177
freeze frames 73
Freytag's pyramid 118
    climax 119
    dénouement 119
    exposition 119
    falling action 119
    inciting incident 119
    resolution 119
    rising action 119
From Ritual to Romance (Weston) 6–7

games 79, **80**
    blocking 73
Gauguin, Paul **289**, **293**
gender and relationships *see* sexual
        issues
gestured dialogue 57, 194
Gittes, J. J. *see Chinatown*
Goethe, Johann von 79
Goldfinger (Maibaum and Dehn) ix,
        109, 110, **110**, **111**, 113, 114, **114**,
        116, 119–20
    action scenes 109–10
    importance 109
    panning shot **110**
    point-of-view shot **110–11**
    tension 109, 111, **111**, 112, **112**, 113,
        113, **114**, 115, **115**, **116**, 116–18,
        119
Goldman, William 241, 242
    on jealousy 241–2
Good Will Hunting (Damon and
        Affleck) 242, **244**, 247, 248, 249,
        249, 250, 252–3, 258, 260, 266
    Academy Award 266
    avoidance **242**, **247**, 248, 260
    conflict 242, **242–3**, **247–8**
    contention 241
    irony **244**, **247**, **249**, 250, 252, **252**
    jealousy 241–2
    monologue 242
    painting **244–6**, 250, **250–1**, 252
    sexual issues **246–7**, **251–2**, 252
    storyline 242, 258
Graduate, The (Willingham and Henry)
        viii, 87, 105, 119, 121, 127, 131–2,
        231
    abridgment 198
    control 128, **128**
    dialogue flow chart 300
    parallel to character 69
    sexual issues 121–2, **122–4**, 123,
        124, **125–7**, 126, 127, 128, **128**,
        129–31, 130, 131
    storyline 132
    succinctness 132, 144, 184, 272, 286
    importance 198
Greenaway, Peter 303
Guimard, Hector **286–7**, **290–1**

Hall, Annie *see Annie Hall*
Harmetz, Aljean 11
Hemingway, Ernest 279
Henry, Buck viii, 119, 121, 298
  succinctness 184, 272, 286
Hero With a Thousand Faces, The
  (Campbell) 6–7, 234
Hirsch, Judd 253
Hitchcock, Alfred
  abridgment by 53
  disparagement from 113, 119
  on MacGuffins 9
  on tension 109
Hold Back the Dawn (Brackett and
  Wilder) 297–8
Hollywood Interview, The 153
hourglass 66
humiliation 199, **203–4**, 204
humor *see* wit
Hutton, Betty **44–5**
Hutton, Timothy 253

Il Postino (Pavignano et al.) 227
imprisonment **94**, 104, **104**, **273**, 276,
  276
incest **162–3**, **164–5**, 165–6
individuality 68, 178, **179**, **181**, **182**,
  212, **215–16**, **220**, 220–1, **221**,
  225
  conflict 178, **180**, **181–2**, **216**, **217**,
    221, **222**, 222–3, **223**
  control and **215**, **220**, 221
  quests **178–9**, **180**, **181**, 182
indulgence 167, 168–9, 172, 175
  ambivalence **167–8**, **171**
  irony **168**, 171–2, 175

jealousy **80**, 103, **228–9**, **230**, **231–4**,
  232, 233, 234, 241–2
Jules & Jim (Truffaut and Gruault) ix,
  66, 68, 71, 74, 78
  Existentialism 68
  freeze frames 73
  games 73, 79, **80**
  hourglass 66
  lies 71
  location 72–3
    control 70

love triangle *see* love triangle
  novels and 69, 79
  old artifacts 72
  paintings 66, 68–9, 73
  parallel to characters 78–9, 80–1, **81**
  peculiarities 65
  plays 74–5, 82
  racing 70
  rapid cuts 65–6
  sexual issues 80–1
  sketch 68, **68**
  statue 69, **69**
  storyline 68–9, 70, 73–4, 75, **75**, 76,
    80–1, 82–4
  voice over 66, **66**, 67, **67**, 68, **76**
  summarization 65–6
    voice over 65, **65**
  time factors 73, **76**, **77**
    control 75, **75**
  voice over 46, 65, 68, **68**, 69, **69**,
    70, **70**, **71**, **74**, 75, **75**, 76, **76**,
    77, **77**, 78, **78**, 79, **79**, 80, **80**,
    81, **81–2**, 82, 83, **83**, **84**, 85, **85**

Kael, Pauline 3, 6, 10
Kane, Charles Foster *see Citizen Kane*
Karnot, Stephen 11
Katz Deli scene *see When Harry Met
  Sally*
Keefe, Terry 153
Khouri, Callie 209, 214
  recognition and 209, 267
  Academy Award 209
Knapp, Laurence 209
Kubla Khan **288**, **292**
Kubrick, Stanley 88, 94, 107
  abridgment by 53
  on length of scene 87
Kulas, Andrea 209

L'Orangerie Museum scene *see
  Midnight in Paris*
Ladd, Alan **36**, 41, **41**, 42
LaGravenese, Richard 197, 202, 203,
  207
  abridgment by 198
  on arrogance 206
Lax, Eric 279

Lehman, Ernest 60, 64
    abridgment by 53
leitmotiv **230**, 234, **234**
letters of transit **16**, **20–1**
    importance 12, **14–15**, 16, **19–20**
    MacGuffin 12
lies and burning 71
Lisbon 22, **22**
Lolita (Nabokov and Kubrick) ix, 87–8,
        92, 94, 95, 96, 100, 101, **101**, 105,
        106, 107
    abridgment 53
    authority and **94**, 104, 105, **105**,
        107
    conflict **88–9**, **91**, **95**, **96**, 100, **100**
    imprisonment **94**, 104, **104**
    length of scene 87
    play **92–4**, 101, **101**, 102, **102**, 103,
        103, 104, **104**, 106
    sexual issues **89–92**, **94**, 96, **96**, 97,
        97–8, 98, 99, **99**, 100, **100**, 104,
        104, 106, 107
    time factors 95, 98, 106
        conflict **88**, **90**, **95**, 98, **98**
Love and Death (Allen) 279
love triangle 68, 70, **70**, **71**, 71, **74**, **75**,
        76, 77, **78**, 78–81, **79**, **80**, **81**, **82**,
        82–3, **83**, 84
    control 70, 71, 72–3, 78, 82
    death 83, 84–5, **85**
    disguise and 70, **70**
    emotional factors 76–7
    jealousy **80**
    schism 72, 76, 77, **77**, 78, **83**, 83–4, **84**
    sexual issues 74–5, 81, **81–2**
    stalemate 73
    time factors **76**, **77**, 81, **82**
        control 75, **75**
Lubitsch, Ernst 33, 133, 298
    recognition and 153–4

Maar, Dora 285
McDonagh, Maitland 209
MacGuffins **9**, 9–10, 12
Machado de Assis, Joachim Maria 267
McLuhan, Marshall 170, 174
    communication and 170, **170**, 171,
        171, **174–5**

macroscripts vii
    microscripts and vii–viii
    see also individual terms
MADE formula viii–ix, 260, 300 *see
    also individual terms*
major and minor ensemble
    films 177
Malick, Terrence 241
Mankiewicz, Herman J. 3, 7, 10, 107,
        240, 297
    on mystery 6
    storyline 297
Manufacturing Consent (Chomsky)
        243, **248**, 249
Medium is the Massage, The
        (McLuhan) 171
Mendes, Sam 267
Michelangelo **288**, **292**
microscripts viii
    macroscripts and vii–viii
    see also individual terms
Midnight Cowboy (Salt) 133, **134**, **136**,
        137–8, 138, **141**, 144, **145**, 147,
        148–9, 151
    abridgment 144, 147
    Academy Award 133
    ancillary dialogue 133–4, **136–7**, 139,
        139–40, 140, **143**, 144
    awareness and **134**
    conflict **146–7**, **150–1**
    deceit **134**, 137, **137**, **141**
    fear **145–6**, **149–50**
    sexual issues **135**, **136–7**, 137, 138,
        138–9, 139, **140**, **141**, **142–4**,
        144, **147**
    storyline 144
    succinctness 144
Midnight in Paris (Allen) 279, 283, 285,
        286, 290, **290**, 295, 297
    conflict 282, 294
    dissolve **281**, **283**
    length of dialogue 286
    paintings 279, **280**, **281–3**, 283–4,
        284–5, 285
    parallel dialogue **280**, **282–3**
    rule breaking 285–6
    storyline 295
    time factors **286**, **290**, 293, 294

awareness and **287**, **288**, **291**, **292**, 293
conflict **286–91**, 292, **292**, 293, **293–4**, 294
Midway Airport (Chicago) 53, 57, 64
gestured dialogue 57
mystery **54–5**
unheard dialogue 57
minor and major ensemble films 177
Miramax 241
Miss Julie (Strindberg) 74
parallel to character 74, 75
sexual issues 74–5
Modigliani, Amedeo **281**, **284**, 285
Monet, Claude **280**, **282**, 283
disparagement **280**, **283**
monologue 242
parallel monologue 131
Moulin Rouge scene *see Midnight in Paris*
movie making 33
disparagement 33–4
Mt. Rushmore **55**, **56**, **60**, **61**
music 267
conflict **275**, 278, **278**

Nabokov, Vladimir
abridgment and 53
on length of scene 87
Name of the Rose, The (Birkin et al.) 227
New York Times 285
"News on the March" segment *see Citizen Kane*
Nichols, Mike 286
Nicholson, Jack 153
North by Northwest (Lehman) 53, 59, **59**, 60, 62, **63**, **64**
abridgment 53
conflict 64
deceit 58, **58–9**, 63, **63–4**, 64
escape **57–8**, 62, **62–3**
location 53, 57, 64
gestured dialogue 57
mystery **54–5**, **56**, **60**, **61**
unheard dialogue 57
mystery **54**, **55–7**, 57, **59–61**, 62
storyline 64

novels 79
autobiographical 69
parallel to character 79

Oddjob 110
Ordinary People (Sargent) 242, 252–3, **253**, **254–6**, 258, 259, **259**, 260, **261**, 262, **262**, 263, **263**, 266
Academy Award 252, 266
avoidance **256**, **258**, 260, 263, **263**, 265, **265**, 266
control and **255**, **257**, 262, **262**, **264**, 264–5, 266
time factors **257–8**, **265**, 265–6
death **254**, **256–7**, 260, **260**, **263**, 263–4, **264**
storyline 258
time factors **253**, 259, **259**
Oscars 133, 209, 252, 266
overlapping dialogue 131, 167, **167–8**, 169, **171**, 172, **198–9**, **202–3**, **216**, **221**
annoyance **274**, **277**
conflict 169, **169**, 170, **170**, **171**, **173**, **174**, 280, **282–3**

paintings 66, 68–9, 73, **244–5**, 250, **250**, 252, 279, **280**, **281**, **282**, 284, **284**, 285
absurdity **280**, **282**, 283
arrogance **280**, **281–2**, 283, **283**, **284–5**, 285
awareness and 283
conflict **281–2**, **284–5**, 285
conflict **245–6**, **250–1**, 252, **280**, **282–3**
disparagement **245**, **250**, 252, **280**, **283**
irony 283–4
panning shot **110**
parallel dialogue 131, 167, **167–8**, 169, **171**, 172, **198–9**, **202–3**, **216**, **221**
annoyance **274**, **277**
conflict 169, **169**, 170, **170**, **171**, **173**, **174**, 280, **282–3**
parallel monologue 131
People's History of the United States, A (Zinn) **243**, **248**

Picasso, Pablo 68–9, 73, **281**, **282**, 284, **284**, 285, **285**
Pinocchio **201**, 202, **205**
Player, The (Tolkin) 34
plays 74, **92–3**, 101, **101**, 102, **102**, 106
　communication and **169**, 173, **173**
　parallel to character 74, 75, 82
　sexual issues 74–5, **93–4**, 103, **103**, 104, **104**, 106
playwriting 177
　listening 177, 185
Poetics (Aristotle) vii, 4, 113, 121
point-of-view shot **110–11**
Polanski, Roman
　changed ending 153
　recognition and 153, 154, 267
Porter, Cole **287**, **291**
Posthumous Memoirs of Brás Cubas, The (Machado de Assis) 267
privacy
　condescension and **199**, **203–4**
　humiliation and **199**, **203**, 204
Psycho (Stefano) 113, 119
Pulp Fiction (Tarantino and Avary) 119

question to be answered (QBA) 2, 3, **4–5**, **7–8**, 10
　quest 4, **5–6**, 6, 7, **8–9**, 9–10
　storyline 2
　points of view 2, 10
quests 4, **5–6**, 6–7, **8–9**, 9–10, **178–9**, **180**, **181**, 182
　indistinctiveness and 4

racing 70
rapid cuts 65–6
Reiner, Rob 242
Renoir, Pierre-Auguste 283
　disparagement **280**, **283**
Rites of Passage, The (Van Gennep) 6–7
Robinson family *see Graduate, The*
Roché, Henri-Pierre 73 *see also Jules & Jim*
Roman Polanski (Cronin) 153
romanticism 23, **27**, **30**, **31** *see also individual terms*
Rosebud 1

importance 4
MacGuffin **9**, 9–10
mystery 2, 3, **5**, **7–8**, 10
　conflict 10
　quest **5–6**, 7, **8–9**, 9–10
Round Up the Usual Suspects (Harmetz) 11

Sabine women 76
Salt, Waldo 133, 140
　abridgment by 147
　Academy Awards 133
　ancillary dialogue 138
　blacklisting 133
Sargent, Alvin 252–3, 266
　Academy Award 252, 266
　on control 262, 265–6
Scott, Ridley 209
　recognition and 209, 267
screenwriting course 177
secrecy 122
　absurdity **122–3**
　alias 122
Serpico (Salt) 133
sexual issues 80–1, **81**, **89**, **91–2**, 96, **96**, 97, 99, 100, **100**, 106, 121, 123, 139, 187, 194, **216**, **219**, **221**, **225**
　absurdity 122, 123, **125–6**, 126, **129–30**
　ambivalence 121
　ancillary dialogue **136–7**, 138, **140**, **141**, **142**, **143–4**, 144
　annoyance **126–7**, 130, **130–1**, 131, **188–90**, 191, **191**, 192, **192**, **193–4**, 194, **195**
　anxiety 122, 124–5, **125**, **126–7**, 128, **129**, **130–1**, 131
　authority and **268–9**, **270–2**, 271, 272
　awareness and **135**, **138–9**, **142–3**
　ambivalence **137**, **141**
　limitations **135**, 137, **139**, **142**
　class issues and 74
　communication and **168**, 169, **169–70**, **173**, 174
　conflict **89–91**, **93–4**, 96, **96**, 97, **97–8**, 98, 99, **99**, 103, **103**, 104,

104, 106–7, 124, **135**, 138, **138**, **142**, **168**, **172**, **187–8**, **190**, 191, 191, **216–17**, **218–19**, **221–2**, 222, **223**, 223–4, **224**, 225, **246–7**, **251–2**, 252
constraint **273**, 276, **276**
contention 74
control **123–4**, 124, **127**, **128**, 131, **131**
death and **82**
disparagement **147**
faking and 195
incest **162–3**, **164–5**, 165–6
individuality and **216**, **217**, **221**, **222**, 222–3, **223**
indulgence and 168–9
ineptness 122, 123, **123–4**, 124, **125**, **129**
    conflict **126–7**, 127, **130–1**, 131
    parallel monologue 131
irony **217**, 222, **222**
jealousy 103
schism 74–5, 122, **122–3**
time factors **81–2**
Simon, Alex 153
sketch 68, **68**
smash cut 6
Speed of Darkness (Tesich) 177
Spirit of St. Louis, The (Wilder and Mayes) 297–8
statue 69, **69**
Strindberg, August 74
Subor, Michel 46
Sunset Boulevard (Wilder) 34–5, **35–6**, 36, 40, 41, 42, **42**, **44**, 46, 52
    conflict **36–7**
    death 49
    escape 52
    Faustian pact 49
    importance 33
    irony 52, **52**
    storyline 34, 40, **40–1**, 41, 46
        voice over 46
    voice over 34, 46, 85
    wit 34, **37–40**, **42–51**, 44, 49

talk show hosts *see Fisher King, The*
tension 109, 111, **111**, 112, **114**, 119

cliff-hanger 113, 116, 118, 119
death **111**, 113, **113**, 115, **115**, **116**
fear **111**, 112, **112**, **113**, 115, **115**
Freytag's pyramid 118–19
ratcheting 116–17, 118
    death 117–18
    trump card **116**
Tesich, Steve viii, 177, 182, 298
    irony 185
    listening 185
    multiple voices 185
    succinctness 184
theater lobby scene *see Annie Hall*
Thelma and Louise (Khouri) 209, **211**, 212, 214, **214**, **215**, **216**, **218**, **219–20**, 225
    control **209–11**, 212, **212**, **213–14**
    individuality and 212, **215–16**, **220**, 220–1, **221**, 225
    irony **210**, 212, **212**
    parallel dialogue **216**, **221**
    recognition and 209, 267
        Academy Award 209
    sexual issues **216–19**, **221–2**, 222–4, **223**, **224–5**, 225
    speed of speech **219**
    voice over **209–10**, 212
Titian **288**, **292**
Towne, Robert 153, 158, 163, 166
    recognition and 153, 154, 267
    on worth 165
Toy Story (Whedon et al.) 227, **228**, **229–30**, 231, **231**, 232, **233**, 234, **234–5**, **236–7**, 237, 238, **239–40**, 240
    committee of writers 227
    conflict **228**, **231**
    jealousy **228–9**, **230**, **231–4**, 232, 233, 234
    leitmotiv **230**, 234, **234**
    self-awareness and **230**, **233–4**
        limitations **229**, 232, **232–3**, 233, 234, **235–6**, **237–9**, 239
        self-pity **235**, **236**, 237, 238, **238**, 239, **239**
Truffaut, François 9, 65
    on voice overs 65, 85
Turner, J. M. W. **280**, **282**, 283

two-hander emphasis *see Good Will
Hunting*; *Ordinary People*

voice overs (VOs) 12, 34, 46, **65**, 66, **66**,
67, **67**, 68, **68**, 69, **69**, 70, **70**, **71**,
74, 75, **75**, 76, **76**, 77, **77**, 78, **78**,
79, **79**, 80, **80**, 81, **81–2**, 82, 83,
83, **84**, 85, **85**, **209–10**, **212**, 297
ambivalence 65

Waiting for Godot (Beckett) 173
Walter, Marie-Thérèse 285
When Harry Met Sally (Ephron) 187,
190, 195–6
sexual issues 187, **187–90**, 191, **191**,
192, **192**, **193–4**, 194, 195, **195**
succinctness 187
Which Lie Did I Tell? (Goldman) 242
jealousy 241–2
Wilder, Billy viii, 33, 46, 52, 297–8
action scenes 297
disparagement from 33–4

storyline 46
succinctness 298
on voice overs 46, 297
wit 33, 49
wit 33, 34, **46–51**, 49, **182–5**, 279
conflict **37–40**, **42–6**, 44
fear and **111**, 115, **115**
death and **112**, 115, **115**
see also Annie Hall; *Midnight in
Paris*; *Toy Story*; *When Harry
Met Sally*
Woody Allen (Lax) 279
World According to Garp, The (Tesich)
177
worth **161**, **164**, 165, 166
Written By 241

Xanadu (*Citizen Kane*) 1

Zanuck, Darryl 44, **44**
Zelig (Allen) 285
Zwick, Ed 241